OUTDOOR SAFETY & SURVIVAL

OUTDOOR SAFETY & SURVIVAL

MIKE NASH

Rocky Mountain Books
www.rmbooks.com

Library and Archives Canada Cataloguing in Publication

Nash, Mike, 1946-
    Outdoor safety & survival / Mike Nash.

Previously published under the title: Outdoor safety and survival in British Columbia's backcountry. Includes bibliographical references and index.
Issued also in electronic format. (ISBN 978-1-927330-02-9)

ISBN 978-1-927330-01-2

    1. Outdoor recreation—British Columbia—Safety measures.
2. Wilderness survival—British Columbia. I. Nash, Mike, 1946- .
Outdoor safety and survival in British Columbia's backcountry.
II. Title. III. Title: Outdoor safety and survival.

GV200.5.N27 2012   613.6'909711   C2011-908609-3

Photo credits: All photographs are by Mike Nash except as noted in the captions
Back cover photo: Valley clouds form in Sugarbowl-Grizzly Den Provincial Park near Prince George, British Columbia.
Frontispiece: Minutes count in the aftermath of a small avalanche

To Judy Lett for shared adventures and helping me to find balance in preparing this book.

Printed in Canada

Rocky Mountain Books acknowledges the financial support for its publishing program from the Government of Canada through the Canada Book Fund (CBF) and the Canada Council for the Arts, and from the province of British Columbia through the British Columbia Arts Council and the Book Publishing Tax Credit.

This book was produced using FSC®-certified, acid-free paper, processed chlorine free and printed with vegetable-based inks.

Disclaimer

The actions described in this book may be considered inherently dangerous activities. Individuals undertake these activities at their own risk. The information put forth in this guide has been collected from a variety of sources and is not guaranteed to be completely accurate or reliable. Many conditions and some information may change owing to weather and numerous other factors beyond the control of the authors and publishers. Individual climbers and/or hikers must determine the risks, use their own judgment, and take full responsibility for their actions. Do not depend on any information found in this book for your own personal safety. Your safety depends on your own good judgment based on your skills, education, and experience.

It is up to the users of this guidebook to acquire the necessary skills for safe experiences and to exercise caution in potentially hazardous areas. The authors and publishers of this guide accept no responsibility for your actions or the results that occur from another's actions, choices, or judgments. If you have any doubt as to your safety or your ability to attempt anything described in this guidebook, do not attempt it.

CONTENTS

CAUTIONARY NOTE

This book presents the outdoor experiences and information gathered by the author over a number of years. It is not a substitute for personal knowledge and skills acquired through hands-on training and experience, moderated by an awareness of current conditions, which are what the reader will require in order to have as safe a trip as possible in the outdoors. There are inherent risks associated with any outdoor activity. You must assess your own skills against each activity and the current conditions you are likely to encounter there, and exercise your own best judgment while in the outdoors. Knowledge, combined with planning, preparation, practice and common sense, are keys to having a safe and enjoyable outdoor experience, but in the end, you use the outdoors and the information contained in this book entirely at your own risk.

PREFACE

This book arose from more than 40 years of exploring Canada's outdoors. My purpose is to alert you to some of the rewards and risks associated with the outdoors and everyday life, and to help you to prepare for and react to situations that can arise. The book is a self-help guide and a checklist for generalized outdoor activities. While it does not address technical aspects of specialized outdoor activities such as motorized sports, water sports, rock and ice climbing, caving and work-related activities, I have drawn on experiences in some of these areas, and the general safety principles outlined in the book will apply in many of these situations. The book was written largely from my experiences in northern British Columbia, but is applicable throughout much of North America, especially with the inclusion of desert safety in this new edition. I have aimed to keep the book interesting by including real-life stories as *Reality Checks*. Some of these are my own; others are ones that caught my interest and were relevant to particular parts of the book. I make no apology for any repetition you might notice as you read through the book – this is unavoidable given the overlaps between otherwise discrete topics. Some repetition also helps to reinforce key ideas, and for those who wish to only read or refer back to particular sections of the book, it is essential.

If you are new to the outdoors, don't be overwhelmed by the number of things to learn, courses to take, equipment to buy and books to read. These represent a lifetime of learning for me and are not something I picked up overnight. Understand the basics and focus on those things that seem most relevant to your chosen outdoor activities. Doing something to increase your knowledge and safety awareness is a lot better than doing nothing; and if you can have fun doing it, you are more likely to continue to expand your knowledge. Aim to continuously improve your outdoor skills, gradually acquire quality equipment as your funds permit, and consciously act to increase your safety awareness in the outdoors and in every aspect of your life.

FORTY DAYS AND FORTY NIGHTS ALONE IN THE WILDERNESS

The following remarkable story covers many aspects of wilderness survival. Fred Van der Post[1] is the most experienced outdoorsman I have known. He appears again later in the book in a *Reality Check* about improvisation during the 800-kilometre, 40-day solo snowshoe trek he undertook in northwestern BC in 1982.

//

REALITY CHECK: As the ice gave way beneath him, the first thought to pass through the legendary woodsman's mind was "okay, Fred, it's happened."

During his famous 1982 walk, hundreds of kilometres and several weeks away from help and with no ready means of communication, Fred Van der Post fell through the ice while crossing Stalk Lakes in the northwest corner of BC's Tatlatui Provincial Park. The small thermometer attached to his pack had been showing an air temperature of −32°C, with a strong wind blowing across the lake ice. Fred had been rehearsing various "what if" scenarios and was ready for what happened next. As he commented many years later with considerable understatement, "There was not a huge element of surprise."

As a precaution, he already had the hip belt of his pack unfastened and his thumbs were hooked under his shoulder straps, such that when he broke through the ice he was able to instantly throw off the pack safely onto the ice, reducing his weight by nearly 40 kilos (88 pounds). "Never have your hip belt fastened while crossing water or ice," he stressed, "especially if the ice is snow-covered and you can't see how secure it is or if the lake is spring fed, as this one was." Without the pack weight, he sank gently, as the snowshoes slowed his descent, giving him a precious few seconds to think through what he was going to do next. If his pack had still been on, he would have sunk like a stone. He recalls feeling no panic or even fear, just the thought that "okay, it's happened," as he moved quickly into survival mode. Sinking up to his chin and not touching bottom, Fred began flapping his arms up and down (his snowshoes would have limited his ability to kick with his feet) to stay afloat, breaking the ice with his elbows until he found ice strong enough to bear his weight. Methodically, he set about bracing himself first on one arm and then the other as he reached down into the water to unbuckle and release first one

9

and then the other snowshoe, carefully throwing them out onto the ice. "This," he said, "was the most difficult thing I had to do." Despite his dire predicament, he maintained the presence of mind to know that his snowshoes would be his lifeline after he had escaped his immediate jam and he could not drop them in the water. Having removed and secured his snowshoes, he was able to kick with his feet into a horizontal position, and with a huge effort he lunged out of the water onto his stomach, a bit like a seal launching out onto ice. He remained horizontal to distribute his weight until he could reach his snowshoes and more secure ice.

The water froze on him immediately, encasing him in a layer of ice like a carapace that temporarily worked to his advantage by breaking the wind. Leaving his gear on the ice, he quickly made for the nearest shore, where by good fortune there was a dry snag and a birch tree with flammable bark. He reached into the pocket of his cruise vest for the waterproof container of matches he always kept there for just this eventuality, and soon had a life-saving fire going. He needed fire quickly to survive, but he also knew he had to take his time to make a good base for the fire. "One match," he said, repeating it several times for emphasis as we talked over coffee at my kitchen table 28 years later. "One match!" Four hours later, having stripped down and dried out, his gear retrieved from the ice, he was on his way.

Fred exhibited the best survivor instincts as well as making full use of his lucky find of dry firewood and fire starter materials. Both are key factors in survival. Perhaps he was also entrenched in the strange beauty of his situation, what US mythologist, writer and lecturer Joseph Campbell once referred to as a sublime experience. Fred described his initial feelings after his escape as some annoyance at losing four hours travel time, followed by a sense of happiness and reward that his mental preparedness and constant "what if" rehearsals had paid off a hundred per cent. Fred stressed that he is never without his cruise vest while in the bush, with enough gear and emergency rations in the pockets to survive for a week if he should ever become separated from his pack by a bear or moose, or, as could have happened in this instance, by falling through the ice.

COMPLACENCY TRAP

No matter how experienced you become, don't allow yourself to slide into the trap of believing yourself to be an expert in the outdoors. As another friend of mine, George Evanoff, used to say about his specialty area of avalanche safety, "There are no experts."[2] He was referring to the words of André Roch, former director of the Swiss Snow & Avalanche Research Institute, who used to remind

Even in the depths of winter, weak ice is a real possibility on spring-fed lakes.

people: "Remember, my friends, the avalanche does not know that you are an expert." Complacency creeps up on all of us, as I was reminded during the course of several adventures while finalizing the first edition of this book. Some of those experiences are included here as *Reality Checks*. As an official of a British Columbia safety council said in early 2010 while testifying about the death of an experienced forest worker: "Death and serious injury in the woods are rarely caused by inexperience. Complacency, often by those who have worked in the bush all their lives, is the deadly enemy." One BC forest company found that the highest death rates were among older, seasoned workers and those with less than two years experience. While the latter was easier to understand, the company attributed the former to complacency and a culture of risk-taking.[3] The bottom line is that we all need to remain vigilant in the outdoors and to keep on refreshing and upgrading our outdoor skills, never forgetting one key mantra above all else: *there is no room for complacency.*

SAFETY AWARENESS

We have some marvellous backcountry in Canada, and the opportunity to experience it is one of the main benefits of living or visiting here. Almost all outdoor activities are safe and enjoyable, but harrowing and sometimes disastrous events do occasionally happen in the backcountry just as with other human endeavours. When things are put in perspective, the risks inherent in backcountry recreation are generally no worse than those of everyday living.

Risk aversion is not a reason to stay away from the outdoors or to discourage young people from undertaking their own journeys of discovery in the natural world and participating in outdoor adventure field trips. There are individual risks, yes; but there are other dangers in life. A generation that is not in tune with the natural world poses an increased threat to the ecology and diversity of life on earth through a lack of connection and understanding. They may also pose a danger to themselves and to the viability of the healthcare system through sedentary lifestyles that contribute to health problems.

As a friend once said to me, "One of the greatest joys of being in the backcountry is the adventure – to go out there and just do it." He went on to emphasize what being in the outdoors meant to him, giving a moderating voice to ideals that are worth keeping in mind as you balance all the do's and don'ts that a treatise on outdoor safety necessarily entails:

> I view backcountry as a passion. I would do it right or wrong. Prepared, I hope, but not always – but always ready to learn. Everyone I have travelled with has taught me something. When I'm in over my head, I look to leadership. Leaders don't expect you to be blind and not voice worried concerns; but at the end of the day, the leader will have my support. Mentorship is really the key – to learn by example and progress up a skill curve. We are blessed to have an incredible group of experienced individuals to guide us.

In considering these passionate thoughts of one of this book's first readers, I hope you will see the book as *handrails* and not *handcuffs*, to quote a favourite expression of an aviation colleague of mine in Toronto in the 1970s. Go out and experience the outdoors with a reasonable level of safety awareness, and strive to develop the knowledge and experience that underlies this, without losing a sense of being on the edge that is an essence of the outdoor experience.

Today, there is hardly a workplace without a safety program, and we are all familiar with the constant emphasis on highway safety. But safety does not begin

"One of the greatest joys of being in the backcountry is the adventure."

and end at the workplace door or when we get out from behind the wheel of a vehicle; it should be a constant throughout all our activities. With this in mind, I will begin with a story about a situation that I found myself in that, while being indoors and ultimately uneventful, astounded me with its implications.

IT CAN'T HAPPEN TO ME
IN EVERYDAY LIFE

REALITY CHECK: A dinner dance was getting underway in a crowded hall on December 31, 1999, the eve of the new millennium. It was difficult to move among the throng of people and closely spaced tables. The latter were covered with paper, and on them were lit candles dressed with coniferous sprigs. The entranceway to the wood-framed hall, for those who might be lucky enough to reach it in a fast-moving fire, was narrow and L-shaped and would likely have bottlenecked in a panic. Even with most people sitting down, it was hard to move around. Uneasy, I squeezed through the jam of revellers and tightly spaced tables and chairs to check out the signed emergency exit. Following the EXIT sign down a wide flight of stairs, I was stunned to find a large chain and padlock on the double exit doors. This was Canada, a so-called first-world country, and among the organizers and guests were members of the medical profession, a community coroner and the head of a large industrial safety program, all of whom, I found out, were completely unconcerned with the situation even after it was brought to their attention.

Why shouldn't we be surprised by this story? It is part of human nature to fall into complacency traps, even those who are professionally involved in safety. No one wanted to make a fuss and risk spoiling the once-in-a-lifetime millennium party, including me, since I didn't immediately call the fire marshal after asking that the chain be removed and being told it would take an hour to get the building owner down to take care of it. At least one other person had found the padlocked emergency exit doors earlier in the evening and had rationalized that there was another way out of the basement through an unmarked side door. Was it reasonable in the circumstances for guests to have done a site inspection? The situation clearly warranted a visual check of the emergency exit, just as when checking into a hotel room or boarding an aircraft. If everything had been okay, then that would have been the end of it.

IN THE OUTDOORS

A similar situation can arise in the outdoors from the assumption that "it can't happen to me," or perhaps an offhand assurance by an experienced member of a group that some situation or other "will be fine." If you've spent any amount of time in the outdoors you will likely have heard it many times and probably said it yourself more than once. These attitudes can be accompanied by peer pressure to "just do it" or perhaps by one's own desire to complete an objective: "summit fever." These drivers aren't necessarily bad, but they must be tempered by knowledge, experience and an aversion to complacency. We all doff our safety hats at one time or another. There used to be a handmade sign beside the logging road to Holberg and Cape Scott on northern Vancouver Island that simply said PAY ATTENTION and was attached to the end of a giant log that had been placed on top of an old car and pressed down hard. A later sign attached to the same artifact read BE PREPARED FOR THE UNEXPECTED.

The nature of many outdoor activities involves taking some unavoidable risk. You might be snowshoeing quietly along on easy ground on a nice spring day when suddenly the snow gives way and you fall into a snow-covered fissure or pothole in the rock and find yourself injured and/or trapped. I came across one of these while snowshoeing in the mountains last year and it gave me pause for reflection. It reminded me of a pothole in the Cariboo Mountains near where I live. We call it Caribou Cave, because at the bottom of the roughly ten-metre-deep pit lie the bones of several long-dead mountain caribou that had the misfortune to

14

walk over the snow-covered entrance. Other risk scenarios are that a bear may be encountered at any time on a spring, summer or fall trail, and the best backcountry skiing and snowmobiling are usually found in avalanche terrain.

The question becomes how to acquire the knowledge and skills that will be needed to prepare for, adequately assess and manage risk. It isn't good enough to take an avalanche course and then just look at a slope when the hazard rating is only "moderate" and assume it is safe without doing a proper risk assessment, or to gamble that you can outrun an avalanche on a high-powered snowmobile. If the trip leaders or organizers in such a situation fail to conduct a reasonable examination of the snowpack and somebody in their party gets injured or killed in an avalanche, there will likely be some legal liability on top of the pain, suffering and grief.

There are many opportunities to learn to do outdoor recreation safely through training courses, often simply by joining knowledgeable groups or clubs. You can manage risk as you continue to enjoy the outdoors, just as you do in the workplace, on the highways and in the home. Look at risks objectively and reasonably. Just because something has never happened to you doesn't mean it won't happen today, especially if you are adding new unknowns on top of situations that have previously made you a little uncomfortable. Conversely, just because something could happen doesn't mean that it will, especially if you manage the risk well and gain experience by pushing your limits in manageable increments. So risk is usually not a reason to stay home. Anticipate the unexpected, like a snow-covered pothole or wildlife on the trail. Consider the possible consequences of each action you are about to undertake, such as what if the ice fails while snowshoeing across a frozen lake as happened to Fred Van der Post in the *Reality Check* above. Then, while you may still decide to cross a steep rock or snow slope, you can choose to minimize the risk by exposing only one person at a time. Or you might pick a different route. Or simply turn around and go home. When assessing the risk, think not just of yourself, but especially of any less-experienced people who may be travelling with you and who are, in effect, in your care. Think also of those who are waiting at home for your safe return. So, prepare for the worst, hope for the best, and then go out and enjoy your chosen outdoor activity!

DEFINITIONS OF SAFETY AND SURVIVAL

Following are definitions that guided me as I prepared the material for this book:

Outdoor safety is the prudent use of the outdoors through knowledge, planning, preparation, practice and experience. Outdoor safety is to be mentally and physically prepared for whatever might happen, and to give first priority to safety and avoid complacency.

A *survival situation* is any circumstance that is beyond the normal experience and has the potential to be life threatening.

PERSPECTIVE

This book has been written from a perspective of mostly self-propelled outdoor recreation activities. If you engage in other types of outdoor pursuits such as working in the bush or motorized recreation, you may wish to vary some of the ideas around clothing and equipment, for example, but the essential principles are the same.

2 INHERENT RISKS AND GOOD JUDGMENT

Before we dig into the fundamentals of outdoor safety, I would like to highlight two concepts that underlie everything covered in the book:

Inherent risks: In deciding to spend time in the outdoors, accept that there are inherent risks involved in all outdoor activities.

Good judgment: Learn to exercise good judgment in order to manage those risks.

This section expands upon these concepts later; but first here are a couple of incidents that happened to me as I was finalizing the first edition of this book:

REALITY CHECK – Loops and encounters of the furry kind: In 2006, several recreation groups combined their resources to build two new mountain trails between Driscoll and Slim Creeks, 100 kilometres east of Prince George in north central British Columbia, later the site of a popular Ancient Forest interpretive trail. On a work-hike in early September, a connecting loop was made when three of us completed a ridgetop traverse between the two trails. After hiking to a subalpine lake on the west end of the ridge, our job was to flag and brush the route across the ridge to connect with the other trail. The roughly seven-kilometre ridgewalk is an up and down mix of open meadows and thick brush through which centuries-old game trails continually start and then vanish. There are periodic views north across the Rocky Mountain Trench to the Rockies and south across Slim and Everett creeks into the Cariboo Mountains. During the five-and-a-half hours it took us to complete brushing and marking the traverse, we had two small adventures.

The first happened halfway from a subalpine lake to the summit when I apparently walked into two bears. I use the word "apparently" because, like another incident described in the section on bear safety, at no time did I hear or see the animals. But my partners 100 metres behind me sure did. Although they had been making a lot of noise chopping with brushing axes and we were shouting back and forth across a gladed gully about route options, the bears had ominously held their ground as I approached to within less than ten metres – too close for safety in the circumstances. My view of the animals was obstructed by bush, but my companions had clear views across the glade. There was no denying the urgency or command in their voices as they yelled at me to back away. The larger bear, which my friends presumed to be a male, appeared to be standing head and shoulders above the tall vegetation while still on all fours. They later estimated it to be a huge 300-kilogram black bear. This was unusual, both because of its apparent size and because we were in higher-elevation grizzly country, which often is out of bounds for black bears. Its companion, which my companions thought was a female, was cinnamon-coloured and smaller. The bears seemed indisposed to leave, but prompted by all the urgent shouting, they eventually did, heading disconcertingly in the same direction where we were laying out the future trail. As we were three people moving slowly and making lots of noise, we decided it was probably safe to continue on, which we did without further incident.

Open gully where the close encounter with two bears took place.

The second and more amusing adventure occurred two-thirds of the way across the traverse when we not only managed to walk in a complete one-kilometre circle using dead reckoning, but also flagged the route with survey tape! All of us were experienced in mountain navigation, but with tantalizing glimpses of the peaks to the north and the south of the ridge, it was easy to get pulled off course by the terrain and accidentally cue in on the wrong mountain range, even in clear weather. We had been trying to avoid what appeared to be an unnecessary descent, and we outsmarted ourselves. One of my companions was the first to question our direction when he noticed a familiar-looking slough. Yet despite his strong suggestion that we had been that way before, and even with my global positioning system (GPS) telling me we had started to increase instead of decrease the distance to our destination, I was so sure we were on course that I did not bother to check the compass bearing. Likewise, my other companion was so convinced we were on track that he read his compass backwards by unconsciously referring to the white end of the needle instead of the red end. It was a classic case of collective tunnel vision! Eventually we spotted red ribbon ahead and wondered who had put it there; it was, of course, us, barely a half-hour before. With mixed feelings of amusement and embarrassment, we retraced our steps and took the extra time needed to repair the newly ribboned route. A few years earlier, I had made a similar mistake on skis on the same ridgetop, and had inadvertently started to descend off the south instead of the north side of the ridge before realizing that something wasn't right. On that occasion, though, my senses were more alert to unfamiliar surroundings, winter conditions and reduced visibility, and I wasn't hampered by overconfidence.

It's easy to get turned around in complex ridge terrain such Driscoll Ridge.

In the first story, we did everything reasonable in the circumstances. We were a group of three; we were fairly close together; we were making lots of noise; we had bear repellent with us; and the animals had left. The lesson was that there are *inherent risks* in the outdoors. The outcome could have gone badly if one of the bears had reacted aggressively to the surprise close encounter; and given their apparent intransigence, the situation could have been even more troubling if I had been alone. It was a good example of the safety benefits of having at least two companions while in the backcountry.

In the second situation, the obvious lesson was to pay better attention to surroundings and compass bearings in the backcountry and heed clues that something was not quite right. The human mind is superbly capable of tunnel vision when convinced of something, and in this case it took the jolt of finding our own ribbon to break us out of it. This was an example of a lapse of *good judgment*. We were not at much risk, as we were well equipped and it was just a matter of time before we sorted it out. If, however, we had been there without navigation aids, or in poor weather or visibility, or late in the day, or in winter, or had been less experienced, or something else had gone wrong to compound things, the situation could have been more serious. A simple navigation error like this could add stress to other risk factors or issues that one might be experiencing, such as the earlier two-bear encounter. Accidents and disasters are often the result of a compounding series of small errors in judgment and missteps, none of which may be individually significant.

REALITY CHECK – Inherent risks and luck: The key to approaching inherent risks in the backcountry, or anywhere else, is risk management: deciding whether and how to approach a situation or possible hazard. But even if you deem the risk to be acceptable or even diminishingly small, you can still be unlucky. There's a cave, high in the Dezaiko Range of the northern Rocky Mountains, known as Close to the Edge. It's the deepest pothole (defined as a continuous freefall) north of Mexico, with a 250-metre freefall. The best place to view or photograph this wonder of the world was from a rocky ledge that projected over the seemingly bottomless shaft. The ledge is no longer there, having one day fallen into the abyss between visits by cavers. I keep a picture on my fridge of me kneeling on that ledge, peering over the edge, to remind me of the capriciousness of life.

KNOWLEDGE

Outdoor knowledge can be developed by taking advantage of safety seminars and courses offered through the continuing education departments of school districts, community colleges, private training institutions, universities, outdoor clubs, volunteer rescue organizations and employers. Any course that encourages safety awareness is valuable. For example, learning in a basic first aid course how to assess an accident scene and follow a priority action approach is likely to be applicable to a range of situations that could arise in the outdoors. As well, specialized seminars and courses are often seasonally available that address specific outdoor skills such as survival, navigation, swift-water rescue, avalanche safety, wildlife safety, wilderness first aid and other sport-specific skills. Learn from mentors and peers, such as experienced members of an outdoors club. As well, while there is no substitute for first-hand teaching and hands-on experience in the outdoors, you can also learn through self-study by reading some of the many excellent texts that are available on the outdoors and outdoor adventure, some of which are listed in the Appendices at the back of this book.

THE FIVE P's
PREPAREDNESS, PREPARATION, PLANNING, PRACTICE AND PREVENTION

Anticipating what might happen is key to prevention. These themes will be developed in the next chapter and throughout the book. Without becoming paranoid and spoiling your own or others' outdoor experience, develop a habit of thinking through "what if" scenarios while you are in the outdoors – mentally prepare yourself for possible eventualities. This practice saved the life of Fred Van der Post after he fell through the ice on a remote northern lake. Avoid the assumption that "it won't happen to me," because if you spend enough time outdoors, something most assuredly will, and probably when you least expect it.

EXPERIENCE

A great way for a novice to gain experience with a particular outdoor activity, while enjoying a good level of security, is to go out with knowledgeable people. If you have the time and the inclination, one of the best ways to learn new outdoor skills quickly, and give back to the community at the same time, is to volunteer with a search and rescue group.

CLOTHING, EQUIPMENT, FOOD AND SHELTER

When venturing into the outdoors, take adequate clothing and equipment as well as sufficient water and food for your planned activity, plus a little extra for the possibility of spending some unplanned time out there. Staying dry and warm is one of your highest priorities in a cool climate, and carrying spare clothing and raingear is the main way to assure that. This is developed further in a later chapter. Maintaining hydration, electrolytes and energy will help stave off cold- and heat-related problems and give you a psychological boost as well. Knowing how to find or build shelter and how to start a fire in the wettest, snowiest and windiest conditions will boost your confidence and margin of safety.

HEALTH, FITNESS, TRAINING

Exercise generally improves physical and mental well-being and fitness, and improved fitness in turn helps you to do those activities more safely. For example, a paper by David C. Nieman in the *British Journal of Sports Medicine* in November 2010 found that increased physical activity and fitness level also correlated with reduced frequency and severity of upper respiratory tract infections. Being physically fit is also likely to make you less injury prone, provided you don't use that heightened fitness to push yourself beyond a safe limit.

If you are undertaking a challenging activity that is outside of your normal fitness regimen and/or experience, first research and then train for it:

REALITY CHECK: Grand Canyon in a day: In the fall of 2010, my wife, Judy, and I had planned a week of hiking in Utah's Zion National Park. Wanting to see and hike the Grand Canyon in nearby Arizona while I was there (my wife had done it two years earlier with friends) and not having an overnight reservation inside the canyon, which generally must be made months in advance, my only recourse was a day hike. Looking at the maps, the approximate distance and elevation change was 30 kilometres and 1,400 vertical metres from the Grand Canyon Village to the Colorado River and back. While daunting, this was comparable to some of my local mountain hikes in north central BC and therefore very doable for me. Or was it?

Some of the challenges I would face would be the intimidating scale, grandeur and deadly reputation of the Grand Canyon, which, along with many well-justified signs warning against hiking to the bottom and back in a day, give pause for sober reflection and exact a psychological price. Added to this, "down first" is very committing compared to climbing a mountain where you can turn around almost anywhere if you are having an off day or the mountain or weather becomes too much. "Down first" is also a potential trap in that you descend in the cool of the morning but ascend in the heat of the day; again, the opposite of mountaineering. In addition, there can be huge environmental differences between the rim and the river. In the fall, for example, this can manifest as subfreezing temperatures and snow on the rim and higher than 30 or 35°C at the bottom. And, if you descend into the Grand Canyon and do not have an overnight reservation, you must make it out the same day. As the warning signs proclaim, "Down Is Optional, Up Is Mandatory." Other issues are the risk of heat exhaustion, heat stroke and hyponatremia (see p. 102), all of which can be deadly, especially in the Grand Canyon from May to September. As well as the heat, the dry desert air further promotes dehydration. The popular trails are wide and have an easy grade, but a century of use by mules has caused a lot of wear such that occasional vertical exposure and a moment's inattention could mean a costly trip or stumble. The Grand Canyon's history and the hundreds of calls for assistance and several fatalities every year should give every visitor pause for thought. In the first seven months of 2011, the official death toll was already six.

For these reasons, I do not advocate that anyone should hike the Grand Canyon in a day, and definitely not in the summer months when many heat-related problems occur – I am just relating my experience and how I prepared for it. Grand Canyon National Park strongly recommends against doing so at any time, with a series of signs such as "DO NOT attempt to hike from the rim to the river and back without being prepared to possibly suffer the following: permanent brain damage, cardiac arrest, death." Warning signs don't get much starker than that!

But the Grand Canyon should also be put into perspective. With five million visitors a year of all ages, fitness levels and experience, a certain number of strokes, heart attacks, suicides, falls, heat-related deaths, drownings, vehicle accidents, plane crashes and even murders are, unfortunately, inevitable. But when I compared the statistics of the last hundred years for the Grand Canyon of the Colorado with British Columbia's little-accessed Grand Canyon of the Fraser, I was surprised to find that on a per capita basis a visitor to the Grand Canyon of the Fraser has 50 times more likelihood of dying than a visitor to the Grand Canyon of the Colorado. And it turns out that lots of people do regularly hike the Colorado Grand Canyon in a day, especially those who are familiar with it, and in the cooler seasons; there were several during my hike. Some even hike or run from one rim to the other and back again in a 24-hour period in one of the world's toughest runs, dubbed "R2R2R": rim-to-rim-to-rim.

To prepare for my hike, I researched what would be involved in order to fully understand the challenges I might face. I trained for 300 vertical metres (1,000 vertical feet) *more* than I would need in the Grand Canyon. I went in the fall season. I carried four litres of water and some electrolytes plus a filter for backup. I carried more food than I would normally take for a comparable mountain hike. I took two cotton shirts for soaking and evaporative cooling. I planned to start no later than first light, and I hiked alone for optimal speed and pacing, bearing in mind that I would be on well-used trails and my wife had my itinerary. The result was that it was probably the best hike I have ever done. I descended the sun-exposed dry South Kaibob Trail in the cool pre-dawn morning into marvellous sunrise vistas on canyon buttes.

Allowing for many photo pauses, my time down to the Colorado River was just 2 hours 40 minutes, affording me a couple of hours in the bottom to enjoy a delicious coffee at the Phantom Ranch, an unexpected liquid and caffeine bonus. After rest, food and an hour's walk along the river, I began my climb of the Bright Angel Trail at 11 a.m. This trail is best for the ascent, as it follows a gully for half its length, with some shade opportunities and a stream, at least in November. In the summer, this lower gully part of the trail is like a reflector

Morning sun on the US Grand Canyon's South Kaibob Trail.

oven and can be dangerous in the heat of the day. Even in early November the temperature at the river was an unseasonably warm 27°c, but by soaking and evaporating dry my cotton shirts no less than five times during the six-hour ascent I kept myself pleasantly cool. One strategy that I improvised partway up was to presoak and wring out my spare shirt and carry it in my pack in a plastic bag for use on the upper part of the climb after I had left the last water behind and after the shirt I was wearing had evaporated dry. In the warmer months of the year, hikers are encouraged to wait out the hot, sunny parts of the day and resume hiking at about, say, 4 or 5 p.m., if necessary using a headlamp for the last part of the trail. Those who ignore this advice do so at their peril, and more than a few have paid the supreme price.

For me in November, though, the hike was a memorable and enjoyable experience made possible by good preparation and training. Except for the final few minutes, I did not want it to end, and I emerged satisfied onto the south rim at Grand Canyon Village just over ten hours after my early start, with still an hour remaining before sunset. You can view a slideshow of the hike at www.youtube.com/watch?v=ZhxNnvVeN0E. See also note on the book *Over the Edge: Death in the Grand Canyon*, in Appendix A at p. 257.

Grand Canyon vista.

WHEN YOU'RE OUT THERE

From a safety perspective, it is not advisable to travel alone. However, if you do find yourself in that situation, or if you are with just one or two other people, make sure you leave a clear itinerary with a trusted contact. Try not to deviate much from the itinerary, and take extra care to avoid injury or becoming lost if you are alone. On the plus side, when you are alone or in a small group you have more control over what you do, such as pace and frequency of stops. You can hear and see more of your surroundings and there is less peer pressure to go beyond your comfort zone or to overextend yourself. On the downside – and it is a big potential downside – there are fewer opportunities to learn from others or to share ideas about courses of action, possibly more chance of a wildlife encounter going wrong and considerably higher stakes if you become lost, stranded, injured or trapped or succumb to hypo- or hyperthermia. On balance, you are much safer in a group than you would be alone, and preferably a group of three or more so that if you have to split up, one can stay with a casualty while the other goes for help. In technical situations such as scrambling, a group size of four is a safer minimum. In wildlife encounters, two people may not offer any more deterrent than one alone. The chance of having a problem with wildlife begins to diminish with three or more people in a group

A group size of four or more provides added security when scrambling.

staying reasonably close together. Some Canadian parks recommend (and in some instances require) groups of four to six people staying close together in places where there is a high probability of encountering grizzly bears.

Whenever people come together, the group itself can present challenges. Whether you are the leader of the group or a participant, consider the responsibilities and consequences of group leadership, group dynamics and group membership. Nothing can induce loss of enjoyment or add risk to a group more than a poor dynamic and/or poor leadership. Indeed, the two usually go together, as a good leader will act quickly to stem bickering and faction-splitting. If good leadership is lacking, there is added onus on participants to recognize what is happening and try to help manage the situation, or at least take more control of their own destiny if things really go off the rails. Individuals may have innate survival instincts that are suppressed while they are part of a dysfunctional group but that can serve them well if the group fractures. Try to resist peer pressure to go beyond your limits of ability, knowledge and comfort; but do learn what your limits are and push your comfort zone a little – especially with the safety advantage of having experienced companions. This is the best way to learn new skills and widen your own experience. For higher-risk activities such as mountain climbing, caving, diving or bush flying, working safely at one's limits can be both a necessity and a matter of life and death. I'll talk more about group leadership in the final chapter, beginning at p. 219.

HOW OLD IS TOO OLD?

When is it time to hang up your hiking boots and backpack and settle for something less demanding? This is obviously a personal choice that is influenced by your physical condition, life choices you have made and any current disabilities or medical conditions. However, I have met several octogenarians who are still very active in the backcountry. And there are studies showing that regular exercise by the elderly benefits not only physical health but also cognitive abilities.[4] Older people can still enjoy the outdoors; they just need to be cognizant of normal age-related changes in their abilities and stay within those new parameters.

REALITY CHECK: One inspiring individual my wife, Judy, and I met a few years ago at Mount Assiniboine was the legendary climber Fred Beckey. Fred has made hundreds of first ascents during his long life, likely more than anyone else, and he was still climbing in 2010 at the age of 87. In July 2006, at age 83, he slept outside near our camp without a tent, and later carried a heavy pack as he slowly made his way up the lower flanks of Mount Assiniboine, Canada's equivalent of the Matterhorn, paying careful attention to pacing and balance on loose rock but moving confidently on secure rock. His progress for his age was impressive, as was his later decision to end his climb because of the unstable rock. We had no trouble passing him on the approach trail, but it was a different story when we reached a rock band. My wife, who ironically was working as a gerontology nurse educator at the time, had the experience of being offered a rope by the famous octogenarian after he shot past us!

Older outdoorspeople have less to prove than their younger cohorts. They make sound decisions based on their considerable experience and the prevailing conditions and can serve as good role models and mentors. There does seem to be a common factor among people who are active in the outdoors at advanced ages: they have not stopped doing it once they began. "Use it or lose it," as the saying goes, and the fact that many doctors subscribe to this principle is pretty significant. It is also never too late to start a physical activity regime to the level of your ability — if necessary, on the advice of your doctor.

Fred Beckey with the author's wife, Judy Lett, on the approach to Mount Assiniboine.

Use it or lose it! An 83-year-old Fred Beckey continues his approach on Mount Assiniboine.

TREAD CAREFULLY

When walking on a trail, and especially if bushwhacking off trail, learn to tread carefully and mindfully in order to avoid a simple but potentially disabling accident. Avoid treading on slippery down-sloping tree roots, for example, or on the bark of a dead tree that may look sound and dry but could slide off a slippery substrate. Avoid touching or leaning on dead snags that may be dangerous. One might think that if you leaned on such a tree, it would just fall over and land harmlessly away to the side, but a rotten treetop can break off and crash down on you or a companion.

Many years ago, a friend I used to hike with in Ontario, who had learned bush skills while training in the military, taught me a basic principle that I have never forgotten and still practise often: don't step on an obstacle if you can step over it; and don't step over it if you can step around it. You might vary this advice if you are working in the bush and wearing caulked boots that are designed for walking on logs, but consider this:

An accident like this can happen to anyone at any time – are you prepared to deal with the consequences if it happens to you or to a travelling companion?

POSITIVE ATTITUDE

If you do find yourself lost or in a hazardous situation, it is essential that you control any panic reaction that may naturally arise and work hard to stay calm and maintain a positive attitude. *This cannot be emphasized enough*; it may make the difference between whether you live or die. Accept whatever circumstances have happened; don't squander your energy in a state of denial or incapacitating fear. Having gained control of any initial panic response, make a quick assessment of your situation and take care of basic survival needs, first ensuring the immediate safety of yourself and your companions by taking care of imminent life-threatening circumstances or injuries. Accept that you are in trouble and that it is up to you whether and how you will survive. If the situation is serious enough, you might have to surrender to the possibility that you will die, but use your energy proactively instead of wasting it by worrying or giving up. Easy to say and tough to do, no doubt, but it could make the difference. Take some time to evaluate, decide and then act; or, following advice used by the military, Stop, Think, Observe and Plan (STOP). Don't be afraid to make decisions and stick with them, or you may find your options disappearing and decisions being made for you. Avoid complaining or blaming others. Believe in your ability to survive, and focus on what best to do next. As the situation progresses you may feel some anger – try and direct that anger toward positive actions. Take any opportunities that arise to celebrate small successes such as building a survival shelter or reaching short, achievable objectives on your journey out. And while complacency is something to avoid in all outdoor circumstances, it is even more important to do so in a survival situation. You might even pause to appreciate the beauty of your circumstance and surroundings. *Do whatever you have to do to survive, and never give up!*

REALITY CHECK: I was with a party of mountaineers halfway along a week-long trek, tent-bound for two days in driving mist and whiteout conditions above treeline, caught in a series of Pacific storms. With more bad weather on the way, we eventually took an escape route that entailed bushwhacking several kilometres down from the mountains via an untried route and then through a lower-elevation coastal rainforest. Toward the end of the day as we traversed the thickest forest with heavy packs and nightfall approaching, we had to resort at times to crawling through tunnels made by animals in the thick West Coast undergrowth. It would have been easy at that stage to become oppressed and overwhelmed by the unending enormity of the bush, but instead I found myself calmed by the beauty of the microflora of mosses and lichens from my unusually close-up vantage point.

After the storm.

PREPAREDNESS

WHEN DISASTER STRIKES

REALITY CHECK: Disaster preparedness seems to have taken on increasing significance in the past decade, beginning with the Year 2000 millennium bug that threatened the world's computerized systems and that became known as Y2K. It was particularly interesting to me, as I had begun working in information technology (IT) in the mid-1960s when computers were still in their infancy and we had to fight for every "bit" of memory space. The future consequences of using only two characters to code the year were seemingly far off and innocuous. It was a strange irony that one of my last jobs before retiring from IT in 2000 was several months spent working on Y2K. Whether it was boondoggle or reality (the truth was likely somewhere in between but leaning toward boondoggle), with years of advance warning and the likelihood of widespread trouble, hundreds of billions of dollars were spent on preparedness, and January 1, 2000, passed with hardly a whimper. Not so some 20 months later, when the world was unprepared for the events of September 11, 2001 – what became known as 9/11.

Even as international terrorism has taken centre stage, human population growth (more than doubling in my lifetime to seven billion in 2011), rising use of fossil fuels, climatic warming, planet-wide loss of biodiversity and impending economic meltdown have begun to vie for our attention. Food shortages, scarcity of fresh water, oceanic dead zones from fertilizer discharge, and disasters such as ice storms, forest fires and floods, insect pests such as the mountain pine beetle, hurricanes and deep-sea oil well blowouts seem to occur with increasing frequency and intensity all around the world. And in the background are the earthquakes, tsunamis and other periodic natural events that have always been there but that growing human population densities make ever more deadly, more economically damaging and harder to relocate away from. I am reminded of the story of a British Columbia family who, in 1981, concerned about increasing tension in the world, moved to the safest place they could find: a small, quiet island colony in the South Atlantic. In March 1982, a few months after their arrival, the Falklands War between Argentina and Britain took place over the sovereignty of the archipelago, and for three months they found themselves in the centre of the world's military hot spot.

An ice jam on British Columbia's Nechako River demonstrates the power of nature.

The grass often looks greener elsewhere, but it seldom is – at least from within one of the more fortunate parts of the world. Instead of looking for escape elsewhere, we should be ready to take care of ourselves and our environment at home. The Canadian Centre for Emergency Preparedness urges all citizens to prepare to take care of their own basic needs for at least the first 72 hours following a major disaster. The Centre recommends that every family create a plan and stock emergency supplies for their home and automobile; practise using these; and work to strengthen preparedness among neighbours. Similar preparedness principles apply to outdoor activities.

EVERYDAY PREPAREDNESS: EVACUATION

Examples of everyday preparedness that we discussed in the opening chapter on safety awareness include taking a few moments to review safety procedures when entering a crowded public space or boarding an aircraft, ferry or other public transportation or when checking in to a hotel. Every hotel room should have a diagram showing the nearest fire escape in relation to your room – get into the habit, before you even unpack your suitcase, of studying the diagram and walking to the exit, trying to imagine what you would need to know in the middle of the night in a dark, smoke-filled corridor. After doing this a few times, it will become second nature. Similarly, when boarding an aircraft, quickly count seat rows to the closest exits, then read the safety features card to review, among other things, how the various exit doors are physically opened. There are often three different kinds of emergency doors and opening mechanisms on one aircraft type, and they may differ on the connecting flight that you catch an hour or two later. I defy you to re-member from one flight to the next how to open a particular door if called upon to do so if you haven't reviewed the safety card. Then, as annoying as it may seem, pay attention to the preflight briefing. Even though you've heard it a thousand times before and you'll likely never need to put it into practice, you will wish you had listened afresh should you be involved in an emergency. Regardless of what you get out of the preflight safety briefing, the flight attendants, if they are alert, may well note those passengers who are paying attention, in the event the crew need help during an evacuation. North American air travellers have an above-average chance of surviving a crash, so it's worthwhile forgoing the fatalistic attitude that some people have about flying and do something to tip the odds in your favour.

Pay attention during safety drills.

the general public. After all, what workplace with more than a few employees does not perform its fire drills?

In the 1990s I led a workplace site evacuation team, and my stipulation to management was that we practise it once a year. If the workplace had been an industrial plant, there would have been no question of practising regularly. But ours was a modern office environment where disaster scenarios (other than fire evacuation, which was practised regularly) weren't as obvious. However, we were situated next to a mainline railway track and a large pulp mill that involved the transportation and use of large quantities of potentially dangerous chemicals.

During our first two site evacuation practices we made many mistakes, which was why we needed to practise. After a couple of years, however, it became a well-oiled event that impacted most people by no more than 15 to 30 minutes a year. This was no mean feat, considering that the evacuation meant not just leaving the building as in a fire drill, but car-pooling off-site in private vehicles. A telling moment came after a few years when a member of the team leading the evacuation missed an important step, and there was a chorus from the assembled staff reminding us what we had missed. They had got it – the whole office was a team. Others have said about similar practices: "We hate the drills every week, but they work!" and "My brain just went on auto and I did what I was supposed to do." To be sure, a real situation would have thrown new curves at us, but we had a well-practised framework, with options that would have allowed us to work different scenarios.

The evacuation test was always mounted as a surprise, but we were sensible about scheduling it to avoid undue business impact, thereby ensuring management's continuing support instead of seeing it as a hit to the bottom line. Twenty years later, and ten years after I had left the company, I visited the same building, now under new ownership, and was delighted to see that the site evacuation procedure and practice were still in effect and being taken seriously.

Historical note: Our site evacuation procedure came about under a directive from one of our parent companies as a result of the industrial disaster at a pesticide plant in Bhopal, India, in December 1984. Half a million people were exposed to a release of poisonous gas and toxins from the plant and up to 15,000 people are estimated to have died from immediate and long-term effects. All too often, safety measures are taken after something has happened, and while it is essential to learn from such experiences, it is better to anticipate and act on safety concerns before problems occur.

REALITY CHECK: In the 1970s, I worked in the Canadian National Telecommunications building on Front Street in downtown Toronto, and my office on the sixth floor overlooked the construction site for the CN Tower. Because of its prominent profile as the world's tallest free-standing structure at that time, its location in the centre of a major city, and the obvious hazards of its construction, a determined effort was made that no lives would be lost building it. Thus, huge safety nets were suspended from the tower as I watched it slowly rise into the sky, and to the best of my knowledge, no lives were lost.

By comparison, until recently, it was accepted that a high number of worker deaths was a normal part of the dangerous business of doing forestry in British Columbia and elsewhere. Now, a significant push toward zero fatalities is starting to have an effect in BC, although there is still a long way to go. It is evident that a high level of safety can be achieved if the will is there; and there is a trend among business executives to view safety as an opportunity for greater productivity rather than an unwarranted expense. Some forest industry leaders have found that where there are safety issues, such as in a wood-processing plant, there are also significant long-term business efficiencies to be had. However, daily productivity achievement is so ingrained in middle managers that it usually takes a strong push from the top to accept short-term productivity loss in order to achieve greater worker safety and the long-term higher productivity that often accompanies it.

OUTDOOR PREPAREDNESS

An important requirement of any outdoor activity is to try to prepare for whatever eventuality might reasonably be expected to happen. This usually means acquiring knowledge through some sort of training, and then developing and applying that knowledge through practice and experience. As suggested earlier, a good way to start is to participate with an organized group or club to gain the basic experience you will need before striking out with just family or friends. Higher-risk sports such as caving (there are many caves in Canada, especially in British Columbia and Alberta) should always be done through a reputable group – underground is never a place to go without experienced companions. You certainly wouldn't go sky diving or scuba diving without training and a support group, and caving is no different. Most large communities have hundreds of clubs of all kinds and there is almost no reason why anyone would have to learn an outdoor pursuit the hard way. Resources can generally be found through a municipal office or city hall, public library, newspapers,

Internet and word of mouth. For those who are visiting or are new to a community, local clubs generally welcome newcomers and ad hoc participants.

Caving should always be done with a knowledgeable group.

A rule of thumb for many outdoor clubs is to allow prospective new members or visitors to participate in one or two trips before asking them to take out a membership. Or there might be a small one-time user fee, perhaps to cover liability insurance. For those who don't have the time, inclination or opportunity to participate in a club, many locales have commercially guided outdoor recreation opportunities. Such resources can easily be researched online, and if you are travelling, they may help you to decide or refine your destination ahead of time.

Both mental and physical preparedness are essential assets in survival situations that may arise in the outdoors. This means thinking through the "what ifs." What if there is an injury or sign of hypothermia or heat exhaustion? What if you are lost or have underestimated the time that is required to return before dark? What if you meet a bear blocking your return trail or capsize a canoe on a lonely stretch of river; or if a member of your party gets trapped in an avalanche, stumbles into a snow or rock crevasse, falls through lake ice or goes missing in a whiteout on a ridgetop? Do you have the self-rescue know-how and gear you may need? Have you made sure a reliable person at home has your itinerary and a list of participants? Does someone in the group have first aid skills and equipment? Does everyone in the party have enough raingear and warm clothing to spend one or two nights out if you can't make it back that day? Does your day pack contain the essentials: raingear, extra clothing, fire-starters, first aid kit, headlamp, food and water?

TECHNOLOGICAL INNOVATION

Weigh the pros and cons of new technology such as synthetic clothing, global positioning systems, wristwatch altimeters, satellite phones and emergency beacons, even portable electric fences to keep wildlife away from your tent at night on remote wilderness canoe trips when gear weight isn't so much of a problem. Cell phones, two-way radios and satellite phones (whichever works best for your budget and your locale) are definitely worthwhile taking along, but except for practising with them to ensure proficiency and coverage in the event of an emergency, and perhaps for updating an itinerary, they are best carried as tools of last resort and not relied on as substitutes for common sense and the ability to self-rescue. If too many people get into trouble in the outdoors and need rescuing, we will inevitably see the evolution of fee-for-service rescue and rescue insurance, as is already the case in some jurisdictions. In my view, it would be a shame if communities lose the volunteer and camaraderie aspect of search and rescue.

REALITY CHECK: One person's idea of common sense can differ from another's, and may depend on an individual's level of skill and experience. A situation that surprised me was seeing two young men set out up a steep, forested trail on mountain bikes wearing very lightweight riding gear. This was a real mountain, not just hilly terrain near the city, and they had almost nothing else with them. They appeared to be equipped for an optimal, all-out cardiovascular effort as if they were at a gym in town. They had made scant provision that I could see for an injury that might occur while riding in the mountains, an undertaking that could hardly be considered low risk. On the same trail a decade earlier I witnessed a young woman sprain both ankles just walking, while descending, tired, late in the day in slippery conditions – she had earlier resisted suggestions that her footwear was not adequate for the terrain, insisting she was a runner and had strong ankles.

PRACTICE

There is no substitute for experience and having good equipment, and I recommend that anyone who spends time in the backcountry take a survival course that includes spending one night, and preferably two, out in the bush. The psychological pressures faced during an unexpected overnighter, and how you deal with them, will make the difference between an adventure that builds confidence and a frightening experience that you may not survive. Having experienced unplanned bivouacs (improvised camps) alone in mountain country, I can attest that having practised in a safe setting made all the difference for me after I made the psychologically difficult decision to stop. I knew from practical experience that I had the skills to do what I had to do instead of worrying or panicking about it.

FIRST AID TRAINING

The same is true for first aid training because of the extensive hands-on practice that usually goes with it. Many people who have taken first aid training will affirm that doing first aid in a classroom or in a certification examination can be more stressful than the real thing. With a real first aid case, not only is all the attention and support directed toward the victim and not the responder, but those around are usually eager to help. A wilderness first aid course is the best type for outdoor activities because of its emphasis on improvisation. But any first aid training is worth having, and the principles involved in the priority assessment of an injured person can be applied to other emergencies as well.

BENEFIT FROM HISTORICAL ACCOUNTS

You can find enjoyment, learning and inspiration in reading some of the great outdoor adventure and survival stories of the past. Then, if you are ever in a tight spot, the knowledge of what others have achieved in far worse situations than you are ever likely to find yourself in will help you to deal with the psychological stressors and your responses to them. Unwarranted despair can quickly lead to disaster, and knowing something of the experiences of others can help you to avoid that consequence. Appendix A lists works I have found inspirational; there are many others and new stories are emerging all the time.

4 PREPARATION, PLANNING AND PRACTICE

There is a difference between general *preparedness* as discussed in the previous section, and specific *preparation* as outlined below. There are overlaps, but the former is more about your approach to the outdoors – your state of mind, training and experience – while the latter is more about actual preparatory steps you can take before a trip. Below are some explicit ways to improve your chance of surviving and perhaps even of enjoying an unexpected problem situation in the outdoors. But first, here is an amusing real-life situation that straddles both sides of the topic:

REALITY CHECK: The occasion was an overnight backpacking trip to the McGregor Mountains in north central British Columbia. One of the participants was a man whose main recreational interest had been private flying and who had little backpacking or backcountry experience. His aim was to gain practical knowledge that might one day help him in the event his aircraft were downed in the bush or mountains. So far, so good: preparation and practice for a possible aviation incident with knowledgeable companions. However, as he did not have much backpacking gear, he went out and bought everything he needed in one fell swoop. The result was that in order to keep his costs reasonable, the new equipment was not of the best quality.

As the man struggled up the steep mountain trail using muscles that weren't yet conditioned to climbing, some of his new gear literally started to come apart at the seams. Somehow he made it to the alpine and passed the night relatively unscathed, as the mild weather was gentle on his cheap sleeping bag and tent. But it turned out the next morning that he was also ill-prepared with food. Over breakfast we saw him looking hungrily at and finally asking for one of the dog biscuits somebody's canine companion was devouring. I don't recall seeing him on another mountain hike, which was a shame because he might have returned if he had had a better first-time experience. But the fact that he achieved what he did with good humour spoke well for his strength of character and his willingness to improvise, and I thought he would likely do well in an aircraft survival situation.

How could this have been approached differently? It would have been better if this man had started with easier hiking trips and then advanced to day trips into the mountains, gradually gaining experience and fitness and slowly acquiring better-quality equipment, beginning with a good backpack and sleeping bag. He could have asked for advice on food and equipment; and perhaps when he was ready for his first overnight mountain trip, he could have shared a tent with someone instead of buying everything at once. Anyone who tries to do too much, too quickly, risks getting turned off the activity for the wrong reasons. If, on the other hand, this individual had simply wanted to gain outdoor survival experience quickly, he could have signed up for a survival course or gone on a trip with a commercial outfitter, where food and equipment would have been supplied.

DOWN TO SPECIFICS

Following are some suggestions for ways to prepare and practise for the outdoors. This list speaks to a range of outdoor experience and activities, so try not to be intimidated by too much information if you are just starting out. Take from it what is most appropriate for you, today, and build on it over time.

- Develop some knowledge and experience through seminars and courses, from mentors and peers, and through the study of texts and resources such as the examples mentioned herein. As a minimum, I recommend that you finish this book and sign up for a basic first aid course.
- Consider group size and group dynamics such as personalities, good sense of humour, likes and dislikes, distances likely to be travelled each day, differences in physical and mental conditioning, personal equipment, outdoor skills and willingness to stay together. Try to avoid macho personalities that may be more prone to get themselves and others into trouble yet prove to be anything but macho in a tight spot. Also avoid chronic complainers, who can drain group energy. That's not to say that difficult personalities can't be changed or managed with good leadership, but choose your companions well! What is the right number of people? The adage that there is safety in numbers does not always apply. For example, in mountaineering a maximum of three to eight people (one or two ropes) may be safest. Similar limitations may apply if you are bushwhacking off trail. Regardless of the type of trip, if there are more than six people, the leader may have to count heads from time to time to keep track of everyone. It depends a lot on the situation, but in my experience of leading many hiking, skiing and snowshoeing trips, ideal group sizes are between three and a dozen people. A group of 20 or more in the backcountry can become nightmarish for the leader and not very appealing for participants. So, if you have more than, say, 15 people

and there is more than one experienced leader available, consider splitting the group along the lines of interests, abilities, fitness and speed.

- Plan your trip carefully, paying attention to road and access conditions, weather reports and forecasts, maps (minimum 1:50,000 scale topographical), terrain, snow conditions and creeks and rivers. Obtain local knowledge whenever you can. Web-based mapping and visualizing tools can also be a great help. Allow sufficient time for planning and preparation that is appropriate to the nature and duration of your trip, and involve everyone in planning for longer trips. Monitor conditions close to the time of the trip and continue to plan ahead and adapt while on the trail.

- Ensure there is a common understanding of the objectives among the participants; try to avoid a situation where individuals create ideas of their own that are in conflict with group objectives. Everyone should also be aware of any likely hazards and of the need for a disciplined approach to safety. In order to keep everyone's experience enjoyable and avoid creating unnecessary risks, look for a balance between expectations, experience, ability and objectives.

- Use only good-quality equipment and take adequate equipment, clothing, food and water. There will be more details on this to follow. If you are short on funds, acquire quality equipment slowly rather than buying cheaper equipment all at once as recounted in the above *Reality Check*. If you are a member of an outdoors club, you may be able to buy or borrow quality used equipment cheaply from somebody who is upgrading or has surplus gear. Other options are to improvise or possibly to rent gear from an outdoor equipment store, which would have the added advantage of allowing you to gain experience while sampling different types and makes of equipment.

- Use only good-quality footwear that is appropriate for both your trip and the weight you are carrying. For heavy loads and/or rough or steep terrain, this means having good ankle support. Break in new boots on shorter trips before wearing them on longer excursions.

- Check, repair or upgrade your equipment before leaving: replace consumables such as batteries in radios, satellite phones, GPS units, avalanche transceivers, flashlights, cameras. It helps if as many of your devices as possible use the same type of batteries, such as AA or AAA, for interchangeability.

- Always try to anticipate what might happen. For example, what if the slowest member of the group slows down even more – will you make it back before dark? What if the leader or guide you are dependent on gets injured? What if you decide to deviate from your stated route and then have the misfortune of being immobilized? What are the possible consequences and what options would you have? As you move along, be mindful that even a very minor injury could be debilitating or spell disaster in the backcountry.

- As you become more independent in the outdoors, practise bush survival shelter construction and spend at least one and preferably two nights in one. Beware of the risk of injury through the unfamiliar and incautious use of an axe, knife or saw while shelter building or of taking a tree branch in the eye if you move around after dark. I've seen these kinds of things happen on supervised survival courses, and it's obviously more serious if you are alone. Practise an overnighter in at least one type of survival shelter to develop skills that will help you to reduce your stress if you are ever caught out unexpectedly. Having rehearsed a bivouac, then you know you can do it, and more than half the battle is won. This can be practised in a safe setting, with ready escape to a nearby building or vehicle and/or as part of a supervised survival course. At the very least, make sure somebody knows where you are and what you are doing.

- Similarly for winter travel, practise different types of snow survival shelter construction and spend at least one night in one. In the mountains, an excavated snowdrift or a quickly dug "foxhole" in the side of a depression in the snowpack around the base of a tree may be the best option. If you are caught out in a prairie winter storm, knowing how to build a powder snow shelter, or quinzhee, may save your life. Because of the risk of suffocation inside an improperly vented snow shelter, or the gradual or sudden collapse of an improperly built one, this is best learned as part of a course or with experienced companions. It may be obvious to say this, but do not build a snow shelter where a snowplow might get it. There is more on snow shelters later in the book.

- Practise a two-nighter. This will take your practical skill to a much higher level, that of dealing with the psychological stress of sitting through an entire day-night cycle with little to do. You'll be surprised at how intense this is for someone used to the bustle and conveniences of the modern world. For added impact, this can be done (preferably in a supervised winter survival course with escape options for safety purposes) where participants are dropped off individually, late in the day, without knowing where they are.

- Anyone can light a fire when conditions are dry, so practise fire lighting in the wettest, windiest, coldest and snowiest conditions. You might, for example, have to cut deeply into a dead tree to find dry kindling after hours or days of steady rain. Once the fire has developed a sufficient bed of hot coals, it should be self-sustaining even with damp fuel. There is little reason to die of exposure in the forested landscape that is never very far away in much of Canada, and this skill will give you the confidence to look upon forests for warmth and shelter. Beware of starting a forest fire when conditions are dry (you shouldn't need a fire in those circumstances); and always clear the ground down to non-combustible mineral soil or bedrock for a good distance around the fire, and fully extinguish it when you leave.
- Develop physical and mental preparedness. Maintaining a positive attitude, regardless of what happens, is crucial.
- Coach and teach your companions while you are on the trail. Apart from any philanthropic considerations, your life may depend on your partner's ability to find his or her way back if you are injured. Lying badly wounded with a compound leg fracture and shock is obviously not the best time to teach your companion how to use a compass or find a back trail!
- If something untoward has happened, stay calm. Secure the scene by ensuring that everyone is safe from immediate further harm. Evaluate the situation and engage your problem-solving skills. Decide on the most feasible options and then act.
- Continually re-evaluate conditions, route, weather and people (whether or not you are the leader) throughout an outdoor trip. Recognize and anticipate changes in the weather.
- Be prepared, if necessary and if possible, to abandon the trip. On a one-way route, it is important, if at all practical, to have preplanned escape routes along the way.
- Always be prepared to improvise in the outdoors.

REALITY CHECK: I first encountered this renowned outdoorsman in the early 1980s during a presentation he gave on his 40-day, 800-kilometre snowshoe trek, alone in the winter wilderness of northern British Columbia. Partway through Fred Van der Post's amazing 1982 solo trek, after he had survived a fall through the ice as described in the *Reality Check* at p. 9, the frame of one of his snowshoes failed across the critical front piece while he was crossing the high, exposed Spatsizi Plateau. Temporarily backtracking to treeline, he ingeniously repaired the snowshoe so that it not only lasted the several hundred more kilometres remaining of that trek, but for a further four years of heavy on-the-job field use before an entirely different part of the shoe failed. Fred knew he had to repair it in such a way that it would not keep failing or promote weakness elsewhere in the snowshoe, so he hunted for several hours for just the right curved piece of dense black spruce, plus the means of leverage to insert it into the tubular frame.

Someone in the audience later asked him a question that has stayed with me for nearly a quarter of a century, "What would you have done if you couldn't have fixed it?" Fred stood transfixed, speechless for a good half minute before answering expressively, "You have to fix it – you have no choice!" The question of not being able to do what he had to do was just not in Fred's vocabulary, and he had struggled to answer a question that he couldn't imagine anyone asking. This is the essential "can do" attitude you must cultivate when you are away from the conveniences and security blanket of modern life.

Snowshoeing on a blustery spring day in the mountains of BC's Sugarbowl/Grizzly Den Provincial Park requires good equipment and the wherewithal to repair it.

WHAT KIND OF PROBLEMS CAN OCCUR?

Although most outdoor trips are enjoyable and uneventful, there are many scenarios where things can go wrong. The following list may alert you to some of these possibilities. I have loosely organized them under the headings People, Equipment and Environment; although there are grey areas and overlaps. Keep these in mind as you prepare for a trip, and continue to re-evaluate risks when you are in the field. Try adding to this list from things that have happened to you or acquaintances of yours.

PEOPLE

- You are lost or not quite where you expected to be.
- You have underestimated the time needed to return to your vehicle and have been caught out by approaching nightfall.
- You or a member of your party has suffered an injury of sufficient severity to slow you down or stop you altogether. In winter, an injury to one member of the party can put everyone at risk if you can't reach your destination before nightfall. It might be as simple as a bad blister, severe cramping, a minor sprain or a recurrent old injury. Or it could be more serious, one of a long list of possibilities: a disabling sprain, dislocation, fracture, compound fracture, severe cut or abrasion, crush injury or concussion resulting from rockfall, bleeding, embedded object, eye injury, snow blindness, cold or heat injury, animal bite, spinal injury, shock (usually accompanying and compounding something else), insect sting with an allergic reaction, snakebite. There are endless possibilities, and it's important to recognize that an injury such as a broken leg is much more serious in the backcountry than in town and may well become life-threatening.
- Someone in your group has a pre-existing medical condition that has suddenly become a problem, such as hypoglycemia (low blood sugar) in a diabetic, a heart ailment, an allergic reaction to an insect sting, epilepsy, asthma.
- When someone in a backcountry party gets sick or injured, no matter how small a matter it might appear at the moment, this is no time for selfish bravado. That person owes it to the group to inform the leader before it possibly becomes a larger problem that could compromise the safety of the group.

47

- Some in the group are exhausted as a result of underestimating the strenuousness of the activity or conditioning for it. Once you have accepted people into your party, you are only as fast as the slowest member.

REALITY CHECK: A small percentage of otherwise healthy people are severely allergic to insect stings, and a few deaths from this occur in the outdoors each year. Most insect stings result in only localized reactions and swellings that may last up to a few days, but in a few people, anaphylactic shock can, within minutes or hours, result in swelling of the tongue, difficulty breathing and swallowing, and dizziness. In such cases, urgent medical attention is required. Individuals already diagnosed with allergies may wear medical alert tags and carry injection adrenaline kits.

EQUIPMENT

- Your equipment has failed. Perhaps you broke a ski or a snowshoe and it has slowed you down or stopped you.
- Your vehicle is stuck or broken in the backcountry. Perhaps you left the lights on and the battery is flat, or it's too cold to start, or you've had two successive flat tires on an unpaved backcountry road, a circumstance that is not uncommon when driving over sharp rock such as shale.
- Your snowmobile has become immobilized and it is too far or the snow is too deep to hike out. Motorized recreationists are likely to have a different problem than self-propelled outdoorspeople, as they may be stranded farther from help and unable to walk out, especially in winter. It is therefore even more essential to have left a detailed itinerary and to have good survival preparation.
- Your boat has capsized, whether in flat or swift water, resulting in wet clothes, delay, or loss of emergency gear, leaving you stranded with no transportation and few supplies. A common accident scenario in wooded country can arise from river canoeing during spring high water and the attendant possibility of losing canoe, gear or life to a sweeper (tree branch hanging low over the water) or logjam.

ENVIRONMENT

- Terrain problems have slowed you down or caused you to take a different, possibly longer and unexpectedly difficult route. Unplanned bushwhacking can easily quadruple the amount of time needed to cover an equivalent distance on a good trail. It only takes one member of a party to start freezing up or, worse, "freaking out" when the bush starts to become nearly impenetrable. Suddenly you've got a more serious problem, with risks of frustration and early signs of panic infecting others. Then, a leader might assign one or two people to work closely with the person having difficulty, and endeavour to lighten or bolster the mood of the party as a whole. If the situation continues to deteriorate, a firmer stance may be required.

- There has been an unexpected change in weather, with rain, snow, wind, poor visibility or lightning.

Poor visibility in complex terrain may slow you down.

- Your clothes have become wet through sweat, rain or immersion in cold water, resulting in discomfort and the risk of hypothermia. High winds may be a contributing factor. You broke through lake or river ice, resulting in wet clothes, possible hypothermia, frostbite, delay or rerouting.
- You slipped while crossing a steep grassy slope made slick by rain, frost or snow and slid downward, hitting rocks or falling over a cliff.
- You are trapped in an ice or snow crevasse or in rough terrain after a boulder moved and pinned you down, or perhaps in a fissure or pothole after ground or

snow cover collapsed under you. People have died when travelling alone (especially when off their planned route) after being caught in this manner.

REALITY CHECK: In August 1998 a man on day four of a nine-day solo backpacking trek in Wyoming's Fitzpatrick Wilderness stepped on a large granite rock that moved and pinned him by the legs. Uninjured, but trapped, there was nothing he could do to move the car-sized boulder. Despite never giving up, and exercising utmost efforts to survive after the incident, he had chosen to backpack alone, without a communications device, and he had deviated from his planned route. He died nine days later, before searchers could find him. A pastor by profession, he kept a journal of his last days. His sobering story was recounted by Jeff Rennicke in a 2002 *Backpacker Magazine* article entitled "Trapped!"

REALITY CHECK: In 2003 another solo mountaineer, Aron Ralston, was pinned by the arm by an estimated 400-kilogram boulder in a remote slot canyon in Utah. After five days, he took the drastic action of amputating his trapped arm below the elbow using a pocket knife, before rappelling to the bottom of the canyon and hiking out. Ralston told his story in his 2004 autobiography *Between a Rock and a Hard Place*, later made into a film called *127 Hours*.

Others who have tried the similar drastic step of amputation to escape entrapment have died of loss of blood and shock, such as the case of an Australian outback worker forced to sever his arm at the shoulder in 1912. Today, a better answer to the risk of entrapment if you must travel alone in the backcountry is to carry a small satellite communications device. (See chapter 20, Communications, at p. 125.)

- You have been delayed by high water causing a diversion. Delay, immersion, or loss of food or gear caused by a flash flood are risks when camped by a mountain creek or in a desert gulch.
- You had a wildlife encounter, resulting in delay, diversion or injury or death of one of your party.
- You were delayed by the need for avalanche avoidance or rescue. You or a member of your party got caught in an avalanche, with resulting hypothermia, trauma injuries or death.

Snowshoeing up onto a flat mountaintop, the author suddenly encountered isothermal snow that collapsed and trapped him by his snowshoes. Even though it only took a few minutes to dig out, it demonstrated what could happen in less forgiving circumstances.

- You were caught in a windstorm, causing delay, route blockage, loss of gear or direct injury caused by flying or falling debris.
- A forest fire blocked your route or, worse, you were trapped in the middle of one as happened to a party of hikers near Vanderhoof, BC, in the spring of 2005.

These possible problem scenarios are not usually reasons to stay home, but they ought to heighten your awareness of what you are undertaking. Thinking about potential consequences of your outdoor situation (and the actions you would then have to take) should become second nature.

PSYCHOLOGY OF SURVIVAL

In order to prepare for and respond to a survival situation, it helps to understand the stressors that are acting on you, and your involuntary and voluntary responses to them. It also helps to know that many of these responses are normal human reactions. What really counts is not so much that you are having stress reactions, but how you deal with them. Mental preparedness and maintaining a positive attitude and the will to live are of paramount importance in a survival situation.

REALITY CHECK: In his book, *Miracle in the Andes* (see Appendix A at p. 256), Nando Parrado describes the way many of his fellow survivors of a 1972 air crash high in the Andes initially drew on their religious faith and the support of their companions to see them through the first few weeks. In time, however, they came to realize that they were entirely reliant on their own resources, and ultimately it was due to the strength, preparation and will of one man, an unlikely hero, that they were rescued. Parrado and one companion endured the most arduous and technically difficult nine-day walk out through high, glaciated mountains. The only thing that kept them going, Parrado said later, was simply that there was no other option. Because of his actions, all of the remaining survivors were rescued ten days later.

POSSIBLE STRESSORS

- The surprise of an unexpected situation.
- Fear of the unknown and an urge to react quickly without thinking things through; an impulse to solve the problem and to get out of a fearful situation as quickly as possible.
- An overwhelming sense of anxiety, panic and even despair.
- Fear of animals and of the dark, especially the prospect of the long, cold, dark night ahead and an uncertain tomorrow.
- You did not leave an itinerary and although this predicament was eminently avoidable (see the section on leaving an itinerary, at p. 56), no one knows where to start looking for you or perhaps even that you are out there. The knowledge that nobody is coming looking for you will add more stress to an already bad situation.

- You are suffering from pain, cold, possible injury, shock and, depending on the season, swarms of biting insects.
- There are insidious problems such as exhaustion, hypothermia or hyperthermia in yourself or other members of your group. This may have led to an inability to self-help if it went undetected or if dealing with it was put off for too long.
- You disregarded advice not to travel alone, giving rise to increased danger, loneliness, a heightened sense of fear, and no one to discuss the situation with.
- You had an earlier problem and did not stay put, with the result that you may have confounded your prospect of finding your own way out, as well as increasing the challenge for searchers.
- You have inadequate shelter for spending a night or two outside, and you may lack knowledge and practice to make one.
- Societal pressures may be causing you to want to push on when really you should stop. These pressures may include disruption of a busy schedule you had planned; embarrassment; or worry caused to family, friends and colleagues.

REALITY CHECK: Aviators sometimes call this "get-home-itis," when they push on into worsening weather and end up crashing into a hillside, as many have done in Canada's mountain provinces.

- After you have stopped, boredom and anxiety may bolster the earlier impulse to move and to try and solve the problem as quickly as possible.

GENERAL RESPONSES

In responding to stressors, and depending on how you use it, your mind is likely to be your best asset or your worst enemy. According to Thomas Homer-Dixon, human intelligence and ingenuity have been powerful aids to our development as a species, and are potent aids for survival.[5] As the celebrated British physicist and philosopher David Deutsch noted in his groundbreaking 2011 work,[6]

> Problems are inevitable. We shall always be faced with the problem of how to plan for an unknowable future. We shall never be able to afford to sit back and hope for the best. And some problems will be hard problems, but it is a mistake to confuse hard problems with problems that are unlikely to be solved. Problems are solvable.

And from political leader Jack Layton's "Letter to Canadians," written on August 20, 2011, two days before his death: "Love is better than anger. Hope is better than fear. Optimism is better than despair. So let us be loving, hopeful and optimistic. And we'll change the world."

- Your initial feelings of surprise, fear and perhaps panic are normal, and knowledge of this fact will help you deal with them. But fear can quickly turn to blind panic and must be controlled. As a former US president, Franklin Delano Roosevelt, famously said, "The greatest thing we have to fear is fear itself."
- There are natural physiological responses to stressful situations that supply needed short term resources, but that can in the long run be physically draining. They include the production of adrenaline, muscles becoming tense and the liver releasing glucose.
- The strongest person can be very quickly weakened by the stressors listed above, and it is sometimes the least expected person in a group who emerges as a mainstay to help steady the others.

REALITY CHECK: On a mountain trek a few years ago, I went through the usual process of sizing up my companions whom I had not known before the trip. I identified one strong-looking individual as someone who would likely be a mainstay if the going got tough. Several days later, the situation did get difficult and after being storm-bound in our tents for 40 hours on an exposed ridge, we decided to bail. The seemingly endless descent through unexplored terrain started in whiteout conditions above treeline and ended in nearly impenetrable underbrush. The person I had earlier identified as a likely source of strength began to show signs of stress, and another member of the party stepped forward to calm the group and support the leader. It was a surprising turn of events, one that brought a fresh dynamic to the group to see us through a difficult day.

- Cultivate survival skills so that you can better direct your response to the stressors. Have confidence in your knowledge and experience; concentrate on the problem; be realistic, decisive, adaptive and patient; be prepared to improvise. Control your fears; remain calm; and *maintain the will to live – regardless of setbacks.* Be mentally and physically prepared for an unexpected survival experience before it happens to you: have a plan and use it.

Forests typically provide all the materials necessary for shelter.

SAFETY PROCEDURES

LEAVE AN ITINERARY

When you are going on a trip, leave an itinerary with a trusted person. This should preferably be someone like a spouse who has a keen vested interest in your safe return.

Prior to filling out your itinerary, check weather, snow conditions (if relevant) and any other special hazards in the area you are going to and include that in the itinerary. Even if you are travelling with a group, an itinerary is still important, since even with good check-in and check-out procedures, someone might slip through the cracks and then become separated from a group without the others being aware of it. Or the whole group may become compromised: for example, a large hiking party nearly became trapped by a fast-moving forest fire at the confluence of the Nechako and Stuart rivers east of Vanderhoof, BC. It would have been useful for fire crews to have had information about the trip and would likely have changed their response priorities. If there are still variables or undetermined route options as you are starting out on your trip, provide details of those in your itinerary. For example, if you are unsure which of several trailheads you will use, provide a list of options (presumably in the same general area) and details of your vehicle(s). It won't take searchers long to establish which of them was your start point. If you have communications capability – satellite phone, cell phone or radio – update your itinerary and status with your contact person in the event of any significant changes to your stated plans, especially on a multi-day trip. This will enhance the effectiveness and reduce the cost of any search and rescue efforts that may become necessary later.

Many organizations have developed itinerary checklists, and government emergency programs and search and rescue organizations sometimes have ready-made checklists that can be downloaded from their websites. Following are some suggestions you can include in your checklist and customize for your personal or group use.

- Planned start: day of the week, date and time.
- Intended return: day of the week, date and time. Having set a return time that includes a reasonable cushion for unforeseen circumstances, you must make every effort to achieve that, barring major problems.
- Length of time your contact should wait beyond your expected return time before notifying the authorities. This will depend on such things as the length of the

trip; how well you know the terrain; food and equipment; weather (major storm); creek crossings (high water); and degree of comfort with your group's skills and strength. For a day trip, this extra wait time may be a few hours; for a multi-day trip it might be 24 hours; and for a major expedition lasting a few weeks, it could be several days or more.

- Information on which authorities to contact (usually the police, except in national parks, where it would more likely be the warden service) and phone number.
- Purpose of the trip and any hazardous techniques to be employed during it such as scrambling, creek-crossing, caving or travelling in avalanche terrain.
- Location of the trip: general area, specific area, intended route in, destination, intended route out.
- Alternative route (plan b) and/or escape route, for example, from a long, exposed ridge traverse.
- Map sheet numbers; any relevant map or GPS coordinates.
- Vehicle(s): make(s) and model(s), colour(s), licence number(s).
- Group equipment and supplies taken; any communication and signalling devices.

For each person on the trip:

- Full name.
- Description: gender, age, height, weight, hair colour, skin colour.
- Vision: any corrective eyeglasses or contact lenses required.
- Disabilities, past injuries, medical conditions, allergies; personal medications such as insulin for a diabetic.
- Description and colour of clothing, especially hat, shirt, coat, pants that are likely to be spotted by a searcher.
- Footwear used – this might provide essential information for a searcher, especially if you deliberately leave tracks when you encounter soft or muddy ground.
- Name and telephone number of contact person.
- General outdoor experience.
- Specific relevant outdoor training and experience such as first aid, navigation, bear safety and avalanche and wilderness survival.
- Personal safety equipment carried, such as first aid kit, avalanche beacon, personal radio or satellite communications device.

This may sound like a lot to do for a day hike in the woods, but it needn't be a difficult chore if you preprint some basic information. Keep a few forms handy at home and in your vehicle and fill out what seems appropriate for the particular trip. Anything is better than nothing, but if something goes wrong and a search party has to look for you, the more information you provide, the greater the likelihood and speed of finding you.

REALITY CHECK: When you fill out your itinerary, try this mind game: imagine you are lying injured and immobile on a mountainside, in dense, wet bush amid clouds of biting mosquitoes. What do you wish you had written down about your trip plans?

Injured or lost, off trail, on an inhospitable mountainside: what is it you wished you had said in your pretrip itinerary?

If you're not sure which trail you are going to hike until you get out there, then at least leave a list of options and a description of your vehicle. If you have failed to leave an itinerary of some sort with someone before leaving home, if nothing else leave an itinerary or even a note on the dashboard of your vehicle at the trailhead. Some (park) jurisdictions recommend that your estimated return time not be visible to the casual passerby to avoid a possible invitation to break into your vehicle.

CHECKING OUT AND CHECKING BACK IN

As with the itinerary, most organizations have formal procedures for checking people out for an activity and checking them back in at the end. Such procedures often include liability waivers in the case of non-profit organizations and commercial recreation ventures. In case of an employer or institution, individual itineraries or personal data sheets may be required. If you are doing fieldwork for a company, government or university, find out about their safety procedures and what is required of both you and your supervisor. Take those requirements seriously because they are for your protection. For the institution it may be due diligence, while for you it's your life on the line. British Columbia's natural resource ministries, for example, require that helicopters flying on government business check in by radio with the ministry office every half hour or so with a current position and their immediate plans. This is especially important in the case of a wildly varying flight plan, such as looking for and counting mountain caribou or chasing radio-collared wolves, as I've been fortunate to be invited to do on several occasions. It was reassuring to hear the position check every half hour, although you can cover a lot of ground in a helicopter in that time. Alternatively, some aircraft now continuously transmit their GPS coordinates so that a flight track can be automatically kept back at the office.

each participant to complete a one-page fieldwork critical data form. As well, for optional or voluntary activities, a one-page liability waiver was required to be signed by each participant. One of the objectives of the seminar was to make people familiar with these very safety requirements. But it's also important that safety forms and procedures be kept as simple as possible consistent with their purpose in order to increase the likelihood of their being used. This one was more suitable to major expeditions and field seasons than to short field trips.

REALITY CHECK: Most non-profit outdoor clubs and for-profit adventure companies require participants to read, understand and sign a liability waiver as part of their safety procedures, due diligence measures and as a requirement for their insurance. If used thoughtfully, this exercise can enhance the safety briefing at the start of the trip.

Checking out at the start of your trip is only half the story – don't forget the equally important obligation to check back in at the end. Some government organizations such as park managers may offer check-out and check-in services to the public, and in some instances they may levy a fine or charge back any search and rescue costs if you fail to check back in. If you use your own check-out and check-in procedures, it's better to develop a standard that you use all the time rather than rely on some ad hoc process. Ad hoc procedures are better than nothing, but they can be fraught with risk, as both I and my contact person found out to our chagrin a few years ago:

REALITY CHECK: Heading out into the mountains on a solo hike, I phoned a friend whom I had never approached for such a purpose before and asked him to be my contact for the day. Travelling solo in the mountains is not recommended, but if you do it, there is all the more reason to leave reliable information. My trip was uneventful, but on returning home that evening I forgot to phone my contact, who, coincidentally, also forgot I was out there. This was a one-off event, and our combined forgetfulness of the ad hoc protocol we had agreed on is evidence of the fallibility of the human mind in the absence of written and tested procedures. This is one reason why aircrews use detailed checklists even though they have gone through the same preflight procedure many hundreds of times before. The consequences of our mutual memory lapse could have had disastrous consequences for me if I had been injured; or it could have caused the embarrassment and cost of an unnecessary search. As it turned out, it was three or four days later that my phone rang. Fortunately I was there to answer it; otherwise a search might have been called. My contact burst out, "Mike! Thank god you're alive!" Apparently he had been out for dinner at a downtown restaurant with his wife and friends when he had suddenly remembered our pact. Jumping up from the table in mid-meal with a sudden cry, he abandoned his astonished companions and dashed off to look for a telephone without further explanation. It was a humorous end to a potentially serious situation, and I had learned a valuable lesson.

A few years ago, a Canadian website began offering a free check-out and check-in service for backcountry recreation. It required preregistering personal details and then entering itineraries for each specific trip. The site presumably looked to advertising revenue as its business model, which struck me as something a bit precarious to hang one's life on. But it was easy to foresee such systems being connected to satellites and GPS for continuous updates. Biologists have been using similar technology for years to track GPS-collared animals such as threatened woodland caribou and grizzly bears and to feed position and status reports to Internet-accessible databases. Although the original website may no longer be there, continuous tracking is now available through GPS personal trackers. (See chapter 20 on Communications, p. 125.)

REALITY CHECK: In his book *Into the Wild* (listed in Appendix A), Jon Krakauer narrates a side-story of a 35-year-old amateur photographer who arranged to be dropped off by floatplane in the spring in Alaska's remote Brooks Range, where he would spend several months alone in the wilderness. The photographer's diary, found with his remains nearly a year later, records that in arranging his itinerary, he simply forgot to arrange for a pickup. In a sobering note for anyone who has ever chartered a floatplane and who has sat waiting for an overdue pickup, he wrote in August: "I think I should have used more foresight about arranging my departure."

Don't make this mistake!

8 EQUIPMENT FOR AN UNEXPECTED OVERNIGHTER

Following are some suggestions for things to carry in a day-use pack, which you can customize for your own experience and preferences. The pack should be large enough for the essential spare clothing, raingear, water and food referred to earlier. A tiny pack may be nice for a walk in the park, but it generally won't cut it in the backcountry in the event of trouble or bad weather.

In general, there are three types of equipment to be carried: personal, leader's and group equipment. Most of this section is devoted to personal equipment. As well, the leader may carry extra items for contingencies, such as a spare toque, mitts, sweater, first aid kit, batteries, sign-in list, logbook and pen, satellite phone. Some of this might be considered group equipment and split among others, but group equipment mainly comes into play on longer trips.

ESSENTIAL EQUIPMENT

- Moderate sized, comfortable day pack capable of carrying adequate spare clothing and equipment. Total weight of pack and contents need not exceed five to eight kg and it can therefore be carried without being too noticeable.
- Waterproof rainwear, preferably of breathable material if you are exercising hard. Note, however, that such materials may not hold up to wet, brushy conditions such as those found on British Columbia's coast, especially in a work environment such as timber cruising or in a marine situation where rubber-lined rainclothes and boots may be required.[7]
- Spare wool or fleece top (sweater, jacket or vest). Generally you will not want to wear too many layers while exercising hard, even in winter, but it is essential to carry warm clothing in your pack for use when you stop or when conditions turn bad. See chapter 12 on Hypothermia at p. 87 for a discussion on dressing in layers and the wicking properties of clothes.
- Wool or fleece hat. For its light weight, this is the best opportunity to reduce major heat loss.
- Gloves or mitts. Take a spare pair for winter or shoulder-season travel because it is easy to get the first pair wet.

- Good quality footwear, as mentioned at p. 43 in the chapter on preparation, planning and practice.
- Bandana. I seldom carry one, as I don't sweat a lot, but many people wear a bandana as a protective and stylish head covering that is multi-purpose and weighs next to nothing.
- Waterproof matches plus alternative fire lighters and fire starters (several preferred).
- Small folding saw for collecting firewood. A good-quality pruning saw works well and is much safer than an axe, especially for occasional users. If you prefer to carry an axe, choose the long-handled variety for safety and effectiveness. If you miss the wood, you are more likely to hit the ground than your leg.
- Basic wilderness first aid kit. Have at least one in the group. See separate list in chapter 9, p. 68.
- Personal supplies, including toilet paper and basic first aid such as band aids, blister prevention, tensor bandage for sprains, and personal medications.
- Lunch, energy bars and/or trail mix and drinking water (typically two litres) for the day, plus some extra. Depending on where you are going and the availability of groundwater, carrying a water filter/purifier may allow you to cut down on the amount of water carried, but two litres is still a good minimum, especially on a hot day.
- Compass and maps and know how to use them. GPS units have become small and affordable and are a worthwhile addition, but do not rely on them as the sole means of navigation. More on this later, at p. 72.
- Bear repellent spray. On balance, this is probably the best choice for bear defence. It must be immediately accessible in a holster attached to your belt or pack.
- Headlamp and batteries. LED lamps have become very small and lightweight, with long battery life.
- Whistle and signalling mirror.
- Sunscreen and insect repellent – seasonal.
- Sunglasses, especially on snow and/or at higher elevation.
- Pocket knife.
- Space blanket.
- Spare batteries for such things as GPS, headlamp, communications devices, avalanche beacons, camera, depending on circumstances. It helps if as many of your gadgets use the same type of batteries, to cut down on the number of spares carried, with AA and AAA being the most common. This should be a consideration at purchase time.

Some typical equipment for a day hike in the mountains. Note the emphasis on clothing.

OPTIONAL EQUIPMENT

Following are some additional items to consider, depending on the nature of your trip and individual preference:

- Second spare wool or fleece top and bottom. Spare clothing is likely to be the most important item in your survival pack. Avoid cotton if you are in a cool climate, since it retains water and takes a long time to dry. Cotton can, however, be an advantage in a hot, dry climate. Dipping a cotton shirt into a stream on a very hot day will lower body temperature quickly and will maintain a moderate temperature through evaporative cooling provided the air is not too humid. Conversely, evaporative cooling is what you must avoid in a cool climate. A long-sleeved shirt and long pants are the best choices for sunburn, cold, insects and bushwhacking. Consider the sun protection factor (spf) of various fabrics when purchasing summer outdoor clothing.
- A second pair of spare mitts and/or spare socks, especially in winter.
- Long underwear, to be worn during winter or carried in your pack during the shoulder seasons. This can also double as warm, comfortable nightwear on extended summer trips, providing four-season usefulness.

- Large sheet of lightweight plastic for waterproofing a bush shelter (seasonal).
- Strong string or parachute cord for repairing gear or constructing a shelter.
- A large, bright-coloured plastic garbage bag is sometimes recommended by safety instructors as optional emergency equipment; some might even put it in the essential category. It's cheap, lightweight, and can serve as improvised raingear, emergency shelter and possibly even a signalling device. It therefore satisfies the important rule of thumb in the backcountry of having multiple possible uses. A serious downside is that condensation will quickly become a problem if the bag is not well vented. As well, there is the danger of suffocation with small children, and for this reason instructors sometimes cut out arm and head holes before handing them out at school presentations.

REALITY CHECK: Many years ago when I was younger and more foolish, and after hearing about the garbage bag option in a survival course, I decided to try it out in what later became Erg Mountain Provincial Park, 160 kilometres east of Prince George. I began hiking up the steep, forested trail quite late in the evening after being delayed for a couple of hours by a torrential rainstorm. As I climbed higher, the forest slowly gave way to subalpine tundra, which helped to compensate for the failing light. As I emerged into meadows, a place frequented by grizzly bears, my surroundings looked decidedly spooky in the dark and I quickly headed into a clump of stunted trees and crawled into the garbage bag. With no sleeping bag, I put on extra clothes and soon fell asleep feeling pleasantly warm. Why, I wondered, hadn't I tried this before – it was so simple and there wasn't much weight to carry. Two hours later, soon after midnight, I woke up in pitch dark, wet and cold from condensation. There wasn't much to be done at that point except put on all my clothes, keep the garbage bag vented as much as possible and just tough it out. By 3 a.m. I'd had enough, so I started brewing water for tea and oatmeal on a small stove. By 4:00 there was barely enough light to travel and I slowly began ascending, first through the meadows, then the ridge and finally the summit, pausing several times as I kept butting up against the slowly rising cloud base. I reached the top before 7:00, fully recovered and set to enjoy a fine day. The verdict: while it could be a lifesaver in torrential rain such as had delayed my start the previous evening, I vowed never again to intentionally spend the night in a garbage bag!

- Ground insulation such as closed-cell foam. This item weighs very little and may be useful for sitting around at lunchtime or in the evening. Alternatively, use tree boughs in an emergency.
- Bush hat for sun and rain and for at least some eye protection when bushwhacking.
- Small cooking pot with oatmeal, soup, teabags and sugar for an unexpected overnighter. In winter, this may also prove useful for melting snow for drinking water.
- Water filter.
- Altimeter and GPS.
- Additional bear repellents and signalling devices such as gas horn, bangers, flares. See chapter 21 on bear safety at p. 135.
- Cell phone, satellite phone, radio, personal locator beacon.
- Repair kit, including pliers, snare or baling wire, duct tape and whatever else you think you might need according to the length and type of activity. Think through "what if" scenarios, considering different possible uses for things in your pack and how you might improvise if necessary.

FOOD AND WATER

The following suggestions are what I have found works well for me; vary them according to your own preferences and needs. See also chapter 23 on native plants, p. 168, and chapter 32 on preparing for an extended outdoor trip, especially the section on food and food dehydrating at p. 217.

- Water. Allow at least 1.5 to 2 litres per day on the trail. Although I still sometimes make the personal choice to drink untreated water from springs and high-elevation seeps, a water filter is now advised for groundwater everywhere in Canada's outdoors. Boiling is an option for overnight trips, but it is time- and fuel-consuming and the result tastes flat. Chemical treatment is another option for short term use. Check on the type of filter or other treatment required for the area you are going to visit. Overseas requirements, especially, may be more stringent. (See the chapter 22 section on water-borne parasites, p. 157.)
- Food types. Carbohydrates provide four calories of energy per gram of food and are a good source of energy for short trips. Fats provide nine calories per gram and are the most concentrated energy source, as well as being a carrier for fat-soluble vitamins and for building bodily insulation. Proteins, like carbohydrates, provide four calories per gram, and build body tissue and supply hormones and energy.

- Breakfast should have high calories, good staying power and be easy to prepare in the field. Favourites are oatmeal, multigrain cereal, granola and dried fruit. The protein from an egg eaten for breakfast may be helpful later in the day.
- Trail snacks should have fast-acting carbohydrates and some fat and protein: for example, trail mix and energy bars.
- Lunches again provide high calories, some fat and some protein: for example, bread, crackers, dried fruit, solid cheese, cream cheese, peanut butter and jam. On a day trip, a wider range of choices and fresh fruit is available than on multi-day trips where weight is key.
- Dinner should be higher in slow-acting proteins and fats. Home-dehydrated food takes advance planning and preparation but it works well for quality and weight.

Some 3,000 to 5,000 calories of food is generally required per person per day while active in the outdoors.

FIRST AID KIT

This section describes a group first aid kit. In addition, each person should carry basic personal first aid items such as those described at p. 62 under "Essential equipment." First aid kits vary a lot, especially according to the type and duration of the activity. The following is aimed at wilderness first aid for backcountry travel. As a minimum, at least one member of the group should have some basic first aid training. Ideally, most members will have some basic training, and one or more people will have taken a wilderness first aid (or ski patrol first aid) course involving field improvisation.

Your kit should contain:
- Assorted band-aids, finger and adhesive dressings.
- Three-inch tensor bandage for minor sprains or joint support. Be careful not to over-tighten and impede circulation when applying tensor bandages.
- Alcohol wipes and/or antiseptic swabs.
- Triangular bandages: as many as six are desirable, since they have multiple uses.
- Roller bandages: one or two three-inch-wide rolls.
- Sterile gauze pads: four-inch-square, non-stick variety.
- Large sterile burn dressings or abdominal pads.
- Pressure dressings with and without tensor bandage.
- Butterfly closures and/or "steri-strips" for field-closing severe cuts that might otherwise require stitches.
- Scissors strong enough to cut clothing or leather away from wounds.
- Penlight, flashlight or headlight (probably already included in other basic equipment as listed beginning at p. 62).
- Tweezers, safety pins.
- Latex or vinyl gloves: three to six pairs recommended. This may seem like overkill, but you will need them if you have copious bleeding to deal with.

REALITY CHECK: I witnessed someone partially sever a finger while cutting cheese at a backcountry campsite. The victim was about 24 hours from medical aid and was lucky not to lose his finger thanks to the intervention of a Scottish mountain rescue paramedic equipped with a good first aid kit who happened to be vacationing at the same camp. There was so much blood that the paramedic used several pairs of latex gloves from his first aid kit before he was finished.

- Pocket mask or microshield barrier for cardiopulmonary resuscitation (CPR) and/or mouth-to-mouth resuscitation.
- "Moleskin" or "Second Skin" for blister prevention. Take the time to stop and apply it as soon as you detect a hot spot and before it develops into a blister.
- Cloth tape: double it up for use in tying splints or for a stretcher. As an alternative (although not as good as cloth tape), the old standby of duct tape may be used for splint and stretcher construction if you are carrying it in your pack for other purposes.

REALITY CHECK: Duct tape and a brilliant case of improvisation got the crew of Apollo 13 safely back to earth from the moon after an explosion in their outbound spacecraft. A similar combination of ingenuity and improvised equipment might get you safely out of the backcountry.

- Folding metal splints. As an alternative, use whatever sticks you can find in your locale.
- Notebook and pencil for recording signs and symptoms and treatments.
- Strong pain killers: discuss with your doctor or pharmacist, but you must be properly trained in using such medicines. As well as easing pain, they may be very useful in reducing shock, which can otherwise become life-threatening.
- If there is a physician in the group, that person might also be carrying a small medical kit with some useful pharmaceuticals, stronger painkillers, surgical instruments and suturing kit. See also Peter Steele's *Backcountry Medical Guide*, listed in Appendix C at p. 263. For longer backcountry trips, especially expeditions to remote places, an accompanying physician and a good medical kit may become more desirable.
- Personal medications: for example, glucose, insulin and glucagon for diabetes or adrenaline for anaphylactic shock (due to insect sting allergy). It is each individual's responsibility to carry any personal medications they may require for their known ailments.

ADDITIONAL EQUIPMENT FOR PLANNED EXTENDED TRIPS

If you plan to be out for one or more nights, you will need more equipment. For example:

- Backpack, with pack cover to keep the contents dry. Make sure the pack is an appropriate size for the activity and a good fit on your body. Practise with it loaded before committing to a long trip.
- Tent or bivouac sack that is suitable for the anticipated conditions. An inexpensive car-camping tent may not survive a severe mountain storm or an overnight summer snowfall, as I have observed more than once.
- Ground insulation: closed-cell foam pad or lightweight, self-inflating mattress. A thick layer of green boughs may be used in an emergency if you are below treeline, but regular day-to-day use of these may result in unacceptable vegetation damage, depending on where you are.
- Lightweight tarp with poles for constructing a kitchen and eating area, especially above treeline. This is not essential for a one- or two-night outing, but it can make a trip much more comfortable in the event of sustained bad weather.
- Cooking stove and fuel: do a test burn with the stove to see how long a measured amount of fuel lasts, and calculate the fuel required before the trip. Allow a 20 per cent margin of error to account for field conditions such as wind or an extra day or two out.
- Cup, bowl and utensil(s): one spoon combined with a pocket knife, a cup and a bowl will usually suffice for backcountry utensils. If there are several people in the party, apportioning rations is a lot easier and less quarrelsome if everyone has the same size bowl and cup.
- Cooking pot(s), pot scrubber and biodegradable soap. I recommend one-pot cooking of simple but wholesome recipes in the outdoors. One pot and a single-burner stove for every two people are adequate. (See also the section at p. 217 on food and food dehydrating.)
- Toothbrush, toothpaste, dental floss, small towel, toilet paper, trowel for burying human waste when there are no latrines. If the area is heavily used and/or you are

going to be there for a few days, build a latrine and rehabilitate it when you leave.

- Gaiters for use in snow, bush, wet vegetation or amid insects. This is a light-weight, multi-use item that is always worth taking.
- Camera, film, binoculars, notebook, pen or pencil, reading material, personal music player/recording devices. These are optional items; consider the added weight and bulk versus the benefits likely to be derived and the record you may want after your trip.
- Specialized repair kits for such items as self-inflating mattresses, eyeglasses and backpacks.
- Down vest (can double as a pillow); long underwear (can double as sleepwear); spare socks (can double as mitts).
- Mosquito jacket and/or mosquito head net, if required, especially in Far North and subarctic regions during the worst of bug season, typically June and July.
- Lightweight camp shoes (can double as stream-crossing shoes).
- Trekking poles, walking stick, ice axe, crampons, as required.
- Food: communal breakfasts and dinners; individual snacks and lunches.

When carrying equipment on your back and weight is at a premium, look for opportunities to get more than one use out of items – examples are indicated above. Some equipment, such as tents, stoves, pots, satellite phone, may be considered group gear and divided among several people. Food should be distributed in such a way as to lessen the chance of too many eggs being in one basket, should a pack be lost.

A good-quality tent will help you stay warm and dry on extended trips, as on this frosty August morning in BC's Monkman Provincial Park.

NAVIGATION

Navigation became simpler a few decades ago with the advent of the orienteering compass, which quickly became the most common type of compass available. Then navigation got even easier with the arrival of the hand-held global positioning system (GPS) to augment (not substitute for) the map and compass. Regardless, when you are setting out into the backcountry, especially where you might end up off trail, in dense bush, thick forest or a whiteout, you should have a navigation plan worked out and stick with it.

USING A COMPASS WITH A MAP

To use an orienteering compass to guide your direction of travel, first set the desired direction (bearing) on the compass. To do this, take the intended direction of travel from a map and set it on the compass, taking into account the current magnetic declination for your locale. I've already introduced four concepts in this paragraph: the orienteering compass, direction of travel, compass bearing and magnetic declination, so let's review those before going further.

- The **orienteering compass** is a device that is typically of rectangular shape, and made of clear plastic so that it can be used as both protractor and ruler on a map. It has a circular, rotating, liquid-filled housing that is usually marked in degrees and that contains a magnetic compass needle. The north end of the needle is usually coloured red, while the south end is usually white. The compass may have a folding lid with a mirror that makes sighting easier and more accurate. High-end models may allow the declination for a particular locale to be preset on the compass, avoiding the need to make declination adjustments each time the compass is used in that general area. This ability to preset declination – usually by means of a small screw located on the back of the compass housing – allows the orienting arrow to be adjusted relative to the orienting lines in the compass housing by the amount of the declination. Note that the basic compass in the following illustration does not have this declination adjustment capability.
- **Direction of travel** is the direction you wish to follow as you move over the landscape. The base plate of the compass will be kept oriented to the direction of travel as you move. A fixed direction-of-travel arrow is usually embossed on the leading part of the compass base plate for that purpose.
- **Compass bearing** is the angle between your target (destination), your present position and north. The bearing is usually measured in degrees, with 0° or 360° being north. Be careful not to accidentally buy a compass that is marked in

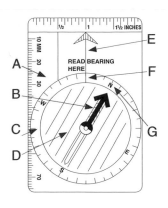

A: Base plate

B: Magnetic compass needle lined up with the orienting arrow

C: Rotating compass housing marked in degrees

D: Orienting lines, which line up with vertical grid lines on your map

E: Direction of travel arrow

F: Read bearing here, in this case 330° magnetic

G: North marker on compass housing (0 or 360°)

mils (6,400 mils equals one revolution, or 360°), which is a system used by the military for artillery purposes. To further complicate matters, as you will learn shortly, there is more than one north to contend with.

- **Magnetic declination** is the deflection of the compass needle from grid north or true north (whichever baseline you are using on the map) to the magnetic north pole.

- **True north** is the direction to the geographic north pole, which is the physical northern end of the axis of rotation of the earth.

- **Magnetic north** is the direction toward the magnetic north pole (actually the earth's south magnetic field, but don't worry about that), a position where the earth's magnetic field lines converge. It is currently located in the Canadian Arctic but it moves around somewhat unpredictably from year to year. To complicate matters further, the compass needle points in the direction of the magnetic field lines at your locale, not directly toward the magnetic north pole.

- **Grid north** is the northerly direction of the grid lines printed on Canada's national topographical maps. In moderate latitudes, the difference between grid north and true north is small, about one degree in north central British Columbia. Grid north varies slightly from true north due to the curvature of the earth's surface and the need to project that curved surface onto a flat map sheet. It varies according to latitude and to the particulars of the map, but all you have to be concerned about is the variance that is printed on the map sheet you are using.

Wow, that's lots to remember. With these definitions in mind, though, let's go back to the basics of using the map and compass.

- **Set the bearing.** Place the compass on the map so that one edge of the base plate is aligned with your intended route, with the direction-of-travel arrow pointing in the direction you wish to go. Then, without moving the compass as a whole, rotate the compass housing so that the north ends of the orienting lines in the compass housing point to north on the map. On Canada's 1:50,000-scale national topographical maps, grid north is the simplest to use, as the vertical grid lines that point to grid north appear every two centimetres on the map, equivalent to each kilometre of distance on the ground. It is therefore easy to line up the orienting lines with the grid lines. On the same maps, the vertical borders of the map point to true north, if you prefer to use true north, but it is much less convenient and more difficult to be accurate, as there are only the two borders.

- **Determine the declination.** On the margins of the map sheet you will find information for calculating the current angle, or declination, between grid north or true north (whichever you are using) and magnetic north. If the map sheet is more than a few years old, the projected magnetic declination will be less reliable due to the unpredictable wandering of the earth's north magnetic pole, and you may need to refer to other sources for the current declination for your location. There are calculators available online, but one novel way that I have used is with a GPS. First set the GPS to magnetic north; then project a new location 0° and 100 kilometres north of you; switch the GPS to grid north or true north; and read the new bearing. This new bearing will be your current declination relative to grid north or true north. Having calculated your declination, you can either set it on your compass, if your instrument provides that option, or you must do the math after you take the bearing from the map and manually adjust that bearing on the compass. The next paragraph refers to the latter case, where your compass does not allow you to preset the declination and you must make the adjustment by hand each time.

- **Adjust for the declination.** Depending on your location (whether you are east or west of the north magnetic pole), you will need to adjust the bearing on your compass by the amount of the declination. In western Canada, we are west of the north magnetic pole and must subtract the declination from the bearing we took from the map relative to grid north or true north. In eastern Canada, it's the opposite. For example, if your intended direction of travel happens to coincide exactly with grid north, you will have set the compass to 0° (or 360°) using the grid lines printed on your map. Then, if the declination from grid north to magnetic north for your location is 21° east, for example, you must reset your compass to 360° minus 21°– that is, to 339°– by rotating the circular part of the compass housing 21° to the right. **Tip:** some people rely on memory or use a rhyming jingle to remember whether to add or subtract the declination. I prefer to figure it out each time by using this simulated special case of travelling north, in order to understand exactly what I'm doing instead of just doing it by rote.

- **Orient the compass, and travel.** With the bearing now set on your compass, orient the base plate (the whole compass, without further adjusting the dial) so that the compass needle lines up with the orienting arrow on the compass housing. Then, keeping this alignment, travel in the direction that the main compass body is pointing, following the direction-of-travel arrow.

- **Reverse the process – triangulate your position.** Having mastered transposing a bearing from map to compass, the next step is to learn the reverse in order to find your position on a map. This is done by taking bearings of two or more distant and recognizable objects using the compass, and then transposing those bearings to a map and seeing where they intersect. This process is called triangulation, and your current position is at the intersection of two bearings or, more accurately, within the tiny polygon formed by the intersection of three or more bearings. You will improve your accuracy by choosing targets that have widely separated lines of sight and by taking more bearings. To take a bearing, first find a good vantage point and aim the direction of travel arrow on the compass base plate to a distant object that you are also able to recognize on the map. Holding the compass steady on the target, rotate the compass housing to line up the orienting arrow with the magnetic compass needle. This is where having a compass that has a mirror in its folding lid helps. Next, adjust for the declination by reversing the procedure described earlier, and transfer the bearing onto the map. Draw a line on the map along this bearing and through the target object using the edge of the base plate as a ruler. Without changing your location, repeat this for one or more other bearings, and where they intersect will be your location on the map. **Tip:** for training purposes, if you have a GPS, confirm your location with the GPS. If the locations differ by more than a few tens of metres, you are doing something wrong, whether with the GPS or the map or the compass or some combination of the three.

- **Handle the compass well.** When aiming your compass in the outdoors, make sure you hold it well away from any metallic object such as an automobile body or metallic parts of clothing or equipment such as buttons, buckles, zippers or knives that could deflect the compass needle if they are slightly magnetic. As well, to ensure you don't lose the critical compass, while keeping it handy for use, pass the lanyard through a button hole and pass the compass through the loop, and then carry the compass in a nearby pocket. This is better than looping the lanyard around your neck, because you can hold the compass farther out at the full length of the lanyard, making it easier to use and keeping it well away from any metal on clothing.

It should be apparent by now that using a map and compass can be both intrinsically easy yet very challenging, especially if you have not practised with it recently. Putting aside for now such issues as magnetic anomalies in the earth, using a map and compass can be prone to human error if you are not practised and careful in its use. For example, you can go wrong if you disregard, miscalculate or misuse the declination or refer to the wrong end of the compass needle or misread the map. To learn how to use a map and compass competently, and especially how to manage declination, I urge you to take a map and compass course. Alternatively, read a book on the subject, such as Björn Kjellström's classic book *Be Expert with Map and Compass*, listed in Appendix C, or at the very least read the directions that came with your compass. And practise with it in the outdoors at every opportunity.

Although a compass can be a valuable tool by itself, in order to get the most out of it you do need to have a topographical map for your location and you must understand such things as magnetic declination, transposing bearings between map and compass, and coordinate systems. Again, some compasses allow you to set your declination right on the instrument, simplifying its use once you under-stand magnetic declination, whereas less expensive models require you to mentally

1:50,000 scale topographical map, compass with adjustable declination and mirror, and GPS.

take account of the declination when transposing bearings to or from your map. I recommend you get a topographical map for the area where you live, and practise with it from a known location that has a good view of surrounding features. If you need accuracy within one or two degrees, choose a compass with a mirror in a folding lid in order to facilitate sighting the compass on a target. And if you use a compass with a map regularly, invest in one that has an adjustable declination.

USING A COMPASS WITHOUT A MAP

Always carry at least a basic compass with you everywhere you go in the outdoors, no matter how easy the undertaking you have planned and regardless of whether you have a map. If you do not develop this as your standard practice, Murphy's law, which broadly states that anything that can go wrong will go wrong, will inevitably catch up with you eventually. For example, a situation could arise as simple as stepping off the trail or away from your camp in order to relieve yourself and then becoming disoriented:

REALITY CHECK: An experienced outdoorsman nearly lost his life while driving alone in the Far North. He stopped on an isolated roadside and walked a short distance into the bush for a toilet break, just out of sight of the highway. He had nothing with him except the clothes he was wearing in the car, and somehow he walked in the wrong direction when he tried to return to it. The bizarre result of his situation was that he wandered the northern bush for over a week with no food or equipment, and wearing only lightweight driving clothes. Fortunately he had a good survival sense, kept his head, and with great good fortune he eventually walked out.

SHOOT A BEARING

You can use the orienteering compass to navigate to a destination without a map, but this only works if you initially know which way you want to go. Perhaps you could see your destination from a clearing or from high ground before entering a forest, or before clouds and mist descend on a mountain ridge that you are on. Keep your compass handy when travelling in such conditions, even if you are not currently using it for direction finding. If a brief opportunity to see a recognizable feature of the landscape suddenly presents itself, you can instantly "shoot a bearing." To take a bearing, simply point the compass base plate (the direction-of-travel arrow) at your intended destination and then rotate the compass housing so that the orienting arrow lines up with the "north" (usually red) end of the magnetic needle. Then all you have to do is walk in the direction the main compass body is pointing, while maintaining the alignment of the compass needle with the orienting arrow in the circular housing and without further rotating the housing. Since you are not using a map in this situation, you don't have to worry about declination – just keep the compass oriented to the bearing you shot as you follow the direction-of-travel arrow.

USE SIMPLE COMPASS TRICKS

"Walk in on the red and out on the white." A simple trick when leaving your vehicle is to take a compass bearing by pointing it in your intended direction of travel and rotating the compass housing to line up the orienting arrow with the north (red) end of the magnetic needle as described above. As long as your route is roughly in a straight line, you can reverse your trip later by walking out using the south (white) end of the magnetic needle lined up with the orienting arrow, without changing the bearing setting. Alternatively, when it comes time to walk out you can reset the compass to the back bearing by rotating the circular housing 180° and continuing to use the north end of the compass needle. With both these, and the methods described in the previous paragraph, make a note of the original bearing you have set, in case you drop or knock the compass and accidentally change its setting. It helps in this situation if your return target is large, such as a road intersecting your direction of travel at roughly 90°. In that circumstance you can improve the likelihood of quickly locating your vehicle by deliberately aiming off by a few degrees to the left or right on the return trip so that you know whether to go right or left to your start point when you hit the highway.

ALWAYS CARRY A COMPASS

Again (I can't stress this too much) while it is best used with a map, a compass has considerable value by itself and should always be with you in the outdoors. Even if you have no idea where you are or which way to go, it will at least enable you to walk in a straight line. This can be of great value given the natural human propensity to walk in a circle in the absence of visible reference points such as distant topographic features or the sun. Then, if you happen to be lost in an area that is bounded by some combination of roads, rivers, lakeshore, fence lines, power lines or other linear features, the compass will enable you to hit a boundary line somewhere and hopefully to walk out along that. Simply pick a direction that will give you the best prospect of getting out, and set the bearing as described above. If you know a major highway lies in a certain direction, say a north/south highway lying to the east of you, simply using the compass to walk in that direction will get you there. Keep in mind, though, that bushwhacking is much slower than walking along a trail and you will have to resist the temptation to mistrust your compass as time passes. A little forethought before your trip should mean you know the rough direction of an escape route.

COMPASS FOLLIES

ALWAYS TRUST YOUR COMPASS

Well, almost always – see the next paragraph. Apart from the human propensity to walk in a circle even on flat ground, terrain variability such as rolling hills intersecting your course at various angles can in short order cause you to walk in a complete circle on a cloudy day if you are using dead reckoning. The shortest time that I have taken to walk in a circle was a shockingly brief ten minutes in such terrain. In that situation, trust your compass, even though your instinct to follow the changing topography will assuredly try to pull you in different directions.

Beware, though, of magnetic anomalies in the ground that deflect the compass needle away from the earth's magnetic field. In my experience these are rare, but they do occur. They are also not usually shown on maps, so it is important to keep your wits about you. If possible, obtain local knowledge before undertaking a trip into a new or remote backcountry area. Having a GPS as a backup is helpful in this situation, but you have to be able to determine which instrument is giving you the wrong information.

REALITY CHECK: I have only encountered one magnetic anomaly that I was aware of, and it was a big one. It was in the volcanic landscape of BC's Mount Edziza Provincial Park, where a presumably iron-rich cinder cone caused a huge 29-degree compass error. To my chagrin, even with good visibility above treeline and many good map references, having just acquired my first GPS for backup on this trip, and even though I knew something was not quite right, I trusted the compass to the point that it took me 24 hours and a climb up the wrong volcanic hill to figure it out. In this case, my ingrained trust in my compass had blinded me to what was staring me in the face. I should add that neither of my two companions realized the error either. If the weather had been socked in, the situation would have been more serious, and I would likely have found myself arguing between the compass and the GPS without any obvious answer. In this case, it would probably be best to defer to technology, although I have also seen GPS units give unreliable results on occasion (see discussion about the pitfalls of GPS, at p. 83). So, ultimately it comes down to experience and judgment.

MORE ON USING A MAP

MAP TYPES

There are many specialized maps available, such as forest cover, soils, geological, highway and guidebook maps, but the best all-round type for backcountry recreation is a 1:50,000-scale (or better) topographical map – that is to say, one that has elevation contour lines and kilometre-scale grid lines printed on it. For concentrated or repeated use in a specific area, it is worthwhile investing in the physical map sheet, even though they're expensive. You should definitely have the sheet for where you live so you can practise with map, compass and GPS. For longer trips (e.g., river trips covering hundreds of kilometres), it may be less costly to purchase a CD or DVD containing wider map coverage and print what you want yourself. If you are using an inkjet type of printer, be sure to plasticize or waterproof the map in some way before taking it outdoors, because the ink will run. In the fall of 2006 the federal government announced that early in 2007 Natural Resources Canada would discontinue the printing of paper topographical maps. This was clearly premature in terms of public accessibility to large printed map sheets, and was later rescinded after widespread outcry. However, as technology evolves and becomes more available, electronic access and/or sourcing of maps will likely be the future. Increasingly, maps are incorporated directly into GPS units, and the temptation will grow to dispense with a physical map and compass backup. Indeed, a GPS with a contour map feature is a very nice tool to have, particularly in featureless bush where creeks, ponds and topography stand out beautifully.

Use the map with compass and GPS. Learn to use your map with both your compass and your GPS. As already discussed, know how to transpose bearings from map to compass and vice versa, taking into account magnetic declination. Know how to use triangulation to locate your position on a map and how to recognize terrain features.

Follow bearings and estimate distances accurately. Practise using bearings in conjunction with estimating distance travelled by means of counting paces. Paces vary by individual and terrain, so find out what yours are for the various types of terrain and bush you typically hike in, by walking a premeasured distance. An alternative but less accurate method is to learn to estimate distance travelled by means of elapsed time in different types of terrain and bush. In the absence of a GPS, counting paces may be the only way to navigate with accuracy if you are caught in a whiteout or you are in a dense, featureless landscape. In such circumstances you can improve your precision with the compass by using a partner as a target. Send him or her out ahead, calling to the person to move right or left to line her up with your compass, then walk up to him. Keep repeating this procedure, taking care to keep in sight of each other.

WHY CARRY AN ALTIMETER?

Using an altimeter can aid navigation in mountain terrain. The intersection of a contour line of known elevation with a single compass bearing taken through a break in the clouds will give you your position, assuming you know generally which mountainside you are on. Take the opportunity to correct your altimeter for changes in barometric pressure from time to time when you are at known positions and therefore at known elevations. An altimeter is another example of a lightweight piece of equipment that has multiple uses, making it worthwhile carrying in the mountains. If it is of the wristwatch variety, it further doubles for timekeeping and other functions. It is especially useful as a barometer to measure sudden changes in atmospheric pressure that may signal big changes in the weather.

GLOBAL POSITIONING SYSTEM, OR GPS

Global positioning system (GPS) units have become affordable, lightweight and reliable, and they are fast becoming a ubiquitous part of recreational navigation. I highly recommend using a GPS, but as an adjunct to, not a substitute for, map and compass. The need for a compass may diminish in the future, just as the calculator has largely replaced the need for mental arithmetic and the now obsolete slide rule of my academic youth; but for the present I would not want to rely solely on GPS. Certainly, if several people in a group have GPS units, the collective dependability may increase. There will probably come a time soon when everyone has a GPS built into their mobile phone, wristwatch or other portable device. Part of the pleasure of being in the outdoors, though, is to understand and relate to the landscape you are travelling through, and having a good understanding of map and compass, as well as the GPS, is an essential part of that.

- **A GPS** can be used by itself, but like a compass it is best used in conjunction with a map. Higher-end units have preloaded maps, providing a powerful and interesting tool to watch one's progress through dense bush or forest on a full-colour topographical map on the small screen. It is hard to get lost with this highly intuitive feature, but beware of the instrument failing, and carry a paper map and a compass as backup. When using a GPS with map coordinates, it is important to configure the correct datum and zone (see next) on the GPS. You can generally find these values printed on the topographical map sheet.
- **Geodetic datum** refers to the system used by mapmakers to project particular parts of the earth's surface onto flat map sheets. These values vary according to time and place. For north central British Columbia, the current standard is NAD83 (North American Datum 1983, which is the same as WGS84, or World Geodetic System 1984), while some older topographical maps are still NAD27 (North American Datum 1927).
- **Map zone** is part of the UTM (Universal Transverse Mercator) coordinate grid system used on maps whereby a location on the earth's surface is given in metres. Confusion can arise because of the large numbers involved and because the zone

usually has to be entered separately on GPS units. There are 60 zones around the earth, starting with zone 1 on the Date Line, at 180° of longitude. Each zone is 6° of longitude wide, or about 667 kilometres wide at the equator. The median line (easting) of each zone is 500000 E. (Northing starts at 0000000 N at the equator, or 10000000 N for locations south of the equator). Zone is not an issue if you are using (and have set your GPS to) degrees and minutes of latitude and longitude as in aviation and marine navigation. Sometimes it is necessary to work in both systems simultaneously, for example, in search and rescue operations where ground personnel must communicate with aircraft.

- For recreational purposes, the GPS is useful for saving and finding locations of your choosing, generally called **waypoints**. For example, pinpointing a good fishing spot in a lake, the location of a cabin or base camp or the point where you left a marked trail, in order to easily find them later. When saving a waypoint, take a moment to type a meaningful name rather than just accepting the next number assigned by the instrument. This may help you to avoid the unhappy consequences of heading toward the wrong waypoint when you are tired and trying to find your way home late in the day, as I have learned the hard way. Apart from specifics already mentioned, the GPS is useful for route finding, estimating travel time and recording the route you have travelled in order to simplify finding your way back. It is nice to have a GPS as a backup in the event you encounter a whiteout in the mountains, and it can be very handy if part of your route entails bushwhacking through a featureless and/or forested landscape, although reception of the satellite signals may be degraded among trees.

- Many GPS units have an optional wide area augmentation system (WAAS) that increases accuracy at the cost of more battery use. Using the unit with WAAS turned OFF provides 15-metre horizontal and 19-metre vertical accuracy, which is ample for most practical purposes. Turning WAAS on provides 3-metre horizontal and 6-metre vertical accuracy. WAAS works by getting correction information sent from various accurately surveyed differential GPS (DGPS) ground sites that has been sent to WAAS satellites. WAAS may not work in all locations, so check your GPS manual so as not to waste battery power unnecessarily.

- Other factors that may affect GPS accuracy include ionospheric interference which slows radio waves, affecting the timings the GPS uses for its calculations and producing 5- to 10-metre error. Poor satellite positions or geometry can produce error in the range of tens to hundreds of metres if the satellites are not reasonably spread out over the sky. At least four satellites must be in sight (3D mode), from which the unit chooses the best four to use, one for time and three for position. If there are only three satellites in sight (2D mode), some 150 to 1500 metres of error will result.

- Some high-end models may have a three-axis accelerometer (acceleration) and gyroscopes (position) so that the unit can continue to provide dead-reckoning travel information while a sufficient number of satellites are temporarily unavailable.
- Although not necessary for everyday use, if you have a scientific or technical curiosity and would like to understand more about how the GPS system works, there is a huge amount of technical information available online. I recently googled the term GPS and got nearly a billion hits! So while this is some indication of the staggering popularity of this technology, clearly it is necessary to refine your search a bit.

PITFALLS OF USING GPS

Technological pitfalls of using a GPS include poor signal strength due to your position relative to surrounding forests, mountains, valleys or other topographical features; temporarily poor satellite configurations in the sky; weak batteries; device failure due to physical damage such as having been dropped; performance-degrading extreme weather; and a very wet forest canopy adversely affecting reception. System downgrading for military reasons is still a possibility, although it has become less of a concern in recent years. A new uncertainty has arisen, though, namely the disruption of GPS services by a storm on the sun directed toward the earth. Solar flares can happen at any time and they peak during solar maxima, which are the high points of the 11-year sunspot cycle. At those times, if a solar flare happens to be oriented toward the earth, charged particles emitted by the sun can hit the atmosphere and create radio noise on the frequency bands used by GPS receivers. Researchers who first noticed this effect have suggested that this could reduce GPS signal strength by up to 90 per cent for several hours at a time during the 2011 to 2013 solar maximum.

Human pitfalls of using a GPS include overreliance on technology without fully understanding its use, accuracy and limitations; not using fully charged or fresh batteries; dead batteries with no spares carried; using the wrong map datum; referencing or entering the wrong map zone into the GPS; and conversion between degrees/minutes/seconds and decimal values. If your GPS unit has a compass feature, find out whether it is the kind that truly detects magnetic fields or whether you need to be in motion in order to obtain a real bearing. Even if your GPS has this enhanced compass feature, carry a basic magnetic compass as a backup.

REALITY CHECK: Don't underestimate the complexity of GPS, especially if you are an occasional user and are in a stressful situation such as being lost or trying to find your way back late in the day. This is not the time to learn how it works. Twice in a four-week period between drafting this section and completing it for the first edition of the book, I found myself in the mountain backcountry with a GPS that was giving me misleading information. In the first instance I was on the boundary between map zones 10 and 11 and had inadvertently entered the wrong zone for several of my preprogrammed destinations. In that case, the large error was obvious, but it had the effect of rendering the GPS useless for the first hour until I figured out the problem.

In the second episode, I was with a group who had targeted a numbered waypoint using a GPS that was giving intermittent and unreliable readings on a north-facing slope during what should have been a relatively easy bushwhacking retreat through mature forest. Not taking the time to label the numerically assigned waypoint on the ascent likely added to the problem. Leaving the old forest, nearly two kilometres off our mark, we had to endure a very tough bushwhack late in the day through a nearly impenetrable jungle of alder, devil's club, young spruce and every other imaginable kind of vegetable that only a 20-year-old wet-belt mountain cutblock can produce. Two members of the party began to show signs of stress, further slowing the descent and adding yet more tension.

Finally, there are behavioural factors such as the ability to acquire spatial knowledge that may be compromised while using a GPS as compared to a map and compass. Research at the University of Tokyo, for example, found that people using GPS devices walked farther, travelled more slowly, made more stops, incurred larger directional errors, had more difficulty relating to surrounding topography and a harder time finding their way than those using traditional maps.[8] As well, GPS users in the study demonstrated poorer knowledge of the route and terrain when asked to draw sketch maps after their walks. Their reduced performance may relate to their being more focused on the GPS display than on their surroundings. It should be qualified that this study was conducted in an urban environment with short walks and lots of turns, but it does strike a note of caution for navigating in the backcountry. While GPS may provide a superior means of navigation for other means of transport such as driving or aviation, this advantage may not always apply to walking.

For all of these reasons, be aware of the pitfalls of using a GPS. Practise with it before you go out, carry a map and compass for backup and cross-checking, and stay focused on your surroundings.

OTHER WAYS OF NAVIGATING

In the absence of a map, compass or GPS, there are some other techniques that can be useful to help you navigate.

- **Sun:** Use the sun in conjunction with the time of day to travel in a straight line or to give an approximate direction of travel. To do this, estimate the sun's apparent westward movement of about 15° each hour. Depending on where you are in your time zone (add or subtract up to half an hour) the sun will be due south at noon, which is 12 p.m. standard time or 1 p.m. daylight saving time. If you have a wristwatch with an analog dial, it is even easier as you can use the combination of the hour hand, the sun's position in the sky, and the dial as a protractor, remembering that one hour on the dial represents 30° of arc and hence two hours of the sun's apparent movement. Thus, orienting the watch so that the small hour hand is pointing directly at the sun, south will be roughly midway between the hour hand and noon on the watch dial.

- **Stars:** Although travelling at night is not recommended, the stars can give you a direction that you can use the following morning. In the northern hemisphere this means referring to the pole star, Polaris, which is the end star of the handle of the Little Dipper (Ursa Minor) and is easily found midway between the Big Dipper (Ursa Major) and the "W" (Cassiopeia). In the southern hemisphere, there is no conveniently bright star at the south celestial pole, but you can locate the approximate pole position using the Southern Cross (Crux Australis) as a pointer. Check out a star map to see how, if you are heading Down Under.

- **Back trail:** On your way in, make it a habit to continually look over your shoulder to check your back trail. What will it look like going the other way? Is your route back well marked?

- **Tracking:** If you are skilled as a tracker – perhaps you took man-tracking training as a volunteer member of a search and rescue group or have been a skilled hunter for many years – sign awareness can be useful to backtrack using marks you left behind in the soil and vegetation on your way in. Note that this is an ability that requires many hundreds of hours of practice to be effective, although there are many degrees of proficiency in between. This is a fun skill to learn, and it will increase your powers of observation, which may prove useful in a tight situation.

- **Tracks in snow:** In the winter it is generally much easier to backtrack by following the tracks you have left in the snow. Some caveats to be aware of are: 1. In the spring, the daily melt-freeze cycle may mean that you leave scant impression in the frozen snow crust in the morning and it may have melted out by afternoon. 2. A snowstorm may have obscured your tracks while you were out, especially if they were faint to start with. 3. Other people may have left a confusing array of tracks behind you, causing you to follow the wrong ones when trying to backtrack.

- **Folklore:** Directions can be derived from the position of mosses and lichens on trees or from the thickness of tree rings. The problem is that when this works at all, it likely varies by location, terrain and species of trees, lichens and mosses. It is therefore not very useful unless you are very familiar with the locale and the orientation of its flora, in which case you are not likely to be lost in the first place.

Game trails can make travel in the bush easy, but they start and stop and are more likely to get you lost than lead you out. Take advantage of game trails if you know where you are at all times and they are going your way.

A hundred kilometres from the nearest road, on the Turnagain River in northern BC's Cassiar Mountains. Good navigation skills are essential if you leave the river this far off the beaten track.

COLD PROBLEMS: HYPOTHERMIA, THE SILENT KILLER

Hypothermia is one of the most prevalent causes of mortality in the outdoors. It often catches people unawares, especially if they have had no training in or experience with what to look for in themselves or others. Fitness and strength are not necessarily indicators of avoidance of hypothermia, since fit people may have less body fat than others and may feel more able to "tough it out" until they pass the point of being able to help themselves. There are other causes and factors in the onset of hypothermia, such as elderly people living in homes that lack adequate heating in cold climates in winter, as well as a range of medical conditions. Starvation and hypothermia can become intertwined in a cold-climate survival situation that is prolonged for more than a few days. In this section, I will be dealing with exposure-induced hypothermia, but keep in mind that trauma injury and other medical conditions may be contributing and confounding factors.

BACKGROUND

Our normal body temperature is roughly between 36° and 38°c, and with normal metabolism, activity levels and clothing (insulation), our environmental comfort zone is between 16° and 25°c.

The body's main temperature control mechanism is provided by a thumb-sized part of the brain called the hypothalamus, tissue that has been evolving in vertebrates for half a billion years. In humans, if the body becomes too hot, the main means of cooling is by sweating, whereby significant amounts of heat are shed through evaporation, enhanced by wind convection or fanning. If the body is too cold, shivering enhances the production of metabolic heat. Insulation provided by clothing, a sleeping bag or huddling with others reduces the loss of heat that otherwise results from the processes of conduction, convection, evaporation, respiration and radiation.

PROGRESSION OF HYPOTHERMIA

Each stage listed below is identified with a core body temperature range as a way of illustrating the progression of hypothermia. You are not likely to have a convenient way to measure core body temperature in the outdoors, and even if you did have one, the way an individual responds at a given temperature will depend on their general health and fitness as well as their state of exhaustion and any traumatic injuries. In a hospital setting, rewarming can be carefully monitored by internal means, but in the outdoors you must pay attention to the signs and symptoms.

- **Normal:** The body's normal temperature varies between 37.5 and 36.5°c.
- **Mild hypothermia:** A core body temperature of between 36° and 34°c is marked by the onset of first symptoms. This is the best time for remedial action! You can easily recognize this first stage in yourself by your feet and hands becoming cold and by the onset of shivering. In non-extreme situations (that is to say you have not suddenly fallen through ice into freezing water and/or you are not completely exhausted) this stage can often be reversed by simply resuming physical activity in order to generate metabolic heat, and/or by putting on extra clothes, toque, gloves, wind jacket or raingear and replacing wet or damp clothing with dry. If possible, take shelter from the wind and rain, although if you are in an exposed position you may not be able to do this right away.
- **Moderate hypothermia:** Core temperature has fallen to between 35° and 32°c and the need for action has become more acute. This stage is marked by uncontrolled and then intense shivering, slowing pace, uncoordinated movements and difficulty speaking. The person suffering from hypothermia may become forgetful – a serious warning sign. Skin is pale and breathing is shallower and slower. As the stage progresses, shivering will diminish and eventually stop, muscles will stiffen and there will be weakness, exhaustion, poor coordination progressing to drowsiness, unusual behaviour and an irregular pulse. The onus has shifted to the hypothermia victim's companions to recognize the problem and insist on or take remedial action immediately. Obviously, if you are by yourself you are now in serious trouble – another reason not to go it alone and/or deal promptly with the first onset of symptoms. Assuming the casualty is not alone, and if it is feasible to do so, his companions should get him to a dry place, remove any wet clothing, dry his skin and replace with dry clothes and a warm blanket or a sleeping bag if available. If you have enough group equipment available, use several sleeping bags and thermal pads and wrap everything up in a tarp. Unless the person is completely exhausted or traumatized, he or she should then be able to passively rewarm herself through her own metabolic heat production, perhaps aided by one or two hot water bottles or donated body heat through huddling with one or more companions. Keep clothing on, though, so as not to cause too rapid rewarming of the victim or excessive cooling of rescuers, who themselves may already be slightly hypothermic. If the person is conscious and able to swallow,

ingestion of warm liquids such as tea or soup might help. Passive rewarming can be a slow process, raising the temperature by as little as half a degree and up to 2°c per hour. In winter conditions, check also for any frostbite and do not rewarm deeply frozen parts prematurely (see chapter 14 on frostbite, p. 99).

- **Serious to severe hypothermia:** At a core temperature of 32° down to 25°c, urgent action is required, but care must be exercised to avoid sudden movements or too rapid rewarming that could trigger death through ventricular fibrillation (rapid and ineffectual vibration or contractions of the heart muscles). The problem with too-rapid externally applied warming is that it could cause rapid dilation of peripheral blood vessels, allowing cool blood to rush back into the body's vital core organs and tip the scale disastrously. Signs and symptoms of this phase are that shivering has stopped, muscles have stiffened and movement may have become erratic and jerky. Pulse and respiration may have slowed and become irregular, progressing to disorientation and a slow loss of consciousness. At first, the afflicted person may still be able to stand and walk, and may appear okay to those not familiar with hypothermia, but in general he will not be able to help himself at this stage and it is up to any companions to intervene. As core temperature falls below 30°c, progressive symptoms include irrationality and slowing pulse and respiration, leading to unconsciousness with no reflexes and an erratic heart beat at around 26°c. Below this temperature, failure of cardiac and respiratory control centres in the brain may occur, followed by likely cardiac fibrillation, possible edema and hemorrhage in lungs, and death. As this stage progresses, the victim requires skilled medical intervention utilizing various active internal rewarming procedures in an appropriately equipped medical facility. Meanwhile, the best thing you may be able to do in the field is to completely insulate the casualty from further heat loss pending medical evacuation, typically by helicopter. It is unlikely at this stage that there will be much residual metabolic heat production for passive rewarming, but the casualty may be stabilized by this action.

REALITY CHECK: Note that even if a person appears to be dead, she may still have a very slow pulse that you can't easily detect. The cooling of vital organs may also increase the chance of resuscitation, for example, in young children after cold water immersion. There is a medical saying that a person "is not dead until they are warm and dead," so don't give up too soon. There are some amazing stories of people being resuscitated from and/or surviving long periods of deep hypothermia and even cold water drowning.

UNDERSTAND HOW YOU LOSE BODY HEAT

Understanding the mechanisms of heat loss will help you prevent hypothermia. There are five ways to lose body heat.

CONDUCTION

Loss due to conduction typically results from such causes as immersion in cold water, wearing wet clothing or prolonged contact with the ground when sitting or reclining without adequate ground insulation. Heat is lost through conduction in a snow burial, meaning rescuers will likely have to deal with hypothermia as well as suffocation and trauma injuries after extricating a buried avalanche victim. Some statistics to keep in mind: the body loses heat up to 30 times faster when wet versus when it is dry; and the thermal conductivity of water is hundreds of times that of air. Therefore it is essential to stay dry in a cold climate. Beware also of freezing injuries caused by skin contact with highly conductive materials such as metal at very low temperatures.

CONVECTION

A key agency of heat loss is wind chill, and when combined with the transfer of heat through wet clothing and the huge loss of heat through evaporation, it can quickly become deadly. Ways you can protect yourself are to wear dry, windproof clothing and especially to protect your head, which can be a major site of heat loss through convection and radiation, as the head tends to be more exposed. A toque is probably the most valuable item by size and weight that you can carry year round in your pack. As the saying goes, put on a hat to warm your feet. (See the *Reality Check* at the bottom of p. 91, opposite, on heat loss by way of the head.)

Remember to avoid cotton clothing in a cool climate, as the thermal conductivity of saturated cotton approaches that of water. (See chapter 8 on clothing and equipment, beginning at p. 62.)

EVAPORATION

This is the big one. To illustrate evaporation's effectiveness in shedding heat, consider that at sea level it requires five times the heat energy to convert water from its liquid to its vapour state (water to steam) as it does to heat water all the way from the freezing to the boiling point. In other words, evaporative cooling is huge, and you lose a large amount of heat energy when water or sweat is evaporated away from you. Evaporation of water produced by the sweat glands and/or from wet clothing is therefore highly beneficial in cooling the body in a hot environment, but it also carries away a good portion of your metabolically produced heat in a cold environment. Evaporative cooling is both key to survival in a hot climate and likely the biggest risk of hypothermia in a cold environment. The huge heat loss associated with converting liquid water to vapour also significantly exaggerates (and is exaggerated by) any wind chill. This is why you should make staying dry a high priority, for example, by wearing windproof, waterproof, breathable outer clothing; dressing in layers and layering up or down as required; and carrying spare dry clothing, particularly if you are prone to sweating. If you are exercising hard, you can get your clothes as wet internally from sweating as you can from external rain.

In very cold conditions, beware of the evaporative cooling effects of getting volatiles such as gasoline on your skin, which could lead to instant frostbite.

RESPIRATION

Everyone has to breathe, and there is therefore an unavoidable loss of body heat from inhaling cold air and exhaling warm air. This effect may be lessened by wearing a scarf, balaclava or face mask when out in extremely cold weather, such as below –20° to –25°c.

REALITY CHECK: Some research has suggested that a reason we become susceptible to cold or flu viruses in winter is that viruses are present in small numbers in the nasal passages much of the time and they may be suddenly free to reproduce when the autonomic vasoconstriction of blood vessels in the nasal passages in response to the cold renders the blood flow, and thereby the body's immune response there, less effective. If this is so, there's another reason to keep warm in the winter outdoors, to avoid catching a cold – your grandmother may have been right after all!

RADIATION

This is another major potential cause of heat loss but it is easily preventable. A key part of the body susceptible to radiative heat loss is the head (and it can account for fully half of the body's heat loss if it is the only part exposed). So, again, wear a toque when it is cold and always carry one with you, even in summer.

REALITY CHECK: It used to be survival lore that an unprotected head affords a disproportionately large heat loss in cold conditions. The US Army field manual recommended that hats be worn because 40 to 45 per cent of body heat escapes through the head, and this was commonly picked up in civilian survival courses (and the first edition of this book). The myth seems to have begun with military experiments conducted in the 1950s that measured heat loss among soldiers in the Arctic. The experiment was flawed, as they wore survival suits but no hats, and it is hardly surprising that they lost more heat through their heads. Research published in 2006[9] reported that heat loss through the head is proportional to the area of skin exposed. The study showed that while an exposed head can certainly radiate a lot of heat, so can an exposed arm or leg, and in an extreme case, if people wear swimsuits, only 10 per cent of heat is lost through the head. Similarly, Ben Sherwood's book *The Survivor's Club* reports, under "Survival Secrets," that only 8 to 10 per cent of heat loss occurs through the head. So while the recommendation to protect the head against cold is still good advice, the underlying mechanism needs clarification.

PREVENTING HYPOTHERMIA

Understanding hypothermia and learning to recognize the signs and symptoms in yourself and your partners is important, of course, but prevention is the key. Following are some pointers for avoiding this dangerous but very preventable condition. You will notice some repetition of what has gone before, but that's okay – this is important stuff.

- A top priority in the outdoors is to stay warm and dry by adding and removing layers of clothing, and to avoid sweating in a cool climate. Use good raingear, have lots of extra clothing in your pack and carry (and when necessary, wear) a warm hat.
- Keep out of the wind and/or use good windproof clothing.
- Dress in layers. Outdoor clothing is comprised of three fundamental layers: a wicking layer next to the skin to draw off perspiration by capillary action; an insulating layer to keep you warm; and a shell layer (breathable if you are going to be exercising hard) to protect you from wind, rain and snow. Despite the shift to synthetic polyester and microfibre-based materials for the wicking layer, wool garments are still a good choice for both the wicking and insulation layers of your kit, as wool retains some of its insulating properties when wet and has reasonable wicking, or water transfer, properties.
- Eat well on the trail – consume high-energy food at regular intervals.
- Drink lots of water or hot and sweet drinks. A small thermos of sweet tea works wonders at lunchtime in the winter, and it doubles as a hand warmer as well. If you don't have access to water, it might be okay to hydrate by eating snow early in the day if you are creating enough metabolic heat through exercise to overcome the cooling effect of the snow, but avoid eating snow late in the day when it may contribute to cooling your body core overnight.
- Avoid getting too tired. Rest as needed and don't overextend yourself, especially in winter.

- Minimize risks and keep safe, since hypothermia can seriously compound other problems such as an injury and shock, especially in winter.
- Use a buddy system in cold conditions. Watch each other for early signs of hypothermia, since it can be insidiously dangerous. Be aware of the capabilities of the weakest member of your group, but also be alert to a strong person who thinks he is immune to hypothermia – he may be the first person to fall victim to it.
- Carry emergency bivouac gear. This is where a small plastic tarp can be most valuable for waterproofing an emergency shelter, especially in spring, summer and fall, the rainy months.
- Keeping active will produce metabolic heat, but activity should not be pursued to the point of exhaustion. Those who are even mildly hypothermic will require more oxygen and use more energy than they would normally need for the same amount of work, creating a "slippery slope." Camp early before the points of exhaustion and related hypothermia are reached. If it is necessary to build an emergency shelter, stop and dig in before hypothermia renders the task too difficult.

for them the night before. This story was featured in a well-known survival training film and dramatically illustrates the benefits of insulation from the cold environment and of passive rewarming.

- Avoid alcohol: it dilates the blood vessels, thereby increasing heat loss, and it interferes with the body's heat-balancing mechanisms.

COLD WATER IMMERSION[10]

In the event of prolonged cold water immersion, such as after a boat capsizing or sinking in the middle of a large lake, you should try to get out of the water as soon as possible while conserving body heat. Hopefully, you will have prepared for this eventuality by wearing thermally protective clothing and a personal flotation device. You may have an emergency position-indicating radio beacon (EPIRB) that is activated by immersion in water or that you can manually activate (see chapter 20 on Communications, beginning at p. 125). Ideally, you will have practised getting back into your boat, and if it has not been lost, you might try to do that next. Perhaps you will have signalling devices such as flares attached to your life jacket. You should wear your life jacket at all times in the boat. After you're in the water is not the time to try to find it and put it on, and may not even be possible. Prevention is always best, and you should maintain awareness that putting yourself far from shore, in a cold water lake, in a remote location, in circumstances where capsize is possible, puts you at high risk of death.

- Your immediate priority after entering the water should be to protect your airway from possible gasping that may result from the shock of sudden cold water immersion, thereby avoiding aspirating and quickly drowning. This may be more easily accomplished if you are wearing a flotation device and if you can remain as still as possible during this initial period. In a few cases, sudden death can also result from cardiac arrhythmias arising from the cold water immersion shock, and the ability to remain still may give rapid breathing and high blood pressure a better chance to stabilize and lessen this possibility.
- Your next priority should be to get as much of you as possible out of the water, either by swimming to shore or pulling yourself as high as possible onto a life raft or boat. This is especially important if rescue is not imminent. Note that you will likely require help to fully re-enter a boat.
- If you cannot escape the water, and if it is too far to swim (you might be able to manage a kilometre or more, depending on the water temperature), you could

try huddling with a companion and/or maintaining a posture that conserves body heat: crossed arms and legs, knees to chest. Note that while moving arms and legs may increase heat loss, it also increases metabolic heat production, so what you do in this respect will depend on circumstances. If rescue is not imminent, you should probably do everything reasonable to self-rescue, and depending on your circumstances, it's possible that keeping moving may be more beneficial than inactivity.

- If you are travelling on a frozen lake, for example, on snowshoes or a snowmobile, and break through the ice, having quickly accessible ice picks with you may enable you to pull yourself out onto the ice before your limbs seize up.

- Eventually, you may not be able to use your limbs, so anything you need to do while they are still functional, such as swimming and/or pulling yourself out of the water, should be done sooner rather than later. If there is a chance of getting out of the water, that may be more important than conserving body heat. Whatever you do, don't give up as long as you are physically and mentally able to continue.

REALITY CHECK: There have been impressive cold water survival stories that were not well understood by attending doctors. One such was a woman who survived through a long night after a boat upset in the middle of a large lake in north central British Columbia. Her partner died some hours after the accident, yet somehow she willed herself to keep going through the night until she finally washed ashore next morning, immobilized with cold. There, with good fortune, a nearby resident happened to be taking an early morning walk and found her still alive. A year or two later I happened to be in a swimming pool with this person during a workshop at a private residence when she suddenly started relating and reliving the story. It was her first time back in the water, and that had a profound effect on her and on those of us who were privileged to be her spontaneous audience.

Anyone who is rescued from cold water in an advanced state of hypothermia should be handled very gently in order to avoid post-rescue collapse. This may entail keeping them in a horizontal position and only passively rewarming them until they reach a medical facility.

HYPOTHERMIA IN SUMMER

Hypothermia occurs in both above-freezing and below-freezing weather. Indeed, summer mountain travel with the risk of cold wind and rain can sometimes be more dangerous than in the cooler but drier conditions of winter. (Water in its liquid form is a great conductor of heat, whereas water as snow is not as likely to cause wet clothing and can be a great insulator in a survival shelter.) The summertime risk is compounded by the temptation to further extend oneself and to pack fewer items of warm clothing and survival gear than in winter.

REALITY CHECK: I witnessed a highly accomplished mountaineer set out alone to run up and down a rarely travelled, steep – but by his standard, easy – mountain (elevation gain over 1,500 metres) as a training exercise, carrying no pack and just wearing shorts, T-shirt and running shoes. He was experienced and fit but could still have been in trouble if he had sprained or broken an ankle on the exposed upper terrain, a not unlikely event given his footwear. For a less experienced or less fit individual, the undertaking would have been foolhardy, but in this case, and not knowing what backup arrangements he had made, there was nothing I cared to say that he didn't already know. Ultimately it is up to each individual to use their judgment, based on their knowledge, experience and individual safety arrangements, to determine what limits are right for them. A few years later I witnessed a comparable incident involving four young men on Vancouver Island. They were lightly equipped and lightly dressed and were descending late in the evening from high, rugged mountain terrain down to the Forbidden Plateau. In this case, the combination of inexperience and bravado of youth clearly put them at risk, and we voiced that concern as they departed our camp heading into the approaching night.

Hypothermia conditions in a fall rain shower in the Rockies.

GIVING AND HEEDING ADVICE WHEN ASSESSING RISK

This is a brief digression from discussing cold problems, but the examples given at the end of the previous section provide a useful segue into the topics of giving and receiving advice, undertakings that are tricky in any circumstance and no less so in the outdoors.

The differences between the situations cited in the last *Reality Check* amount to risk assessment. In the first case, the individual clearly understood the risks he was taking and had made an informed decision to continue. In the second case, the young men did not fully understand the risks they were taking and had made their decisions in ignorance. In the first instance, the decision to comment was a personal choice; in the second it was an obligation.

Now let's turn this around. If you meet someone on the trail who thinks you need advice, is it worthwhile to listen to them and factor their opinions into your decision making? It may seem natural to resist advice you have not asked for. But perhaps this person may offer experiences you do not have or a perspective you had not considered. They might add weight to doubts you were already entertaining or impart local knowledge you weren't aware of. If nothing else, it will cost you nothing but a little time to hear them out, and you will have a better appreciation of how others see you as you continue on your way. A possible bonus, if you do subsequently get into trouble, is that the person might serve as a valuable witness or last contact, helping searchers to find you sooner.

REALITY CHECK: Two very different scenarios on Mount Robson:

1. Two mountaineers were descending Mount Robson Glacier from the highest peak in the Canadian Rockies. Partway down they passed a climber who was going up alone and appeared to be relatively ill-equipped for this dangerous peak. Concerned, they counselled him to return with them. He declined their offer and was never seen again; the two climbers later became key witnesses in an unsuccessful search.

2. Many years earlier, in October 1978, I had just made my first overnight trek in to Berg Lake, below the northwest side of Robson. I was with a friend, a former climber from France. After supper we met a lone individual, an

American I think, who camped with us on the beach. We were the only three people at Berg Lake that evening. He told us he was going to try and solo Mount Robson starting early the next morning to cap off a climbing season in the Canadian Rockies. Because he was alone, and because of the lateness of the season, my friend argued strongly for him to give up his plan. The next morning we awoke to find a note saying that he had heeded the advice and hiked out.

The Robson River and the north side of Mount Robson.

Mount Robson from Berg Lake in winter.

MORE COLD PROBLEMS: FROSTBITE

Frostbite is the actual freezing of bodily tissues and is therefore quite different from hypothermia. Since both occur in a cold environment, however, they can occur at the same time and compound each other. There are three main stages of frostbite:

- **Superficial frostbite** affects the body no deeper than the thickness of the skin. Signs and symptoms are pain followed by numbness, and a white and waxy appearance of the skin, typically affecting the ears, tip of the nose and cheeks. The treatment is to first prevent further heat loss, perhaps by getting out of the wind or putting on additional clothing, and rewarming gradually, possibly by immersion in cool water. Note that previously frost-bitten skin may be more susceptible to further frostbite.
- **Deep frostbite** affects both the skin and the tissues underneath. This is much more serious and may involve an entire hand or foot, with risk of gangrene and eventual amputation. Treatment is to handle gently to prevent further damage and to get to medical aid as soon as possible. Do not thaw frozen parts unless medical aid is immediately available and there is no danger of refreezing.
- **Frozen skin and tissues** appear to be frozen solid. Get urgent medical aid and remember the adage "not dead until warm and dead."

HEAT PROBLEMS: HYPERTHERMIA

Hyperthermia is less of a problem in Canada's cold northern climes, but it does occur here, the main contributing factors being insufficient hydration, excessive heat and humidity and insufficient cooling. The human body is capable of responding both physiologically and behaviourally. The first physiological autonomic cooling mechanism is to direct blood to the skin, where, if the environment temperature is lower than the body temperature, heat will be radiated away. The second physiological cooling mechanism is through the secretion of sweat, where, if the air is not saturated with water vapour, the highly effective mechanism of evaporative cooling will take place. These two mechanisms are not always enough to ward off hyperthermia, however, especially while exercising hard in hot, humid conditions. This is where behavioural responses come into play. These include monitoring the signs and symptoms discussed below, as well as voluntary actions taken to ward off or recover from hyperthermia.

Hyperthermia is very preventable, provided you are in reasonable physical shape, drink sufficient appropriate fluids even if you are not thirsty, and take some initiative to keep cool. This can be as simple as wearing loose-fitting, lightweight, light-coloured clothing; wearing a shade hat; and avoiding the hottest part of the day, which is generally between noon and 4 p.m. General health, weight and age are also factors in the onset of hyperthermia, and some medications affect the body's ability to sweat. When moving from a cooler environment to a hotter one, the body does adapt on cellular and molecular levels, with significant adaptation occurring within one to two weeks. Therefore, as with climbing to high altitude, acclimatization for heat tolerance can be accommodated into one's travel schedule when going to a hotter clime.

REALITY CHECK: In extreme situations such as in the Sahara desert, a person just sitting in the shade can lose several litres of body fluid per day, and much more while doing moderate exercise. Critical factors are not just the temperature, but especially the dryness of the air. In this circumstance, there is a need to continually replenish fluid, and extreme exercise becomes dangerous or impossible. Beware, though, of consuming too much water – see the discussion on hyponatremia, at p. 102. An effective way that I have found to stay cool while exercising hard on a hot day in is simply to soak a cotton shirt in a stream from time to time and utilize the effect of evaporative cooling without having to first get soaked with sweat. This only works if the ambient air is relatively dry. See also the *Reality Check* about the US Grand Canyon, at p. 23.

THERE ARE THREE STAGES OF HYPERTHERMIA:

- **Mild or onset hyperthermia** may be marked by excessive sweating, muscle cramps, fatigue, headache and nausea. Sometimes the nausea is an after-effect and can linger for a few hours. The response is to rest in a cool place and to drink plenty of water.

- **Heat exhaustion** is a more serious stage where your body is warning you that it is getting too hot. You may become thirsty, although your body's thirst response alone is not very effective in telling you when to drink, which is why you should be drinking long before you get thirsty. The main symptoms include profuse sweating, becoming weak and uncoordinated, nausea and vomiting, and light-headedness leading to unconsciousness. Your skin will be cold and clammy, your pulse slightly weaker and faster than normal. As you sweat you will lose salt along with water. Salt supplements were once part of standard backcountry first aid, but current recommendations are that they should only be taken on the advice of a doctor. Heat exhaustion often results from loss of body fluids through exercise in a hot or humid environment, with humidity reducing the effectiveness of evaporative cooling, as the air is already saturated. Appropriate responses are to find a cool place to rest, remove or loosen clothing and drink lots of water.

- **Heat stroke** is a life-threatening condition where the body's temperature has risen above 40°c, either as a result of the body's temperature control mechanism failing (called classic heatstroke, with very young, elderly and sick people being the most susceptible), and/or continued heavy exercise in a very hot environment beyond the point of heat exhaustion (called exertional heatstroke). Symptoms include a flushed and hot skin that will be dry in the case of classic heatstroke and sweaty in the case of exertional heatstroke. Other symptoms may include headache, confusion, combativeness or unusual behavior, restlessness, nausea and vomiting, faintness or dizziness, strong and rapid pulse progressively becoming weaker, delirium, unconsciousness and possible coma. Heat stroke victims often die, so immediate medical attention is essential. If obtaining urgent medical aid is not possible – as may be the case in the backcountry – the victim should immediately be moved to a shaded place and cooled by means of complete immersion and/or sponging in cool water while maintaining a clear airway.

The body has an amazing ability to generate metabolic heat. Only 25 per cent of metabolic energy production typically goes into the physical work, while 75 per cent is surplus body heat. This has plusses and minuses in a cold climate, through desirable heat production to stay warm or getting dangerously wet from sweating if you have too many clothes on. In a hot environment, it can lead to heat exhaustion or heat stroke.

REALITY CHECK: A cyclist who was able to race all day with the cooling benefit of a 20 km/h road breeze collapsed after only one hour on an equivalent laboratory treadmill. He had the same metabolic heat production, but without the evaporative cooling effect. Conversely, there have been many times when I have winter-climbed a mountain on skis or snowshoes in subfreezing temperatures on a sunny, windless day and experienced the comfortable effects of metabolic heat production while wearing only a thin undershirt. In such circumstances, it is essential to put on extra clothes as soon as you stop, in order to prevent rapid cooling.

HYPONATREMIA

Hyponatremia, or water intoxication, is the opposite of dehydration and is sometimes associated with extreme sports in hot environments where large amounts of water are consumed to prevent dehydration and hyperthermia. The problem is that in addition to the loss of electrolytes, primarily sodium from sweating, the large volume of water that has been consumed dilutes the remaining salt content of the blood. In extreme cases, this can cause problems with muscles, heart and brain, causing confusion, nausea and fatigue, and if left untreated, can quickly lead to coma and death. Since both the environment in which they are manifest and the symptoms themselves are similar to those of hyperthermia, a misdiagnosis that results only in more water being consumed could be catastrophic. The solution, if you plan to exercise hard in a hot environment where you will be sweating a lot, is to drink fluids that contain a good combination of electrolytes. Your pharmacist or physician can advise you on what is available. Avoid drinks such as soda, iced tea, coffee or alcohol that may contain excess sugar or insufficient electrolytes and that are diuretics. A snack of a banana will provide a quickly digested, fast-acting energy boost, with the added bonus of containing potassium. You can minimize sweating in the first place by periodically soaking or misting cotton clothing with water in order to reduce the volume of water required to be consumed. A long-sleeved cotton shirt works better than a T-shirt, as it provides more sun protection and a larger evaporative area. You can extend your evaporation time between water sources by carrying a spare wet cotton shirt in a waterproof bag in your pack.

Hyperthermia or hyponatremia can be a problem in a hot, sun-exposed place if hydration and/or electrolytes are not well maintained.

DESERT AND ARID ENVIRONMENTS

There are no real deserts in Canada, at least as deserts are usually understood, although there are semi-arid areas in British Columbia and Alberta, notably along the Thompson River west of Kamloops, Osoyoos in the southern Okanagan Valley and the badlands of southeastern Alberta. Canada also has polar deserts in such places as Bathurst and Ellesmere islands in the High Arctic. More relevant to Canadians are the deserts of the us southwest, which are readily accessible from Canada by road and by air. Las Vegas, for example, because of its gaming and entertainment focus, is well and inexpensively served by Canadian airlines and is a convenient place from which to stage a trip into surrounding desert lands. The main deserts of the southwest are the hot Sonoran Desert of southern Arizona and southeast California, which extends down into Mexico; the Mojave Desert around Las Vegas in southern Nevada, also extending into California; the Great Basin Desert, covering much of Nevada and extending into southern and western Utah and north into Oregon and Idaho; and the Chihuahuan Desert in south central New Mexico and southwest Texas that extends mostly into Mexico.

Most of my backcountry know-how has come from the hinterlands of Canada. However, as I was preparing the new edition of the book, my wife, Judy, and I took a two week trip to Nevada, Arizona and Utah, where we spent time hiking in the Grand Canyon in Arizona and later in Zion National Park, where we had a chance to see and experience some desert environments – albeit in the fall – as well as being able to talk to park rangers and read guides and books written from local experience. I saw enough to better understand that deserts are not necessarily harsh, empty, forbidding places as many of us who are used to bushier lands may sometimes think. Deserts are full of life and beauty and sometimes of wonderful flower displays. And they invariably offer unending vistas and freedom from the bush and bugs that are an inevitable part of the Canadian backcountry experience.

Like anywhere, deserts have their own particular challenges and dangers, most of which relate to heat and water. As the saying goes, there are two ways to die in the desert: from the heat and by drowning. Why drowning? Take a look out the aircraft window as you fly over Nevada into Las Vegas – the landscape is covered with dry river and stream beds (dry washes) and runnels from almost every ridge. Water has been and still is a big factor in shaping the desert landscape in the us southwest, going back to the inland seas of geological time and the great lakes and floods that followed the end of the last ice age, of which the Great Salt Lake is a remnant. Today, fierce summer thunderstorms of late July and August over the western mountains cause flash floods a great distance away as water runs off impermeable rocky ground. Even as I was writing this part of the book in December 2010, there were major storms in California that caused flooding in Las Vegas and northeast into Utah. Parts of the desert city of St. George in southwest Utah that we drove through in November 2010 were underwater a month later.

For other desert-related information in this book, please review chapter 15 on heat-related problems, beginning at p. 100, and chapter 22, "Other Wildlife Encounters," at p. 150. As well, I have described my Grand Canyon hike in an earlier *Reality Check*, at p. 23 under "Health, fitness, training."

As a final introductory note, desert skills are transferable to other environments. These include minimum-impact dry camping (which opens up new camping opportunities where random camping is allowed); navigation in featureless landscapes; avoiding heat problems; preserving fragile vegetation; avoiding scarring the landscape with vehicle tracks or fire-blackened rocks; and, since desert areas are sparsely populated, off-highway driving.

WATER

The maxim that you can go several weeks without food but only a few days without water applies even more so in the desert. Since hypothermia may be less of a problem in the southwest deserts of the US (although temperatures there can still drop below freezing at night), food consumption for metabolic heat production may be less of an issue than in the Canadian backcountry. Water, on the other hand, and maintaining a proper electrolyte balance, is likely to be a greater challenge due to the daytime heat and the dryness of the air. Even in winter the air here will dehydrate you faster than in moister climates, and two days without water would likely be problematic. In the extreme heat of summer, survival time without water might be measured in hours, not days, especially if you are unable to find shade during peak sunlight hours. Nearly every summer, there are heat-related deaths in Grand Canyon National Park despite many signs warning of the risks.

Water controls most aspects of desert travel: where you go; how much water you can carry; the availability of groundwater and your skills at finding it, especially on multi-day trips; dry camping skills; distant thunderstorms and risk of flash floods, especially if you are exploring some of the many canyons Utah is famous for, or you incautiously find yourself in a dry wash at the wrong time.

Watch for changing weather, sudden changes in water clarity or the approach of floating debris, increasing sounds of water upstream and rising water or stronger currents. It is generally best not to try to outrun rapidly rising water in canyons – instead, seek higher ground by whatever means you can, or as a last resort seek shelter behind a large rock to help break the force of water and debris. On the plus side, flash floods subside as fast as they arise, usually within 24 hours.

Carry enough water to reach the next water source or to return to the last one, and learn what your own particular water needs are. As a general rule, this might be as little as one or two litres for an easy walk on a cool winter day, to eight litres (with electrolytes) for a long hike on a hot day. Since water is used to metabolize food, you could also try eating less if you run low on water, keeping in mind that both food and water are important in a colder climate to help ward off hypothermia.

The various water sources that can be found in the southwestern deserts include permanent and seasonal streams, lakes and ponds; springs; wells; reservoirs; and natural rock tanks, which are deep cavities in impervious rock that catch and hold sparse rainfall. To locate natural desert water sources, look for green vegetation indicating that a spring is nearby; a clump of water-loving trees such as willow or cottonwood that could mean an open stream; small water pockets on sandstone that can be best seen early or late in the day when low sunlight glints off the surface; upstream in shaded canyons; and where there are signs of wildlife.

Because of the scarcity of open water, it is even more important in desert environments than in wetter ecosystems to camp well away from water sources. As a general rule, camp at least 400 metres away, which may be a legal requirement in some jurisdictions.

HEAT

Some of the advice in this section can be extended to northern climes as well, such as when I once found myself in BC's Northern Rocky Mountains Park on a hot summer day, well above treeline with no natural shade from an unrelenting sun that became nearly intolerable; or mountain hiking near Lillooet, BC, at 38°C. But mostly this section applies to the hot deserts of the US southwest.

Whatever you take on in a desert or a hot environment, use moderation and balance your food and water intake to the situation. It is best to reduce or cease physical activity during the hottest part of the day in the summer. This might mean between 10 or 11 a.m. through to 4 or 5 p.m. During that hot period, seek shade under a large rock or tree, or if none are available, erect a tarp or tent fly for shade. The tarp needs to be open and breezy (inside a tent is worse than no protection, akin to an oven) and doubling the tarp or tent fly will block more sunlight and heat. Even when you are away from the direct sunlight, the arid environment will cause you to lose a lot of water through respiration and evaporation, which may not be apparent, as it disappears quickly. Try to avoid gullies that reflect and concentrate sunlight like a reflector oven. An example is the lower section of the Grand Canyon's popular Bright Angel Trail, where some people get into trouble in the summer. If there is open water nearby or if you have a misting bottle, soak or mist a cotton shirt and/or hat to enable the powerful effect of evaporative cooling to take place without the need to sweat. Resume travelling in the early morning, late afternoon, evening and possibly by night, using a headlamp to find your way and to watch for possibly poisonous nocturnal critters.

REALITY CHECK: Two very fit hikers in the Grand Canyon ran out of water and were stricken with hyperthermia. One of them went for help, while the other was unable to travel farther. She, who went for help and was likely the strongest, died, while he, unable to continue, lived. The message is clear: wait for the cool of the evening.

If you are caught out in the desert with a broken-down or stuck vehicle, you can use the vehicle for shade. The best refuge may be to excavate a space in the soil underneath the vehicle (assuming you are off pavement, obviously), making sure the parking brake is on and all wheels are blocked to prevent rolling.

Little Colorado River canyon in Arizona's Painted Desert.

OTHER DESERT CONCERNS

- **Desert plants:** Be aware that the spines of some cacti and other desert plants, especially when they fall off and turn to a desert-colour on the ground, can puncture bike tires and inflatable sleeping pads. Some desert plants are poisonous, so don't eat anything you are not absolutely sure is safe.
- **Sun protection:** Use good sun protection, including a broad-brimmed hat, good SPF sunscreen and UV-blocking sunglasses.
- **Wind:** Watch out for high winds when hiking in the desert in order to avoid dust or sand storms. Stay off particularly susceptible places such as the tops of sand dunes on windy days. This can also be a problem when driving in the desert, even on paved highways, with reduced visibility and especially in agricultural areas prone to topsoil erosion. Apart from the risk of collisions, a full-blown sandstorm can seriously damage vehicle glass and paint, not to mention what it might do to people.
- **Quicksand:** Sand that is saturated with water or is lying on top of water-saturated ground might not be obvious, but if you suddenly find yourself sinking farther into sand with each footstep, and if you can't back out the way you came, fall forward on your stomach and use swimming motions. Quicksand is dense and you shouldn't sink.
- **Walking on sand:** Conserve energy by walking more flat-footedly than you normally would. The same technique probably works for loose snow.
- **Valley fever, or coccidioidomycosis:** See the section on fungal lung infections, at p. 169.

In the desert as elsewhere, **plan ahead** and always have an alternative plan.

Badlands in Alberta.

ELECTRICAL STORM, LIGHTNING

What should you do if you are caught outdoors in an electrical storm? Lightning storms come in different forms. Some approach quickly, while others take hours to build. Some last for hours, while others are over in minutes. Sometimes lightning will strike with no warning whatsoever, as happened to me a few years ago at midnight while tenting in a remote mountain setting. There's not much you can do to avoid that scenario, but fortunately it's rare.

If you are caught by an approaching storm, how much time do you have to react and what action should you take? The easiest approach is to count the seconds between lightning flashes and the accompanying thunder: three seconds equals one kilometre. By this means you can judge whether the storm is coming toward you and how fast it's approaching. If you can, take shelter in a building or vehicle, but not under an isolated tree, especially if it's in an open meadow or field. In that situation, it's better to don raingear and crouch out in the open as described next. If you are on a summit, a mountain ridge, a pinnacle or other exposed place, get off as quickly as you can, as lightning strikes are frequent in such places that provide the shortest distance to ground. Be alert for any signs of charge buildup around you, such as buzzing and sparks, and act quickly. If there is no time to retreat and it is necessary to sit out the storm in the open, put aside anything metal such as an ice axe or aluminum trekking poles and minimize your height, ground contact and chance of an electrical current flowing through you from one limb to another. Crouch down low on a piece of insulating material such as a packsack or sleeping pad, with your feet close together, knees to your chest and hands wrapped around your knees and minimize contact with the ground.

Scrambling or climbing can be especially hazardous, as you may not be able to evacuate the route quickly or find a safe refuge, and a nearby strike could also dislodge rocks or you from your perch. Therefore, allow an extra margin of safety if electrical storms are forecast or you see thunderclouds developing, preferably by staying off steep terrain or at least by starting early to avoid likely danger periods as the day heats up. Avoid rappelling during an electrical storm, as the wet rope could be a conductor.

There are several different kinds of lightning strikes that affect people, of which a direct strike, although violent and often fatal, may be the least common. One type is a lateral strike from an object to you. Another is electrical current induced in the ground from a nearby strike. To avoid lateral strikes and ground currents, stay clear of small lakes, wet open meadows, trees and shallow caves or overhangs that the current could arc across. To avoid direct strikes, stay off ridges and other convex topography such as knolls during electrical activity. A concave slope or good-size hollow may be your best choice, or in the open near the bottom of a good-size cliff or pinnacle, staying within a radius roughly equivalent to the height of the pinnacle and a few metres away from the base. When an electrical storm hits, split up the group to lessen the chance of the whole party being struck and ensure that help will be available for any who do get hit. If someone in your party is struck by lightning, follow the ABCs of first aid and be prepared to administer CPR if needed; then treat other injuries such as burns. Recovery is common after a lightning strike and you should be prepared to do everything possible to help someone who has been struck. Don't be concerned about getting an electrical shock from a lightning strike victim; that's generally only an issue in an electrical emergency for someone in contact with an energized transmission line.

If you are thinking of camping on a ridge or mountain top to be closer to the stars, check the weather forecast very carefully to be sure there is little chance of lightning that night.

A rapidly approaching electrical storm.

REALITY CHECK: My childhood introduction to the outdoors was in Leicestershire's Charnwood Forest, in the heart of the English Midlands. A centrepiece of Charnwood Forest is a wild deer park, which loomed large in my eyes as a kid, walking through tall bracken ferns, climbing to the landmark Old John Tower on the park's prominent hilltop and down to the ruins where the nine-day Queen of England, Lady Jane Grey, spent her formative years before briefly taking the throne in 1553 as the shortest-reigning English monarch. Through many return visits over half a century, I watched the 340-hectare Bradgate Country Park (now part of Britain's National Forest) gradually diminish in stature to a simple hill, overrun with too many visitors, that could be traversed in half an hour of easy walking. Not so, however, in the summer of 2009, when I went for a walk there and found myself in the epicentre of the most violent electrical storm I have ever experienced. The skies raged for two hours, and since I was ill-equipped, with light summer clothes and an old breathable raincoat that had long since given up being waterproof, I was soon soaked through and fast becoming hypothermic as I

There is never any room for complacency, as the author found out in Bradgate Country Park, UK, where he took shelter from a fierce electrical storm. The ruins in the background were once the home of Lady Jane Grey, Queen of England for nine days, July 10–19, 1553.

sought refuge from intense lightning strikes that were now all around. First, I crouched beside a stone wall near Lady Jane Grey's old house, then out in the open and finally in a copse of ancient oaks. I wasn't sure what to do, as there were at least as many strikes in the open as among the centuries-old oak trees, some of which I knew to have blackened interiors from past lightning strikes. Deer ran this way and that, equally confused, which was not very comforting, as you at least expect the wildlife to know what to do in the outdoors. Large clouds of birds were periodically blasted out of nearby trees where they had sought refuge. The roof of a house in a nearby village was blown off and a small tornado was seen in another, an event almost unheard of in the English countryside. As the intensity of the storm exploded into the second hour, one thought kept occurring to me: how ironic to have survived decades of exploring Canada's mountain backcountry only to succumb to the elements in Bradgate Park. The moral of this tale is: *Complacency – Always leave home without it!*

BORDERLINE MOUNTAINEERING

Hiking trips in the mountains can sometimes stray into what might be called borderline mountaineering, where higher standards of care are required by people who may not be skilled in, properly equipped for or being led in accordance with technical mountaineering standards.

ROCKFALL

Mountaineers, especially rock climbers, generally wear climbing helmets for protection from falling rocks, and they follow protocols such as small group sizes and careful positioning on the slope to minimize the risk of injury to themselves or others below. Before climbing helmets came into use, early mountaineers would sometimes hold their packs over their heads when hearing rocks falling from above, not always to good effect. But rockfall does not happen only on climbing routes; it can occur on easy ground below rock faces and on non-technical slopes too, and it can be a considerable hazard if a large group of people are ascending a slope that is littered with loose rock. Even a small rock accidentally dislodged by an incautious footstep could have potentially deadly consequences to those below as it quickly gathers speed. It is easy for non-mountaineers to stray into borderline territory without realizing the danger they have suddenly exposed themselves to. The situation can be exacerbated if the group is in a laid-back hiking mode without a clearly defined leader close by. In such a circumstance, it is especially important to have identified the leader and to have a group size sufficiently small that the leader can observe and communicate with everyone. When a difficult piece of ground is encountered, the leader should pause and discuss with the group how they will proceed. Where rockfall is likely, one approach is to ascend or descend the slope at an angle or one person at a time, avoiding chutes and concave terrain.

REALITY CHECK: In August 2006 a large group of hikers was starting to ascend the upper slopes of the recently dedicated Mount Pierre Elliott Trudeau above Valemount, BC. It wasn't clear at that point who was actually leading the group, which was spread out over the slope, with everyone more or less doing their own thing. Adding to the confusion, a loud disagreement broke out between two members of the party as to whether or not a rockfall hazard existed. The slope, while steep, did not appear to be a technical climb and it was not obvious to most of the people in the party that there was a danger. Suddenly, someone dislodged a large, flat, circular rock that, because of its shape and the smooth nature of the shale slope, rapidly gained speed as it cart-wheeled down, skipping in ever higher bounds as it reached a high rate of speed. It was headed straight at a member of the party, who waited until the last instant to be sure where it was going before leaping out of its way. A catastrophe was narrowly averted and the club later held an incident review meeting with an independent expert present to review its procedures and learn from the event.

Mount Pierre Elliott Trudeau shortly before a rockfall incident took place on its upper slopes.

GLACIERS AND SNOWFIELDS

It may be tempting for a party of hikers to venture onto a snowfield or glacier, perhaps just for the experience of doing so or to reach an objective above or on the far side. Depending on the situation and time of year (and local knowledge is key) the route may be fairly safe or it may require ice axes for self arrest, crampons for grip on exposed ice, and harnesses, ropes and slings for a possible crevasse rescue. In the latter situation – more likely to be found in convex, or bulging, terrain, where crevasses are more prevalent – just having the gear may not be enough. Crevasse rescue requires specialized knowledge and practice to set up the belay

114

and pulley systems for the necessary mechanical advantage. Similarly, anyone using an ice axe on steep ice or snow should have some practice at self arrest and be aware of the pitfalls of getting it wrong, namely injury and/or ineffectiveness. A good rule, therefore, is to stay off glaciers and snowfields unless you are part of an experienced and properly equipped team. If you must cross a snow-covered glacier, the party should usually be roped together. This also applies to snowfields and sometimes even to rock and scree slopes, as the transition to snow or debris-covered glacier may not be apparent.

REALITY CHECK: I know of several hikers who have fallen through crevasses in snow or ice where none were expected, and it was only by good fortune that none of those who found themselves in that predicament were seriously hurt or killed.

Glacier in BC's Monkman Provincial Park.

SWIFT WATER AND OCEAN SHORELINE

Swift water can present many challenges in the backcountry. Here are some suggestions for staying out of trouble in a variety of situations in creeks and rivers.

BOATS

This section is mainly directed at recreational canoeing and kayaking, but most of it applies as well to other craft such as rafts, tubes and power boats. Note that operators of powered watercraft used for recreational purposes in Canada now require a Pleasure Craft Operator Card certifying that they have passed a Transport Canada accredited exam.

- Always wear a life jacket or personal flotation device (PFD), and carry a bailing device, line and spare paddle in the boat. You will have even less chance of donning a life jacket after capsizing in a river than you would in a lake, and you will have quite enough to do in a very dynamic situation without having to worry about your PFD as well.

- Watch out for and avoid logjams, overhanging sweepers, and strainers, especially on fast rivers in wooded country. Sweepers and strainers are most often found on outside bends where the river has undercut the bank and caused trees that are still rooted in the bank to topple into the river. If there are a lot of branches remaining on the tree, it forms a strainer that can stop a person while allowing the water to flow through, forcing the person underwater with a high likelihood of fatality. If you have no way of avoiding a strainer or logjam, try to climb out of the boat or the river and onto the obstacle before you get caught. Be especially vigilant during and after the spring freshet, and try to talk with someone who has been down the river recently. Logjams, sweepers and strainers change from year to year, and the river you canoed without incident just a few months earlier may now have new and potentially deadly obstructions where your canoe and gear – and yourself if you are unable to scramble clear of the boat in time – could be trapped or sucked under by the irresistible force of the water. Keep your attention on the river at least 100 metres ahead to give you time to avoid an obstacle and if necessary either land the boat or ferry it to the other side. If you are the skipper of a boat on swift water your attention should always be on the river ahead, not on a fishing float or the passing scenery.

- Avoid having a loose rope trailing the boat in the water: it can drop to the bottom and become entangled; or worse, attach itself to a person by wrapping around an arm or leg. If you are in moving water and caught by a rope like this, the tendency will be for it to dive you underwater like a fishing lure. Be wary of tying two or more boats, rafts or tubes together, especially in a river with bridges: the combined craft will be much harder to steer and could wrap around a bridge piling with disastrous results.

- Take a swift-water canoeing or kayaking course and learn the river rating system:[11]

  Class 1 (easy, no manoeuvring required)

  Class 2 (novice or basic paddling skill – some rocks, small drops and some manoeuvring necessary)

  Class 3 (intermediate or experienced paddling skill – medium-sized waves and drops with more significant manoeuvring)

  Class 4 (advanced or whitewater skill – larger waves, rocks and drops and tight manoeuvring)

  Class 5 (expert or advanced whitewater skill – continuous rapids with large waves, rocks, drops and other hazards and exact manoeuvring)

  Class 6 (expert – extreme and exploratory with huge hazards, hydraulics and unknown dangers; hazardous or life-threatening even for experts)

- If you are river canoeing, it's best to travel in groups of three or more craft, ideally with a paddling club and/or with experienced companions, some of whom should have experience with a swift water rescue course. Techniques learned on such a course may include approaching an incident from downstream and the use of throw bags or getting a line across the river to reach a victim in the water quickly. For experienced river travellers there are advanced techniques for situations such as rescuing people trapped in a logjam.

- Practise rescuing an overturned canoe in safe water, for example, by lifting the stricken boat out of the water and across your boat, righting it after it has drained, then stabilizing the two craft side by side to enable the other canoe's occupants to reboard. This, again, is best learned through taking a canoeing course.

- Practise righting and/or exiting from an overturned kayak, also in a safety-supervised setting. Some municipal swimming pools set aside times when people can practise with their craft in the pool.
- Protect yourself when approaching a victim in the water whom you suspect might panic and endanger you as well. If unsure, offer the person the end of a spare paddle, but be prepared to release it should you become imperilled by their having a panic reaction.
- Beware of and avoid perpetual circular currents below a low drop, whether natural shelf or artificial weir. These often appear to be harmless but can sometimes entrap a person in the circular hydraulics.
- There are many other hazards that may be encountered on rivers. As well as logjams, sweepers and strainers already mentioned, smaller rivers often contain obvious visible hazards such as rocks, falls and turbulent water. Larger rivers have these hazards as well, but you also have to be careful of powerful hydraulics at such places as eddy lines, headwalls and sharp corners. Again, travel with experienced companions and take some training.

Paddling the Arctic–Pacific Divide at Summit Lake, north of Prince George, BC.

- If there are two or more of you in cold water and help is not imminent, huddling together may help reduce heat loss and postpone the onset of hypothermia. See also the section on cold water immersion, at p. 94.
- For rescuers dealing with apparent drowning victims in cold water, be aware of a possible anti-drowning reflex whereby water may be prevented from entering the lungs, especially in very young infants. That, and attendant hypothermia, may offer a greater possibility of resuscitation, even after an extended period in cold water.

WADING AND FORDING

- Avoid standing alone in swift water that is much greater than knee deep. Unstable footing could lead to your feet becoming trapped and/or to loss of balance causing you to fall into the water and the force of the water to pull you under. A safe depth for fording depends on the size of the individual, the speed of the current and possible footing hazards that could trap you. For example, if the water is thigh deep with a safe footing, the maximum safe current speed might be around eight kilometres per hour.
- If you are using hip or chest waders while working (e.g., aquatic sampling) or playing (e.g., fly-fishing) in swift water, beware of the danger of the waders becoming flooded and holding you under the water. Tree-planting bags may create a similar hazard. Chest waders, while providing more clearance from the water, are likely to be more dangerous than hip waders if they fill with water. Wear a life jacket and carry a knife similar to those carried by divers to give you a chance of cutting yourself free.
- While fording swift-moving creeks, for example, on a mountain trek, wear your hiking boots or change into sturdy creek-crossing shoes, and use a pole for support on your downstream side. If you have trekking poles with you, two poles may work better than one. Choose a crossing place where the creek or river is wider and shallower and there are no deep holes. If there are shorter and/or less secure people in the group, they may need assistance to cross. One method that works well is to have several people in a diagonal line support each other with linked arms or poles, with a strong person in the leading, or upstream, position breaking the water flow and the others taking advantage of slipstream effects and upstream support. A variation is a "football huddle" of three people supporting each other.
- On more serious, expedition-style crossings, you may have no choice but to use a rope, but watch out for the possibility of slipping while tied to or caught in a rope and being pulled under the water by a tied or snagged rope and the force of the current. It might be better to have someone on shore belay the rope to the

person in the water rather than tying the rope to a fixed object such as a tree; that way the rope can be slackened or, in dire circumstances, released as needed. Persons doing the belaying can attach themselves securely to trees or rocks to avoid being pulled into the water.

Fording a mountain creek at the end of a long hike.

- If you fall or slip into fast-moving water and are unable to regain your footing, swim diagonally with the current to the nearest shore. Do not try to stand up until the water is very shallow.
- Before fording a creek, ask yourself whether you really have to cross. If the water is above the knees of the shortest person in the group, seriously consider not doing it. Where do I cross? How do I cross? Is the water likely to rise (rain, afternoon snow or glacier melt) such that I might be prevented from returning?
- If you decide you must ford a creek, some places to avoid are at bends, above rapids or waterfalls, above a confluence, places with poor visibility, downstream obstacles or debris carried by current, or during floods. Better places to cross might be where the riverbed is smooth and in the middle of an S-curve between bends.
- Before you cross, unfasten your hip belt and any other buckles and pack straps or other gear that could hold you under if you can't quickly get rid of them. Similar action is recommended if you must cross a snow slope that is at risk of avalanching

Four people support each other, with the tallest breaking the force of the current for the others.

and especially for crossing a snow- and ice-covered lake. In the latter case, keep your thumbs hooked under your pack's shoulder straps so you can instantly throw it backward onto the ice to reduce your weight and encumbrance if you break through. See, for example, the *Reality Check* about Fred Van der Post, at p. 9.

- When you cross, take short, shuffling steps; avoid hanging on to or leaning against underwater obstacles; move with the current; and use a chain of people, with the strongest person upstream to break the current.

REALITY CHECK: A young woman, backpacking in a remote part of Jasper National Park a few years ago, drowned after she fell into a creek wearing a pack that she was unable to release.

VEHICLES IN WATER

This section applies to both moving and flat water: What do you do if your vehicle inadvertently and suddenly leaves the road and enters the water? First, it will most likely be a total surprise — most people who find themselves in a deadly

British Columbia's Grand Canyon of the Fraser River, 75 km east of Prince George, is reputed to have claimed over 200 lives in its rapids and whirlpools.

circumstance had no idea it was coming three seconds before it happened; otherwise they would have taken evasive action. Therefore, it's good to think through circumstances like this ahead of time, especially if you are on a little-travelled, unpaved road in the backcountry.

Entering a river or lake might happen by going off a bend in the road while driving on ice, loose gravel or other slippery surface or on a wet road in the dark or by falling asleep at the wheel. It might be a failed bridge deck, especially off-highway during a stormy night. Your actions in the first minutes are going to be critical to your survival, as the average float time of a car is just one to four minutes before it sinks, nose down. Stay calm and immediately open a window or door. Once the vehicle has started to submerge, it may be impossible to open a door until the vehicle has flooded and the water pressure has equalized. Most modern vehicles have electric windows which may remain operable for only a few seconds; if you're lucky they may last a few minutes, but don't count on it. The next option is to break a side window. The windshield may be impossible to break, as it is laminated glass designed to withstand impacts. Even side windows in modern vehicles can be tough to break. I once heard several people trying to break a side window of a modern pickup truck while we were camped near a northern community in the middle of the night. It took repeated blows over several minutes with what sounded like a sledgehammer, and the process was sufficiently protracted to give the police time to be called, respond and give chase. To stand the best chance of breaking the side window, you need to keep a sharp tool handy in the vehicle (sometimes called a safety hammer or life hammer) and strike the glass in a corner next to the window frame. The tool must be sharp – discard if is has dulled or been used more than a couple of times. To recap: stay calm; immediately get a door and/ or window open; release your seatbelt; get out!

It may take only two feet to float a truck and as little as six inches to float a car, which could be enough to quickly carry the vehicle into deeper water. If an all-terrain vehicle (ATV) flips and pins you underneath, it may be impossible to move it by yourself and you could drown even in a shallow creek. Therefore, it is a good idea to check out crossing points in advance; it's a little-known and unfortunate fact that many industrial fatalities in remote settings are water-related.

OCEAN SHORE HAZARDS

An ocean beach is often thought of as one of the most benign and relaxed places in which to enjoy the outdoors, but it comes with its own special hazards.

TSUNAMI

During a recent tour up the coasts of Oregon and Washington's Olympic Peninsula, I was interested to see how seriously the threat of tsunami is being taken there. Hazard zones and tsunami evacuation routes are routinely signed in many places, and in one place in Oregon I was surprised and pleased to see a temporary highway sign warning of traffic slowdowns the next day for a tsunami evacuation practice. The Cascadia subduction zone of western North America (which, in Canada, includes Vancouver and the Fraser Valley) regularly experiences the largest earthquakes on earth, the last one being a little over 300 years ago, and we may be getting close to the next one: most authorities say there is a 20 per cent probability in the next 50 years. If you are living in this part of the world, it's a good idea to try and prepare for the big earthquake, and if you are living or recreating close to the ocean, you should also be aware of and prepared for tsunamis by knowing local tsunami warning signals and where the evacuation routes are. Tsunamis are associated with earthquakes, and the west coast of North America experiences two types: those resulting from distant earthquakes, in which case you will likely have many hours of warning to seek higher ground or move inland; and those associated with local earthquakes, where you have little warning and may not be able to count on your vehicle for evacuation, due to infrastructure damage. In the latter case, especially for permanent residents in a tsunami zone, you should both know and practise your evacuation route(s) on foot and at night. Higher ground means at least 15 metres, or 50 feet, above sea level. If you are on an extended shoreline hike, especially away from populated areas, you might consider carrying an inexpensive all-hazards weather radio.

After a disaster of the magnitude likely to accompany either of these earthquake/tsunami scenarios, you may have to be self-sufficient for at least a few days. A final note: when a tsunami wave is imminent, you might see the ocean draining rapidly away. This would be a good time to run for higher ground and/or inland. After the first tsunami wave has passed, there may be follow-up surges for many more hours, especially as a result of aftershocks and related submarine landslides.

OTHER SHORELINE HAZARDS TO WATCH OUT FOR

- Avoid becoming stranded by rising tides isolating parts of beaches, cliffs and rocks; carry local tide tables with you and refer to them.
- Watch for unusually high waves, especially where they may swamp rocks and jetties you might be walking on. This is an obvious danger during storms, but watch out for so-called sneaker waves even on less stormy days.
- If you choose to swim (or even wade) in the ocean, watch out for strong outflowing rip currents. They can be too strong to swim against, resulting in exhaustion and death by drowning. Wearing a personal flotation device is a good idea, especially for children or non-swimmers who are wading in waist-deep water and who risk being swept off their feet and pulled out to sea. If you are caught in a rip current, stay calm and swim parallel to the shoreline until you are out of the usually narrow flow. Then swim diagonally back to shore, aiming for breakers if possible to help push you ashore.
- High cliffs and falling rocks are common on shorelines and must be respected just as in the high mountains.
- Watch out for large drift logs that can roll in the surf and entrap or crush you.

Oregon coast in the fall of 2011.

COMMUNICATIONS

There are many communication options you can consider for backcountry use. Being in a remote place without any means of communication adds a dimension to the experience, but if you should find yourself in a tough situation, the lack of communications may mean the difference between life and death.

REALITY CHECK: In the mid-1990s, two companions and I were 14 days, 110 kilometres and several mountain ranges away from the possibility of help in a remote part of northern BC. Unarmed and without communications, we were being stalked by a large grizzly bear. I would not recommend the experience, nor would I wish to repeat it, yet I am not sorry I had it. Apart from our modern gear and an eventual prearranged pickup by floatplane, the experience was not unlike that of our ancestors throughout human history. It also resembled what soldiers sometimes describe about combat as a sublime or transcendent experience; we too were utterly absorbed in the moment. Although it appeared that we were facing an imminent charge, we were fortunate in being able to take control of the situation by simply retreating behind the mountain the bear had claimed. After a tense hour circumnavigating three-quarters of the mountain, we spent an anxious night camped on a knoll hardly two kilometres from the place of the original encounter. The next afternoon, we spotted another grizzly blocking our way in a valley bottom we had to cross, and after working our way carefully around, we opted to camp on a ledge high on the mountainside above. Throughout both of these encounters, we were all too aware of having no means of summoning help.

It was easier to justify not having communications capability even as late as the mid-1990s, as lightweight, affordable satellite phones were only then starting to become available. It was just part of the backcountry experience to be out of contact for a few days. Today, that window has largely closed and it is now hard to rationalize (especially to loved ones and dependents) not taking a satellite communication device on a long backcountry trip to a remote place where you are unlikely to meet anyone. As technology continues its rapid development, more options are becoming available and existing systems are evolving every year.

Regardless of the type of communications equipment you take with you, make sure everyone in the group knows how to operate it in an emergency.

SATELLITE PHONE

This is a great option to have with you. Weighing only a few hundred grams, including a battery that will give several hours of talk time, a hand-held satellite phone can now be purchased for a few hundred dollars and rented for much less. Unfortunately, some of the satellite availability has degraded such that many sat-phone users now carry satellite availability tables that can be downloaded from the Internet for a particular time and place, rather like carrying tide tables for marine or coastal travel. Hopefully this is a transient problem that will diminish as aging satellites are replaced. The weight and cost of a satellite phone are now trivial compared to the security provided, especially when divided among a group of people and used sparingly. The phone can be used to update your itinerary if circumstances in the field have caused you to make changes. It can also be used to give highly specific information in the event of a problem, thereby minimizing and confining search and rescue costs to perhaps a single helicopter flight to a specific location.

REALITY CHECK: A dramatic rescue was mounted following a serious accident in Fang Cave in Evanoff Provincial Park in north central BC in the fall of 2009. Several factors made the difference between life and death in a cliffhanger of an operation. The first critical success factor was getting a satellite phone connection from the cave entrance high on the mountainside – it was literally a lifesaver. One key lesson learned the hard way in the Fang Cave rescue is the value of carrying local emergency phone numbers to avoid going through an international call centre with the attendant risk of losing critical time and key information not being relayed properly. This incident is described in more detail in chapter 24, "After something has happened," beginning at p. 171.

In my view, the key to taking a satellite phone and still having a great wilderness experience is to avoid using the phone except to test it and to report significant itinerary changes to your contact, and of course as a last resort to ask for help in the event of a serious problem. The satellite phone (or any telecommunications device, for that matter) should not be viewed as a substitute for self-sufficiency.

The phone should be carried in a waterproof container or packaging. Make a few calls before leaving in order to make sure it is working and to become familiar with it in a variety of situations. Carry along or preprogram the phone numbers you may need, and ensure that others in the group know how to operate the device. Be aware that the terrain you are travelling in may limit the phone's efficiency and require you to move to different or higher ground. As mentioned above, satellite availability may also be an issue, depending on which network you are using, and it might be helpful to know when a working satellite will be in range. If you are travelling far from your home, especially overseas, ensure that you have the ground-station access you will need in order to make contact from where you will be. Also, in the Far North (above 70° latitude) some satellite phone systems may not provide coverage at all and it might be necessary to use a different network. It may also be helpful to carry a GPS with you in order to be able to give accurate coordinates when changing an itinerary or requesting assistance. The downsides of a satellite phone versus a personal locator beacon or a personal satellite tracker (described below) are that it may be less reliable in terms of satellite availability; it requires dialogue (usually a plus), which might not always be possible; and it is likely to be more complicated to operate than simply pushing a button. These are actions that could be compromised by an injury or by urgency of response time in the face of an impending disaster.

EMERGENCY LOCATOR TRANSMITTER

An emergency locator transmitter (ELT) is a device required to be carried in all aircraft that is automatically, and if necessary manually, activated in the event of an air crash to transmit a distress signal on the 406 MHz international search and rescue frequency. Some pilots also carry a second, portable unit as a backup. If you are flying in a bush plane or helicopter, ask the pilot where the ELT is located before you take off and how to activate it manually in the event it doesn't trigger automatically. You may be the only one able to do so in the aftermath of an accident. The ELT signal will be picked up by SARSAT, the search and rescue satellite-aided tracking system, and after confirmation a search and rescue response will be initiated. This will typically involve an armed forces fixed-wing aircraft and/or a helicopter crewed with search and rescue technicians (SARTECHS) with parachute capability to provide immediate assistance. This is obviously a very big deal, as an air search can quickly run into the tens of thousands or even millions of dollars, so the use of an ELT is strictly controlled, by law, for aviation use only. See also SARSAT, below.

EMERGENCY POSITION-
INDICATING RADIO BEACON

An emergency position-indicating radio beacon (EPIRB) is the marine equivalent of an ELT, also operating on 406 MHz. The best models are designed to automatically activate and float free if submerged. A GPS option is almost essential, especially on the open ocean, and could be a lifesaver to better pinpoint the position and reduce rescue time in stormy waters.

PERSONAL LOCATOR BEACON

A personal locator beacon (PLB) works like an ELT in that it sends a signal to a satellite network, but is designed for personal rather than aviation use. Like the ELT, it transmits on the 406 MHZ international search and rescue frequency, and some models may also use the 121.5 MHZ aircraft distress frequency. The PLB is similar in size, weight and cost to a satellite phone and works anywhere in the world, which not all satphones do. It is likely to be more robust, failsafe and powerful than a satphone or other personal satellite communication device, but it lacks the means to provide much personalized information beyond a unique identifier (which keys to whatever data you supplied when you last registered or updated your personal information for the device) and, in many models, your GPS location. All you can basically say through a PLB – mind you, it's a powerful "all" – is "Help! Come and get me!" You can't use it just to update your position or itinerary or to request some lesser action than a full-on emergency response. A PLB may require servicing by the manufacturer after it has been deployed. Some models have an optional GPS that instantly transmits your coordinates with the distress signal, potentially cutting down response time. Planned upgrades to the SARSAT system (see below) may eventually lessen this advantage. Use of a PLB requires preregistering with the nearest (military) rescue coordination centre, with periodic updates recommended. The response to a PLB activation will be similar to that of an ELT, except that the search will not necessarily be for a downed aircraft.

Since satellite phones have become lightweight and affordable and allow the versatility of a telephone, you might prefer to carry a satphone rather than a PLB. But if you are travelling in remote or higher-risk areas, choosing a PLB as well as or instead of a satellite phone might make sense. Even closer to home, if you don't know where you are or you are unable to communicate because of injuries, or you are in a poor location and unable to move, and you can't get a satellite phone signal, a PLB is likely to raise an alarm and locate you. All you have to be able to do is deploy the antenna and push the SEND button. Other personal satellite tracking devices described in this chapter would likely serve a similar purpose, perhaps trading more versatility for slightly less certainty that your signal will be heard. If you are immobilized in a place without a good signal or if time is of the essence and you can't wait for a satellite to be acquired, a PLB might be the best choice. A final word: dispose of your old PLB properly by removing the battery to avoid another accidental activation in a waste disposal dump (as has happened a few times), which could have monetary and legal implications.

SARSAT AND DASS

The search and rescue satellite aided tracking system (SARSAT) was originally established in 1982 by the US, Canada, France and the USSR, and since that time the system has been responsible for 27,000 people being rescued worldwide as of 2010. Previously, the system used 121.5 MHZ and 243 MHZ international distress frequencies, but as of February 2009 these are no longer being monitored by satellites, although cockpit air crew may still routinely monitor 121.5 MHZ for other aircraft in distress. ELTS, PLBS and EPIRBS now transmit on 406 MHZ at 5 or more watts instead of 121.5 MHZ at 75 milliwatts as on the old system. This has drastically reduced the number (and cost) of false alarms while cutting the potential search area from 1,260 square kilometres to only 13 and reducing response time in that the more powerful signal can reach geostationary satellites that are always in view. In the original system, search and rescue satellites were in low earth orbit, requiring an orbital delay of 45 to 90 minutes plus perhaps additional delay to get a confirmation from the next orbit, followed by an aircraft search to pinpoint the signal location. Now, the National Oceanic & Atmospheric Administration (NOAA) is the lead agency in the US for SARSAT, as it carries search and rescue instruments on its satellites. A high-orbit geostationary operational environmental satellite (GEOS) picks up a distress signal immediately and stores and forwards it to a response centre within ten minutes. If the transmitting device has a GPS option, the position within 100 metres is known immediately. Otherwise, a low polar orbiting environmental satellite (POES) acquires the signal on its next pass overhead, and because it is a satellite that moves relative to the ground, it can determine a 13-square-kilometre approximate location using the Doppler effect. In May 2010 NOAA and NASA announced the development of the distress alerting satellite system (DASS), which will eventually have search and rescue instruments installed on all 24 of its next-generation GPS satellites. Whenever a distress signal goes off, six satellites will be in view and an exact position can be calculated almost immediately. The aim, according to the lead agencies, is to take the "search" out of search and rescue. Other countries with their own versions of GPS systems, including Russia, Europe and China, will have similar capabilities.

OTHER PERSONAL SATELLITE COMMUNICATION DEVICES

In recent years, other small, inexpensive devices incorporating GPS receivers are becoming available, marketed as satellite GPS messengers or personal trackers. The forerunner of these was the Spot device, which, at the push of a button, sends an sos alarm and your GPS coordinates to an international response centre. This is similar to a PLB, except that it uses a commercial satellite phone network instead of the search and rescue system. It has options to send a non-life-threatening help message or a check-in/okay message to designated contacts, typically by email, and to create a track of your progress. It can also send a prewritten short text message. This is a marvellous device that combines features of a satellite phone and a PLB. It is not as versatile as a satellite phone and probably not as failsafe as a PLB, but it's a powerful tool nonetheless. Although it uses one of the satellite phone systems, it is not as sensitive to aging satellites, as it uses different instrumentation on the satellites. It is not as expensive to buy as a PLB, but it does have an annual operating fee. It can be used as often as required, whereas the PLB may be designed for a one-time activation, after which it may require servicing by the manufacturer.

REALITY CHECK: A friend of mine bought one of these when they first came out. He found it to be a reliable tool and his wife was able to track his progress whenever he was out in the backcountry, even when she was away travelling.

Like anything else, test out new gear in the conditions in which you intend to use it, to become familiar with its operation and effectiveness.

TWO-WAY RADIO

A two-way radio is more likely to be used in work-related situations where an employer or government agency provides repeater stations and monitored frequencies in the area you are working in. Radios can be highly portable and can sometimes be used to patch into a telephone network, thus giving the advantages of a satellite phone in limited areas of use. A two-way radio can require specific knowledge to use and programmed access to local private frequencies and infrastructure. A VHF radio also requires line of sight to a repeater station, meaning that it may not be as versatile as a satellite phone.

HAM RADIO

If there is someone in your party who is trained and qualified as an amateur radio operator, that person may be able to offer a good, portable, inexpensive alternative to a satellite phone. Local amateur radio, or "ham radio," clubs offer training and also volunteer their time to search and rescue and other emergency planning and response organizations. With the advance of technology, however, there are far fewer people involved in amateur radio today, and those who remain are generally part of an aging demographic, suggesting a continuing decline. In recognition of these changes, and the continuing importance of amateur radio in times of emergency, the federal government has relaxed entry requirements, recognizing that there is little need anymore for the average user to understand the inner electronic workings of radio sets or to be able to communicate in Morse code. Perhaps there is also less fear of uninformed disruptions to radio communications. What used to take a year of study and an examination can now be done in a weekend for the basics, with a little more study required for access to a wider range of frequencies (and reach). Other factors to consider are that on the plus side, significantly less use of ham radio frequencies means easier access to airtime for scheduled calls, while on the downside there are fewer people on the air to hear an unscheduled distress call. One aspect of the now pervasive use of satellite technology is the possible effect of a large solar storm on satellite networks during periods of solar maxima, which happen every 11 years. Amateur radio may therefore still have a societal role to play vis-à-vis natural disasters, human conflicts and possible disruptions to satellite networks; and as long as it's there, it can potentially be used for backcountry communication and emergencies.

REALITY CHECK: One of the largest searches ever to be conducted around my home town of Prince George in north central BC took place in September 1980. Continuing throughout the three-day Labour Day weekend and attracting national and international media attention, it later became known as the "Hoax Search" because of its eventual outcome. Intermittent calls for help were heard through a radio telephone repeater station from a child who was supposedly trapped with his critically injured or possibly already dead parents in an overturned pickup truck somewhere in the bush within an approximate 100-kilometre radius. With over 30,000 square kilometres to search and a faint and highly intermittent radio signal providing the only clues, ham radio operators became the stars of that weekend, supplying technical help that neither the department of communications nor the telephone company could provide during the holiday weekend. The hams set up mobile, manned radio stations on high ground around the city with the aim of triangulating the source (not the repeater) signal. Apart from time spent on the search itself, I spent one night helping man one such station, west of the city. I was there when an American tourist in a ham-equipped motor home offered to interrupt his journey home from Alaska and stay as long as it took to help in the search, amply demonstrating the camaraderie of the ham community. The search was ultimately determined to be a hoax after the ham volunteers succeeded in locating the source signal, but the episode served to illustrate the resourcefulness of ham radio operators in emergencies.

GMRS AND FRS RADIOS

Inexpensive, small, hand-held GMRS (general mobile radio service) and FRS (family radio service) radios may be useful for communicating between separated parts of a group over distances of up to a few kilometres, depending on the power of the radio and line-of-sight limitations of the UHF (ultra high frequency) band. However, these units are not always dependable, due to terrain difficulties in hilly and forested country, and they should be used with that in mind. These radios may also be useful for communicating between members of a party in an emergency where direct voice communication is difficult due to background wind or stream noise. While these are obviously intended for parties of two or more people, they might still have value for a person who has gone out alone in that a search party could listen on a designated channel if it was known that the missing person was carrying a GMRS or FRS radio.

REALITY CHECK: I was once repeatedly unable to contact another member of a party I was hiking with, using a GMRS radio that was supposed to have a 25-kilometre range. I finally made radio contact, only to look up and see the individual a mere 200 metres away in open subalpine forest, by which time we could communicate just by shouting across the clearing!

MOBILE (CELL) PHONE

A mobile phone offers similar benefits as a satellite phone but with much less certain coverage outside of metropolitan areas and away from major highways. On the other hand, mobile phones are extremely lightweight and they have become almost ubiquitous, so it probably wouldn't hurt to carry one when you are in the backcountry. If you are high on a mountainside, with line of sight to a mobile phone tower, you might get a signal even if you are outside the normal coverage area. Try yours on local hikes and see how effective it is. If you are far from the coverage area or in complex, steep terrain, do not rely on a mobile phone; and, as with the satellite phone, never substitute the mobile phone for common sense and self-sufficiency. They do, however, come in handy for ordering pizza for pickup on the way into town after a backcountry trip!

LOW-TECH COMMUNICATION
SIGNALLING MIRROR

A signalling mirror is small and inexpensive and can be quite visible from the air on a sunny day. It is useless, of course, if there is nobody overhead to see it, or on a cloudy day or at night. For its size, though, it is definitely worth at least one member of your group carrying one. Although any mirror, such as that found in an orienteering compass may suffice, it is better to have a signalling mirror that is designed for the purpose. It will have optically flat glass for a tighter beam, with a hole and a grating in the centre for better aiming. If you don't have the grating in your mirror, hold your fingertip out at arm's length over the target and flash the reflected sunlight across your fingertip in order to crudely guide it on target.

WHISTLE

A whistle is another small, lightweight and inexpensive signalling device that is always worth carrying. It could be useful to attract searchers on the ground if they are just outside voice range, and it is definitely useful for a group travelling in thick bush or above treeline in the mist, to stay in contact. Ideally, every member of the group will carry a whistle.

SIGNAL FIRE

If you are in a survival camp, it may be helpful to have a signal fire burning or ready to ignite quickly. By daylight it should be smoky, and if you are in a forested area the smoke should rise above the treetops. At night it should burn brightly.

REALITY CHECK: Two people failed to show up for an agreed rendezvous at the end of a day of hiking in which we had split the group. After sending other members of the party back to town with instructions to call the police if they had not heard from us by a certain time that evening, I reascended the mountain with one companion together with food and gear for an overnight stay. Our hope was to spot a bivouac fire during the darkness of night, or for the missing people to spot ours. Fortunately it wasn't needed, as we met the missing people on our ascent – they had simply misunderstood our rendezvous time by two hours. This was a good reminder to double check communications to make sure both parties have the same information. It was also a novel way to deal with the situation while allowing most people to return to town. A signal fire may double as a fire for warmth, especially in winter, but take care to avoid starting a forest fire, by keeping it reasonably sized and well clear of other combustible materials.

FLARES

Pen-sized bear bangers usually also come with flares, and both flares and bangers can serve as signalling devices. (See the cautionary note about the use of bear bangers in bear encounters in the next chapter.) Be aware that these are quite short-range devices that will generally just clear the treetops. Practise with one of each when you first buy them and again later when they near their expiry date, in order to get a good feel for their usefulness. When practising, take care not to cause a false alarm, or ignite a forest fire by sending it into combustible materials. Larger flares are commercially available for creating light or smoke, but these will depend on your specific needs.

GROUND-TO-AIR SIGNALS

Learn a few key ground-to-air emergency signals. Although these follow international standards, they may not be as commonly used today as in the early years of aviation and may vary by locale. Ask the pilot who flies you into a remote spot what is the best local signal for declaring an emergency. If nothing else, spell out the letters sos with sticks or brush or stamped in the snow – this has worked for some.

REALITY CHECK: In the section on safety procedures, at p. 61, I related the account of the amateur photographer who was dropped off by floatplane in Alaska's remote Brooks Range and who neglected to arrange for a pickup. During the course of his ultimately fatal ordeal, he had one chance to save himself when the pilot of a fixed wing aircraft spotted his camp. Having no floats and being unable to land, the pilot circled low several times to check him out. Unfortunately, in his frantic waving at the plane, the desperate photographer inadvertently gave the pilot the okay signal.

LIGHTS

Other signalling aids for mainly nighttime use could include a powerful spotlight (limited battery life, so use wisely) or electronic strobe light. Headlamps of the LED variety sometimes have a strobe feature.

SAFETY AROUND BEARS

Whenever one thinks of outdoor safety in the context of wildlife encounters in Canada, the tendency is to think first of bears. This is a topic that is close to home for me, as both black bears and grizzly bears are common in northwestern Canada. I have had many encounters with both species, and a friend of mine died in a grizzly bear encounter in the mountains east of Prince George in 1998 (see note regarding George Evanoff at p. 10 and the *Reality Check* at p. 137). I also addressed the topic of bears anecdotally in my first book.[12]

INTRODUCTION

Some key points to consider that are further developed later in this section are:

- **Understand** animal signs and behaviour and learn to differentiate between grizzly bears and black bears.
- **Assess** your situation when you encounter a bear. Differentiate between defensive-aggressive bear behaviour resulting from a surprise encounter, possibly aggravated by the presence of cubs or your proximity to a kill that the bear feels obliged to defend; and straight aggressive behaviour arising from curiosity, opportunism, annoyance, hunger and/or predatory stalking.
- **Respond appropriately** to a bear encounter: know when best to hold your ground, retreat, play dead or fight back.
- **Use bear repellents wisely:** pepper spray, bear bangers, air horns and firearms.
- **Practise prevention** by hanging and cooking food well away from tents; avoiding areas showing recent bear sign; travelling in groups of three or more; making noise; keeping any dogs securely on leash; and avoiding habituating bears to humans by keeping garbage and human food out of reach of bears. In urban areas situated near to bear habitat, this also applies to compost and fruit trees.

In my experience, both black and grizzly bears generally avoid people.

REALITY CHECK: With only three exceptions (one black bear and two grizzlies) all of the hundreds of bears I have met quickly went the other way as soon as they knew what I was. And all but one of these went quietly, the exception being a large male grizzly that pounded the ground in such an impressive display of annoyance that we were sure we could feel the ground shaking 50 metres away as he whirled around. Even if I could have reached it in time, my bear spray felt utterly insignificant in that moment as the bear did an angry 360-degree pirouette AFTER it had pinpointed us. I don't know what decided it to flee rather than charge; perhaps it was just chance, a quantum firing of a single neuron somewhere in its brain.

Subadult males that are newly on their own may push the limits and may need to be discouraged. Older, malnourished bears may be inclined to predatory behaviour if they are hungry. Bears that have become habituated to humans and humans' food may become dangerous. Barring surprise encounters, though, most non-habituated bears shun contact with humans unless they feel it necessary to defend cubs, a mate or a carcass they are feeding on, or they find themselves too close for comfort and feel threatened or trapped.

UNDERSTANDING BEAR BEHAVIOUR

Bear safety begins by learning about the habits and behaviour of bears, especially differentiating between defensive and aggressive (possibly predatory) hostility by a bear. See also Appendix C on information resources, at p. 261, for more detailed behavioural information about bears. The probability of having a problem with a bear in the first place is very slight, but in the event that you do, you can significantly increase your chance of surviving the encounter through knowledge and choice of action.

First, it may be helpful to understand some evolutionary differences between the two species of bears. The grizzly's long claws, as well as the muscle mass that makes up the prominent shoulder hump, appear to have developed for digging in the open alpine, the plains and the Arctic tundra for roots and small mammals, and for den building. As a grizzly bear matures, its long claws become poorly suited for climbing trees, since it has little need to do that; but you should know, if you do seek refuge in a tree, that some grizzlies can climb trees. Also, because it has evolved in mainly open habitat, a grizzly is more likely than a black bear to defend personal space, cubs or food. The black bear, by comparison, has evolved mainly in forested country and, as a result, can climb trees very well. Indeed, it is not uncommon for black bears, especially cubs, to seek refuge in a tree from humans, and black bears can sometimes be seen high in aspen trees in the spring, feeding on new leaf growth. A black bear is also more likely to retreat to the abundant shelter that is available in the forest. If a black bear does not flee, its intentions may be something other than defensive; that is to say, the bear may be predatory, curious or habituated to humans and/or humans' food. Sometimes, a bear may not yet have recognized its intended prey as human, and simply standing up to identify yourself may be sufficient to cause it to turn and run. If it knows you are human and continues to approach, you will need to take more assertive action to discourage it.

A key factor in determining your response to an aggressive bear is to know whether its behaviour is defensive or aggressive in nature. It is the behaviour, rather than the species, that is crucial in making this determination, but knowing the species may be helpful. There is anecdotal evidence suggesting that defensive aggression may be more common in grizzly bears, while aggressive behaviour in black bears is more likely to be predatory. A study by Stephen Herrero and others confirmed that the majority of the fatal black bear attacks on people in North America in the past 110 years resulted from male black bears targeting people as food.[13] Complicating this determination is the fact that it is not always obvious which species you have met. I have been unsure a few times, and I have seen a seasoned biologist be unable to make a definite identification. Size and colour don't necessarily help. Although black bears are predominantly black and most grizzlies are brown, there are large, brown-coloured black bears and small, dark-coloured grizzly bears. And of course, size varies by age and locale. If you are in a good position to see it, the characteristic shoulder hump, dish-shaped nose and long claws distinguish the grizzly from the black bear. Your location, such as in the alpine tundra, where grizzlies predominate, may also help in the determination. Grizzly bear attacks, then, tend to be defensive in nature, resulting from a surprise encounter when a person gets too close for the bear's comfort. Possibly the most dangerous and least predictable situation is in getting close to a kill that is in the possession of a grizzly bear. Nearly as dangerous is getting between a female grizzly and her cubs or between a male and female mating pair. Persistent black bear aggression, when it occurs, may be more likely to be predatory.

REALITY CHECK: A close friend of mine *(see note 2 regarding George Evanoff, at p. 10)* died while out for a day hike alone in the mountains in late October 1998 after encountering a grizzly bear that was defending a moose kill. He was one of the most competent outdoorsmen I have met and was well experienced around bears, but he had the misfortune to walk into one of the most dangerous situations in the Canadian backcountry. Injured after the initial attack, he apparently made several attempts to use the two-way radio that he had with him before the bear resumed the attack. It's hard to second-guess an incident like this – perhaps if he had heeded the fresh bear tracks in the snow sooner or had been carrying bear spray or had been hiking with a companion or had carried a PLB with him, the outcome might have been different. Or more likely this simply fell under the "inherent risks" category, such as a freak accident while crossing a city street.

The bear was still close by the next morning when we found our friend as part of the ensuing search effort. We spent a very tense half-hour piecing together what had happened until armed police and conservation officers arrived and we were evacuated by helicopter. As this was an isolated occurrence in an off-trail wilderness setting and there was no evidence that the bear was habituated or otherwise acting out of character, no attempt was made to hunt it down.

ASSESSING AND RESPONDING TO A BEAR ENCOUNTER

There are no definitive right and wrong things to do, and recommendations tend to evolve over time. The following suggestions are therefore offered only as a guide. The best advice is to seek as many and varied opportunities as you can to learn about bears, and use your judgment in the situation in which you find yourself.

- If you come across a bear, and it does not appear to have noticed you, retreat quietly the way you came. If the bear immediately retreats from you, go quietly in the other direction.
- Do not run unless you are sure of reaching safety, as it may trigger an automatic chase response. You are unlikely to be able to outrun a bear, as it can run several times faster than you and can probably climb trees much better than you.

REALITY CHECK: A few years ago I watched a large grizzly run across an alpine meadow below me as fast as a race horse. It was probably moving at about 15 metres per second – faster than your normal residential-street speed limit of 50 km/h. How many seconds would it take you to reach a good climbing tree and then get at least five metres up it?

- If the bear is blocking your way home and there are no alternative routes, it may be best to retreat and wait a while for the bear to leave the area. Alternatively, you may be able to make a wide detour around it. If the bear is travelling on the trail when you meet, another option is to get off the trail a safe distance and allow it to pass. This may have the added benefit of avoiding stressing the bear by not disrupting its intended foraging route.

- There is increasing safety in numbers (three or more people), and some park jurisdictions now restrict human access in places where there is potential for human–grizzly bear conflict to groups of four or more people who must stay within a certain distance of each other.

- If you are caught in a situation where the bear (or any wild animal, for that matter, but especially a grizzly) feels trapped, this is not good news. This could occur when members of a group of people become separated when their numbers ought to give them a high degree of safety. A bear, fleeing from an encounter with one part of a group, might feel trapped if it runs into the others and could attack defensively. So keep your party together, especially if grizzly bears are known to be in the area.

REALITY CHECK: In August 2011 I was hiking with a friend in BC's Erg Mountain Provincial Park. As we were approaching the final summit climb, we saw two large mountain goats just ahead of us also starting toward the top. One held back watching us, while the other climbed. Then, to our astonishment, the first mountain goat surprised a grizzly bear that leapt out of a hidden hollow on the ascent line. It had likely been taking an early afternoon siesta, perhaps to avoid the plentiful mosquitoes that had plagued us earlier in the meadows. This demonstrated how readily grizzly bears can disappear in apparently open terrain and was a sharp reminder that constant vigilance is a good idea. As the drama unfolded, the bear retreated a short distance from the goat, then held its ground near the edge of a precipice. It is also possible that our scent was by now confusing the situation. If it hadn't been for the goats, we would likely have surprised the bear instead of them; disconcertingly this was near the edge of a cliff where the bear may have felt trapped. The first goat appeared unconcerned with its situation and continued to approach the bear until it was quite close, comfortable with the steep escape terrain immediately available to it. At this point, encouraged by a little adrenaline, we decided that the marvellous wildlife encounter and drama we were witnessing and were part of more than compensated for the summit, and we turned around. As we retreated, we watched the stand-off between the bear and the goats continue for several more minutes until all disappeared from sight. Warily keeping an eye backward, we stopped for lunch a little farther down the ridge before descending to the meadows where we encountered more fresh grizzly sign that hadn't been there a couple of hours before. Erg Mountain was living up to its reputation!

- If you come across a bear that has seen you but does not immediately retreat, and if you think you are within its "personal zone," one strategy recommended by researchers is to hold your ground, analyze your options quickly and prepare any defences at hand – bear spray, air horn, bear banger, knife, firearm or even a large stick. If the bear advances toward you, continue to hold your ground. If the bear stops advancing, take the opportunity to retreat, without running. If the bear advances again, stop and hold your ground.
- If the bear advances calmly and purposefully, making no attempt to avoid eye contact and showing no sign of stress, it may see you as food. In this case, be prepared, if necessary, to fight for your life with whatever is at hand. This may be the time to use a bear banger if you have one, preferably before the animal gets too close. (See cautionary notes on the use of bear bangers, below.)

REALITY CHECK: Wildlife biologist Karsten Heuer, in his book *Being Caribou*, described a frightening incident in 2003 in the Far North when he and his wife, Leanne Allison, were stalked by what appeared to be a predatory grizzly bear. After all other deterrents had failed, Heuer picked up the free-standing tent he had just erected and waved the flimsy but large object at the bear, causing the animal to finally hesitate and leave. Taking advantage of the bear's retreat, they broke camp and moved and the bear did not follow. This was an excellent example of improvisation in a difficult situation.

This young grizzly bear was fishing for salmon north of Haines, Alaska, when it got a little too close to the author for comfort.

- If the bear attacks suddenly and you believe the behaviour is defensive, such as when the animal is protecting its cubs or food, fall to the ground at the last possible moment with your face and stomach down and your hands behind your neck to protect your head, neck and vital organs. Spread your legs to make it harder for the bear to roll you over, and if it does succeed in doing this, try and complete the roll to end up face down again. Do not give the bear your pack – keep it on to help protect your back. Stay very still and quiet as long as is necessary until you are absolutely sure that the bear has left the area. If the attack turns predatory, fight for your life.

- Perhaps the ultimate nightmare is an attack at night when you are in your tent. To prepare for this eventuality, take your bear spray into the tent and be prepared to fight for your life if you are attacked there, keeping in mind the effect of the spray on you as well as the bear in the confined space of the tent. Both grizzly and black bears attacking a tent at night could become predatory as an opportunistic response to stumbling into your camp. This is a situation where it might help to have a dog tied up in camp as a warning and as a deterrent. Wilderness canoeists (where weight is less of a problem than with backpacking) sometimes carry a battery-powered portable electric fence to erect around their tent at night to deter wildlife.

Every situation is different and has to be assessed and acted upon according to your knowledge, experience and the situation. Usually this means getting a sense of what the bear is going to do before you react. As a general guide, avoid direct eye contact and aggressive body language unless you are dealing with a predatory bear (usually a black bear) and retreat slowly when you have the chance.

REALITY CHECK: After a long hike into Lake Magog at the foot of BC's Mount Assiniboine on a hot day in July 2006, our party of eight were descending, tired, from Assiniboine Pass to O'Brien Meadows, only a few kilometres from our destination. Although camping for the week, we were not well equipped to spend the night out, as we had flown most of our gear in to Assiniboine Lodge by helicopter earlier in the day. The trail led right across the meadows, and in the middle of it I spotted a large, blond-coloured grizzly bear. The wind was in our favour and the bear had not scented us, so we stood around talking for a while so as to allow the bear to become aware of our presence, and enjoying the moment from a safe vantage point. The grizzly was still several hundred metres away. When it heard us, however, instead of fleeing, it first stood its ground and then bluff-charged us, crossing the meadow at an impressive speed. Stopping well short of us, it retreated and then reared up in the classic stance that looks frighteningly aggressive but usually is just a sign of curiosity. For some in the group, it was their first grizzly encounter and there was a fair amount of excitement and trepidation, especially after the charge. Some even rated it (in hindsight) as their favourite moment of a fine week of hiking. Over the next half hour, the bear stayed mostly in the meadow, alternately disappearing into the forest on the far side and reappearing. This was a "park bear," habituated to and unafraid of people. During the hike in, we had twice passed signs warning of prior grizzly attacks on hikers on the trail. This bear appeared to be exhibiting territorial behaviour and was clearly reluctant to vacate its meadow and our trail. What to do? Most of our gear and food lay across the meadow; but although we were well over the magic number of four to six generally considered safe for travel in grizzly country, it did not feel right to push the bear in these circumstances. Our first strategy of waiting it out hadn't produced any results after half an hour, so we decided to retreat and try and find a way around. Although some felt we were being overly cautious, retreat has always worked for me in this type of situation. At worst, it would inconvenience us, whereas the alternative had a small chance of ending in disaster. As we began climbing back toward the pass, however, we met four more people returning to the lodge from a day hike. With 12 people, we now felt confident to cross the meadow and did so as a tight group without further incident. Still, the bear only retreated a few hundred metres to one side, where it remained in view, and it was still there an hour later to challenge two more hikers.

USE OF BEAR REPELLENTS

PEPPER SPRAY

Most people now carry pepper spray, and the statistics citing its effectiveness, especially against grizzly bears, suggests good (although not certain) deterrent value. Carry the spray in a readily available holster and practise with it when you get the chance, for example, by discharging a recently expired canister, so that your actions will be instinctive in a real situation. Do not keep the product past its expiry date; it will eventually lose effectiveness over time, especially in cool temperatures. Don't think in terms of throwing out a perfectly good $45 canister when it is three years old. Think instead of depreciating it at the rate of $15 per year, and anticipate the day when you and your partner can practise with it. The same principle of depreciation and replacement applies to other deterrents that have shelf lives, such as bear bangers. Keep the bear spray handy at all times – it won't do you much good in your pack. Do not discharge the spray on your clothes or tent as a preventive measure – it doesn't work that way and there have been suggestions that the active ingredient may serve as a food attractant. If you get a chance, back up to or get behind a tree or a large rock so that the bear has to slow its charge before reaching you. Remember that the spray has a very limited range of up to four metres, and that many grizzly bear charges are initiated as a bluff or to find out what you are. Get well back from a lake, creek or river that a bear is emerging from, as pepper spray may not be as effective on a wet bear.

BEAR BANGERS

Another defensive option to consider is the use of bear bangers, especially to deter a bear that is showing an unhealthy interest or is intent on stalking you. There are, however, some pitfalls to consider with this option. There is anecdotal evidence that a bear, especially a grizzly, may attack in response to the sound of a firearm or to the launch and/or subsequent explosion of a bear banger. This happened to a British Columbia forestry worker in 2003.

REALITY CHECK: A man and his wife were doing silviculture work in a cutblock in the mountains east of Prince George in 2003. They were working in different parts of the block when the man spotted a female grizzly with cubs. The bear was neither close nor threatening, but, concerned about his wife's safety elsewhere in the block, he decided to scare it off with a bear banger. The resulting "bang" had exactly the opposite effect, and the man was instantly charged and knocked down by the grizzly bear. It was a defensive attack that likely would not have happened if the bear banger had not been fired. Fortunately, after knocking him down, the bear apparently felt that the threat had been alleviated and left without causing too much harm, but the incident illustrated the possible consequences of using a bear banger.

Tree planters sometimes use bear bangers to deter bears that persistently hang around planting sites or camps. This may be a situation where the use of a bear banger is appropriate, especially if backed up by a firearm in the camp or at the worksite. Others in similar circumstances have told me that in their experience bear bangers are ineffectual – see next reality check. And if meeting a bear is a chance encounter without any apparent opportunistic or stalking behaviour by the bear (the usual recreational experience), I would be very cautious about using a bear banger lest you trigger an attack that would not otherwise have happened.

REALITY CHECK: I once used a bear banger in a safe situation to test the reactions of a black bear. The bear reacted more annoyed than alarmed.

Even when a bear is frightened by the sound of a bear banger, there is little control over the direction it will run, particularly if you drop the charge behind or above the animal instead of in front of it – both are easy to do. On the other hand, firing the charge short may not work if it hits the ground before exploding.

REALITY CHECK: I test fired a bear banger toward the ground, and the charge simply buried itself and did not explode. Others have reported a similar effect if the bear banger did not travel far enough in order to explode while still airborne. The small initial crack of the shell discharging from the launcher would probably not frighten a bear away but it may still be enough to trigger a charge.

Bear bangers, like bear spray, require safe storage and handling. You must periodically check cartridges for the discoloration and sweating that indicate the possibility of a premature ignition that could result in an injury or burn. Transportation of both bear spray and bear bangers in chartered bush planes and helicopters requires special safety considerations, usually storage in a separate baggage compartment or float. Scheduled commercial flights do not allow either one. Aircrew will usually advise you of the requirements for safe carriage, but in case they don't, it is well to be familiar with safety rules and insist they be followed, as your life is on the line as well as theirs. Safety guidelines for using bear bangers indicate the need to hold the launcher at arm's length and above the head when firing, and not to screw a cartridge into the launcher until ready to use. This last suggestion, of course, would limit its effectiveness in a sudden bear encounter, so use your judgment on this. I usually arm my bear banger only while travelling in what I consider to be a high risk situation. So, there are lots of reasons to be wary of using a bear banger, but the devices are small and probably a worthwhile addition to your emergency gear. The bangers, and the small flares that come with them, can serve double duty as signalling devices.

One last point about bear bangers: there seems to be anecdotal evidence that they are more effective against polar bears. Perhaps this is because polar bears are almost always encountered in open terrain, where the bangers can be used to deter the bears from approaching too close in the first place. Unless they are in a national park where firearms are prohibited, many people travelling in polar bear country also carry a shotgun or rifle for protection, and the bear banger is a good first line of defence that reduces the danger to both bears and humans by warning them off without having to fire a real shot.

FLARE
Some people have used flares to deter bears, either the kind that often come with bear bangers or perhaps highway or railroad flares that you strike and place on the ground. I can't speak to the efficacy of either, but if you have nothing else at hand, it might be worth trying. Again, be careful not to start a forest fire in dry conditions – out of the frying pan into the fire!

AIR HORN
An alternative sound deterrent to a bear banger is a horn, powered by a small cylinder of compressed gas.

REALITY CHECK: I have seen one of these used effectively against an overly curious black bear that had approached a group of hikers who were sitting eating lunch on a riverbank. A gas horn is safer to handle and may be less likely than a bear banger to trigger the attack you are trying to prevent.

FIREARM

Should you carry a firearm? If you are hiking in a national park the question is moot, since they are generally not allowed there. If you are travelling in an area where firearms are permitted, consider the following. In the event of a sudden bear attack, is it likely you will have time to use a firearm effectively? How competent and practised are you with the weapon in a moment of sudden and extreme stress? Will a warning shot from a firearm or bear banger provoke a violent response from a bear that wouldn't have happened otherwise? Bears can be hard to stop even with a large-calibre rifle – what is the likelihood that you will wound a bear or cause an attack that wasn't going to happen otherwise? Are you prepared for the moral and legal implications of needlessly killing or wounding an animal that may be a member of an at-risk species when bear spray or simply retreating may have sufficed? Have you considered the danger to human life of carrying a possibly loaded firearm in the group? Do you mind carrying an extra three or four kilograms of weight?

Having said all this, there are situations where a firearm may be the only thing that could save your life, and I have heard of several such circumstances since moving to north central British Columbia. I have been with a party carrying a firearm in a few situations, but these were rare exceptions, and in my view carrying a gun changes the dynamic between man and bear, and for most people it is more likely to cause a problem than to be of any real help. If you are in an Arctic region, with the possibility of encountering a polar bear, carrying a shotgun or high-powered rifle is usually advised, with non-lethal bear bangers as a first deterrent. If you do carry a weapon, ensure that anyone who might handle it is both trained in and practises firearm safety.

PREVENTION

There are some things one can do to help avoid conflict in the first place. They include making a lot of noise, preferably by talking or singing. Personally I dislike the noise of bear bells disturbing the natural sounds of the woods, although that might be preferable to someone's rendition of opera. If bells are your choice, lower-pitched cowbells carry for a long distance and they avoid the suggestion some have made that higher pitch bells might arouse a bear's interest – dinner bells as the joke goes. If you travel with a party of four or more people, you will naturally make so much noise that your chance of any kind of wildlife encounter is vanishingly small. Two people may be the most vulnerable size of group, possibly because two are less likely to be aware of their surroundings than one, while not offering much more deterrence than a person alone.

On encountering fresh bear sign, take a different route if possible. A judicious retreat has worked for me many times, with both grizzly and black bears. A bear that shows no sign of fear may simply be curious or it may be sizing you up as a prospective meal. Either way, it may become opportunistic if you stick around too long. Leaving may return control to you before the bear has made up its mind. If the bear follows, you may have to consider other, more assertive measures.

Other preventive tactics are to camp well away from fresh bear sign and avoid arranging tents in a circle such that an intruding bear might feel trapped. Cook well away from tents and avoid getting any food odours on either tents or clothes. While in camp, store both food and white gas securely and well away from the tents, preferably by hoisting them from a high tree branch with a cord and pulley system. There is plenty of anecdotal evidence that grizzly bears and other wildlife are attracted to gasoline. If this isn't possible (for example, above treeline), place them under a rock cairn well away from the tents and preferably in two or more locations so that all your eggs aren't in one basket. I generally use two layers of heavy-duty plastic, zippered food storage bags, which I then put in two or three larger waterproof gear bags or dry bags. Some jurisdictions, notably Kluane National Park in the Yukon, mandate the use of cylindrical plastic containers that a bear supposedly cannot get its teeth into. These are currently loaned free to backcountry travellers there, the park's interest being not only to encourage hiker safety but to avoid getting bears habituated.

Avoid using scented soaps, deodorants, cosmetics and perfumes, and only use unscented sunscreen. A commonly asked question is whether women who are menstruating are at risk of attracting bears, especially at night while in a tent. This is a situation of interest both to women campers and their male tent partners. There does not appear to have been a lot of research done on this, but what is known, from US and Canadian park studies, suggests that there is no evidence of a problem with either grizzly bears or black bears. One study did suggest a possible risk with polar bears. Even though the risk may be slight, common sense recommendations include using internal tampons, double bagging with zippered plastic bags after use, and taking similar storage precautions as you would with food. Then, either pack it out or burn it completely in a hot fire. Do not bury it, as this could lead to a problem for later campers.

If you are travelling with a dog, keep it on a leash and tie it up in camp. A dog in camp may be beneficial in deterring a bear from entering the camp, or at least it will raise the alarm if one does. A free-running dog is a definite liability to other wildlife and could bring a bear back to you.

This large black bear grazing in open tundra just south of the Yukon was first mistaken for a grizzly. Either way, it deserved plenty of space.

frightening experience that took several months to get over, but the biologist had the presence of mind to press and hold the transmit button on the radio, which had the effect of both preventing incoming calls and also broadcasting the frightening sounds of the attack to the other workers, who were then able to come to his aid. The other incident was defused by the forestry worker quietly switching off the radio and talking softly to the female bear, who eventually withdrew. Therefore, if you are carrying a two-way radio and you are suddenly faced with a bear encounter, consider switching off your radio if you're not going to use it to call for help, or at least be prepared to press and hold the TRANSMIT key.

SUMMARY

When you are travelling in bear country, practise reasonable bear safety, but keep an open mind about one of the planet's truly magnificent animals. Almost every human–grizzly encounter is told as a "life and death" story, but the reality may be quite different. Considering its size and immense power, the grizzly bear is a secretive and tolerant animal. Make no mistake about its speed and power and show it the respect it deserves, but also think of all the encounters you and your acquaintances have had that you survived unscathed.

REALITY CHECK: I once walked within four metres of a female grizzly bear that was hiding in bushes with three small cubs. Had it not been for other members of the party who were just emerging from the forest 100 or so metres behind me, I would have known nothing of the encounter, as she took the cubs and silently ran up the mountainside away from me. How many times, I found myself wondering, has that happened to me before? Research with automatic, motion-activated cameras has also shown that human–grizzly encounters are a lot more common than we know or might like to think about.

So, learn about bears, take reasonable precautions and prepare yourself for an experience that is as old as mankind!

OTHER WILDLIFE ENCOUNTERS

Whenever we think of safety with respect to wild animals, a common tendency is to think of bears. But any wild animal in Canada can be dangerous, especially if it is hungry, feels cornered or threatened, perceives its young to be in danger, is diseased or rabid or is in any way habituated to people. In short, all wildlife should be respected, including those that we normally think of as harmless. They are best enjoyed from a distance, and (need it be said) never feed a wild animal unless you are part of an officially sanctioned wildlife rehabilitation or emergency feeding program. Apart from the harm caused to animals and the danger posed to humans, it is illegal to feed wildlife in most jurisdictions.

Even a habituated squirrel can cause serious harm, especially if you are several days from medical aid; and it could carry rabies. The moral: stay clear of all wildlife, for their sake and yours.

COUGARS

Cougars, or mountain lions, are powerful predators, next in size among Canadian carnivores after bears. They are secretive, seldom-seen animals and encounters with them are rare. Yet they inhabit many parts of British Columbia and Alberta and historically they ranged across the southern parts of most Canadian provinces. They are common on Vancouver Island and the Gulf Islands, throughout the Rocky Mountains and along the Rocky Mountain Trench north into the Yukon.

In parts of British Columbia such as the Robson Valley, cougars are common enough to have been a nuisance, preying on domestic farm animals. They are also seen in cities from time to time, including my home town:

REALITY CHECK: During the winter of 2007/08 there were an unusual number of reports of cougars in and around the city of Prince George, including several attacks on pets. Twice in a two-week period around Christmas, my wife and I came across the fresh tracks of an adult male cougar in the woods a few hundred metres behind our house. On the second occasion, I discovered (after circling around) that the cougar had been just seconds behind us before cutting across below where we had crested a small treed ridge. First it had been behind us, and then, just a few minutes later, we crossed its just-made tracks where it had gone ahead. Perhaps it had been following us before continuing on its way. An adult male cougar will cover its hunting territory every two weeks or so, which was consistent with the timing of our two near encounters.

Fresh tracks of a male cougar in the city of Prince George.

Cougars do attack and sometimes kill humans as well as domestic animals and pets, especially if food is scarce and they are hungry or starving. It's common to hear of incidents in western Canada every year involving people or pets. Smaller people, especially children, are at greater risk, but adult women and even large men have also been attacked by cougars. Attacks on adult men are rarely fatal if the victims fight back, but the animal can still do a lot of damage. Cougars are very fast, with strong hind legs adapted for leaping. They usually hunt by stalking close to the ground, leaping on their prey from the side or behind from a range of a few metres and biting the neck or throat. As with bears, learn to recognize the habits and signs of cougars. Be especially cautious around dawn or dusk when cougars are more active. Make lots of noise and/or walk in groups to reduce the chance of encountering a cougar or at least give it the opportunity to retreat. Avoid places where there are signs of an animal feeding on a carcass (such as crows flying around), as cougars, like grizzly bears, will defend a kill. Cougars are generally well able to sense the presence of humans, and under normal circumstances you will not see them even if they are around. If you do encounter a cougar that does not flee from you, here are some actions to consider:

- Do not run, make sudden movements or turn your back on a cougar, as this may trigger or encourage an attack.
- Cougars do not bluff charge like some bears; assume that a cougar charge is an attack.
- Face the cougar and retreat slowly while keeping direct eye contact with the animal. Know where it is and give it room to escape. If you have a chance to move behind something to get out of the cougar's sight, that might help.
- Otherwise make yourself appear to be larger than normal, for example, by raising your arms above your head and perhaps holding up something large. If a log, rock or rising ground is close by, try standing on it to enhance your effective size and increase your chance of intimidating the cougar.
- Try talking to the cougar in a calm but strong voice.
- If the cougar is being aggressive, try throwing rocks and yelling at it as your aggression may scare it off.

- Pick up small children to discourage an attack on them. Don't let your children play unattended when cougars are known to be in the area, and keep them away from bush that the cougar might use for cover.
- Fight for your life if you are attacked by a cougar. Do not play dead!
- Bear spray, a walking stick or a belt knife may be useful for defence against a cougar. Following recent attacks on people in the area of Banff, Alberta, bear spray is being recommended there as a possible defence against cougars.
- Dogs may have deterrent value (trained dogs are often used to hunt cougars), but small dogs are sometimes seen as prey.
- To keep things in perspective, as with bears, anyone who frequents the outdoors has probably walked right past a cougar many times without realizing it – likely a lot closer than we might like to think. The chance of an attack happening is low but cannot be dismissed.

MOOSE AND ELK

Moose are the largest member of the deer family and can be very dangerous, especially bulls in the fall rutting season and cows with calves, and perhaps also when stressed with ticks in late winter.

REALITY CHECK: There were two dangerous moose attacks on people in Prince George early in 2007, which also happened to be a high tick-infestation year.

Moose are strong and fast-moving and have caused human fatalities. One of their attack strategies is to knock you over and kick you with either their front or hind feet. According to Les Stroud, speaking from personal experience in his book *Will to Live*, nothing compares to being chased by an angry bull moose in rut. Some strategies you might consider are:

- Do not approach a moose or get between a cow and her calf. If you meet one on the trail and it shows no inclination to move, turn around and find another way.
- As with bears, keep any dogs under control in order to avoid the potentially disastrous situation of your dog chasing after a moose and then bringing the angry animal back to you. A dog could, however, be useful to distract an attacking moose.
- Try to get behind a tree if a moose charges toward you. This will afford some protection and should give you an agility advantage, as you should be able to dodge around the tree better than the moose can. I have met people who used this strategy successfully upon encountering an aggressive moose on an urban trail.

Cow and calf moose feeding in a popular Prince George park at a safe distance from onlookers.

Moose encounter, too close for comfort.

- Watch for signs of an impending charge such as ears laid back or raised hair on the moose's back.

Elk are another large member of the deer family and can be similarly dangerous, especially when they are in rut, so keep your distance and try to avoid getting either yourself or your vehicle between a male and females. Elk can become a problem when they move into protected townsites, such as Banff, where they may have taken refuge from wolves from the surrounding wildlands. They are becoming common in some Rocky Mountain national park campgrounds. Try and stay at least 30 metres away from elk and if necessary seek protection behind a vehicle or tree. Move away while maintaining eye contact, and do not play dead.

WILDLIFE ON THE HIGHWAY

A major cause of property damage, injury and death in many parts of British Columbia is the result of vehicle collisions with moose, elk, deer and even buffalo (northern BC) on the highways, especially at dusk or night and especially in the spring when the roadsides are replete with fresh green forage. Indeed, this may be the greatest risk you will ever face from wildlife, so slow down when driving at night and pay special attention to roadsigns warning of the possibility of wildlife on the highway. Remember that your chances of seeing and avoiding wildlife are improved with reduced speed. Keep your windshield and headlights clean to help with visibility. Slow down even more when you actually see an animal, since even during daylight hours, animals (especially members of the deer family) can move suddenly and unpredictably. If you see an animal by the roadside, assume there are others nearby. If an animal suddenly runs across the road in front of you, consider that it might have a companion poised to follow. Where there are deep roadside ditches or embankments, a moose or deer could be standing right next to the road, ready to spring out, but invisible until you are almost upon it. Travelling behind another vehicle provides no assurance of avoiding a collision with wildlife; animal collisions can happen anywhere and at any time.

REALITY CHECK: A colleague of mine was driving on a major highway in British Columbia in the middle of the day, following behind a large truck, when suddenly a moose ran out between the truck and his new car. He hit it squarely, totalling the car, and survived the impact only because the animal did not penetrate the windshield, a fortuitous circumstance that he put down to the make of vehicle.

Utilize passengers to help you scan both sides of the road. Having had a couple of very close nighttime near misses when I had not seen a moose standing on the highway until I was actually passing it, I urge you to take this seriously and slow down – even a 10-km/h reduction in speed may make the difference between life and death. From what I have observed, many drivers pay lip service to this risk, rationalizing either that it won't happen to them or that they will see an animal on the road in time to avoid it. Every year, the toll of highway fatalities from animal collisions continues, and the evidence of animal bloodstains and carcasses is there for all to see, especially on northern highways.

REALITY CHECK: If, for example, you have to make a 150-kilometre nighttime drive on an unlit highway known for its wildlife, driving at 80 km/h instead of 110 km/h will cost you half an hour and you will have a greatly reduced chance of hitting a moose. As a bonus, you will also use less fuel. How much is your time worth? It takes a lot of self-control to ease the pressure on the gas pedal, especially on an empty road when you just want to get home.

REALITY CHECK: Even birds can be dangerous, as I found out one day when I was cruising along a West Coast highway at mid-day and suddenly struck a hefty, low-flying goose that had just taken off from the shoreline. Hit at more than 100 km/h, the unfortunate bird bounced off the top of the driver's side windshield frame and ripped the securely attached roof rack from my car. A few centimetres lower and it could have come through the glass, with potentially disastrous consequences.

WATER-BORNE DISEASE

With the possible exception of springs and snowmelt in relatively pristine areas, water-borne protozoa such as *Giardia lamblia* (found almost everywhere) and *Cryptosporidium parvum* (associated more with agricultural areas) can be assumed to exist in much of the groundwater in Canada and elsewhere in North America and can cause discomfort and illness. As well, there may be parasite cysts in the water, symptoms of which may take years to manifest, as well as bacteria that can cause more immediate illness. Fortunately, most of what you are likely to encounter in the Canadian or US backcountry can be easily removed using microfilters that are readily available from quality outdoors stores. A low-tech but less convenient alternative is to boil water for several minutes before consuming it. Groundwater in areas frequented by people, such as a provincial park campsite, should definitely be considered suspect and filtered unless specifically posted as being potable. Viruses are too small to be removed by a filter, so if you are travelling in an area where they are likely to be a concern, you will need to further treat the water chemically, for example, with iodine. In the case of salt (some desert locales) or chemical contaminants, the water may simply be undrinkable. The weight of a filter or purifier in your pack should be more than offset by the reduced amount of bottled drinking water you need to carry and/or fuel to boil water.

If you are faced with an imminent threat to life due to lack of water in a hot environment (see chapter 15 on heat-related problems, beginning at p. 100 and chapter 16 on desert safety, starting at p. 104 and you have access only to untreated groundwater, choose life over the possibility of water-borne sickness.

MOSQUITOES AND WEST NILE

Historically, mosquitoes and other biting insects have mainly been an annoyance in western Canada, rarely carrying life-threatening diseases. This is changing with the rapid westward spread of the West Nile virus (WNV) across North America. West Nile is spread by birds and mosquitoes and can infect humans through bites from mosquitoes that are carrying the virus. To put this into perspective, only a small percentage of people exposed to mosquitoes will likely be infected by WNV. Of those, only about 20 per cent will get sick, displaying flu-like symptoms such as a headache, fever and a stiff neck for a week or more. Only 1 to 2 per cent of human infections may result in a severe illness such as encephalitis, and an even smaller percentage will cause paralysis or death. As with most infectious illnesses, those with a weakened immune system are more at risk. As WNV spreads to become endemic in North America, resistance will likely develop in the human population, and there are suggestions that it may become less infectious over time. However, as the climate warms in the north, other mosquito-transmitted diseases will likely be introduced and/or become more common here.

It is nearly impossible to avoid mosquito bites while living in northern parts of Canada and recreating or working in the outdoors, but you can do some things to lessen your exposure. Try covering yourself with light-coloured protective clothing with long sleeves and long pants, using insect repellents (in moderation, noting possible side effects of the active ingredients), and where possible, avoid being outside at dusk, when mosquitoes are the most active. The higher risk period for WNV is reported to be later in the season, from July or August.

SNAKES

Venomous snakes are uncommon in Canada, and even when snakebites happen, they are rarely fatal to humans. There may be a greater risk of a deadly bite in urban centres from an exotic pet snake that has escaped than from wild snakes in the outdoors. In British Columbia, for example, the only native venomous snake is the northern Pacific rattlesnake, which is found in the Thompson–Okanagan region of the province. This species is not aggressive by nature, and unless you are unfortunate enough to trip over or step on one, it prefers to use its rattle to warn you to stay back, instead of just striking. If you do hear a rattlesnake, stop, visually locate the snake, and if you are very close to it, remain still and allow it to back away. When it is a few feet away (at least four feet), step back and go around it.

In the event you are bitten by a venomous snake, try to remain as still as you can, and keep the part where you were bitten below heart level to minimize the spread of venom through the body. Have someone get you to medical aid; or if you are alone, on foot and have no other recourse, walk slowly to avoid moving the injured part as much as possible. Don't touch dead snakes, as a bite reflex could still be functional. Lastly, note that if you are in British Columbia, all snakes are protected in the province – it is illegal to harm them or remove them from the wild.

If you are travelling in the desert lands of the US southwest there are many species of snakes and several venomous species to watch out for, including several species of rattlesnakes as well as Sonoran coral snakes and copperhead pit vipers. As in Canada, rattlesnake bites require serious medical attention but are rarely fatal. Snakes may be out sunning themselves on the trail in cool weather like one we saw in Zion National Park late in the day. In hot weather they take refuge in shady spots, so it's good to stay at least two to four feet away from blind spots on trails. Also in hot weather, snakes can be nocturnal, so use a flashlight if you are hiking or walking around in the dark.

Unidentified snake sunning itself on a trail in Utah's Zion National Park.

TICKS, LYME DISEASE AND RMS

Historically, ticks do not seem to have been much of a problem for humans in northern parts of the western provinces, but they are prevalent in the southern, drier areas such as British Columbia's southern interior, especially in the spring. A report by Gwen Barlee and Jim Wilson in the *Vancouver Sun* in April 2011 went further, suggesting that Lyme disease is now one of the fastest-growing infectious diseases in North America, and ticks carrying this infection are found throughout British Columbia. With climatic warming, we are sure to see more of them farther north. A big problem in diagnosing Lyme disease has been that it has symptoms that mimic other diseases, such as multiple sclerosis. This is compounded by the previous rarity of Lyme disease, although this might be changing, especially in eastern Canada, with increasing numbers of Lyme disease cases and better diagnostic tools.

If you are in an area and at a time of year (generally spring) where ticks are plentiful, you can reduce your risk of exposure by wearing long sleeves, long pants and a hat. Make frequent body checks to find any ticks, not only in the field but also when you return home. In particular, check your hair and scalp and tight places such as underarms and groin. Wearing light-coloured clothing might make it easier to spot and remove ticks before they reach your skin – check each other frequently on the trail while hiking in tick country. If you find a tick that has bitten into you and become embedded, grasp it gently near your skin with tweezers or tick-removing pliers, pull it clear, taking care not to break off the head, and keep it for a few days in case testing is required. Do not use petroleum jelly or heat to kill the tick, as you may cause it to burrow more deeply and increase the risk of infection. Watch for symptoms of infection over the next few days and weeks, such as a red circle around the bite, red streaks or flu-like symptoms, and if necessary see your doctor. Although rare, ticks can carry Lyme disease and Rocky Mountain spotted fever (RMS).

BEES AND WASPS

Given the number of people that are allergic to insect stings, it is bees and wasps that have the potential to be among the most dangerous creatures in North America, especially the Africanized bees (or so-called killer bees) that have moved into the US south from South America. Although I have never had to try it, apparently dropping one's pack and running (if you are out on open ground) can be a good strategy if attacked by a swarm of angry bees. Most reasonably fit people are apparently capable of outrunning a swarm of bees over a distance of 800 metres or so. This, of course, is the opposite advice from dealing with most wildlife encounters, where running can trigger an instinctive attack response. If you are in thick bush, seeking refuge there might confuse a swarm of bees. Either way, don't swat them, as the chemicals released from the crushed bodies will likely induce an even angrier response from the swarm.

SCORPIONS AND SPIDERS

If you are hiking in the desert states of the US southwest, you might encounter several dangerous species of scorpions and spiders. It's best to consult local information for details, depending on where you are going, but here are some general tips:

- Scorpions kill more people than snakes do in the US southwest, and one species, one of the smallest, can be lethal.
- Scorpions are nocturnal, so sleep inside a tent or net tent when you are in scorpion country, not outside on the open ground.
- To avoid unwelcome guests, keep your sleeping bag stuffed until ready to use, and/or secure inside a zipped-up tent.

RODENTS AND HPS

Another disease that is still rare in Canada but appears to be moving north is a serious lung disease called hantavirus pulmonary syndrome, or HPS. In the unlikely event that you become infected, it may be bad news, since 50 per cent or more of people infected with HPS die within a few days. Hantavirus is found in the droppings and other excretions of mice, especially deer mice, as well as some other wild rodents. The main way that HPS is contracted by humans is by inhaling dust from the dried feces of infected rodents or microscopic droplets of their saliva or urine. Although there are occupational risks of contracting HPS, such as biologists studying wild deer mice or workers cleaning out a barn or sawmill, one of the main risks to recreationists may be in entering a backcountry cabin or other structure that has been unoccupied for a while. Most rustic buildings are not mouse-proof, and it is common to find droppings all over the place. I've even had mice run across my head in one popular recreational mountain cabin. Rather than sweeping out the droppings as we used to do when entering a cabin that had been vacant for a while, with the risk of raising contaminated dust into the air, it may be safer to wipe them up with a wet cloth. Other, more stringent preventive measures may be necessary in an occupational setting.

BATS AND RABIES

The principal wild animals known to regularly carry rabies in Canada are bats. While rates of infection in the general bat population are probably below 1 per cent, as many as 10 per cent of bats tested after biting people may test positive.

Since bats are largely nocturnal, they are rarely seen or encountered by most humans, but you may come across them in the lofts of buildings and in caves, such as Cadomin Cave on the east slope of the Rockies, south of Hinton, Alberta. Rabies is transmitted by the saliva of an infected animal, usually by means of a bite. Although very rare, there is also a slim possibility of transmission through the inhalation of airborne droplets, two cases having been reported from a US cave many years ago. If left untreated for too long, rabies is fatal in humans. Any wild animal that is acting strangely, and that bites you for no apparent reason, should be suspected of rabies. Take the animal in for testing; and if that is not possible, get treated as a precaution. By the time rabies symptoms become obvious, it will likely be too late to save your life.

REALITY CHECK: Be especially careful if travelling overseas to places where rabies is endemic. A biologist I know was staying with a friend in Africa, where he played with and was likely exposed to the saliva of a domestic dog. Later, after the biologist had resumed his travels and could not be reached, the dog was diagnosed with rabies. In a life and death cliffhanger, the individual was intercepted on about the last possible day that treatment could be started, at Vancouver International Airport when he arrived back in Canada, and he began treatment immediately.

WOLVES

Before 2005 it used to be claimed there was no record of a human having been killed by wild wolves in North America. There were recorded attacks by habituated wolves, at least one by a rabid wolf and several by wolf/dog crosses, and there have been anecdotal accounts of potential predatory behaviour in wolves. There have been many people who have disappeared in the bush throughout Canadian history, some of them undoubtedly killed by wolves.

REALITY CHECK: In my first book I described an account told to me by a respected outdoorsman who had been treed for two days by wolves when he was a teenager in the Ootsa Lake area of west central BC.[14] He was saved only when his dad returned from a separate part of their trapline and drove the animals away with rifle fire. He told me this story more than 25 years ago as he and I were lying in our bunks late one night on a Provincial Emergency Program-sponsored man-tracking course. There was no denying the intensity and conviction of his account.

> To hear a pack of wolves close by in the bush, and especially to come face to face with them, evokes some of the most primitive feelings of both exhilaration and fear. It is one of the finest and scariest outdoor experiences one can have, and I relish the several I have been privileged to have had, while treating the wolves with the utmost respect.

Historically, wolves have an undeservedly fearsome reputation, but it was likely also a myth to believe they are harmless to humans. Certainly they have a great deal of respect for people, but if they are hungry enough, and especially if they have become habituated to humans' food or garbage, there is little doubt that they could become dangerous. Such was the case in 2005 when a pack of wild but possibly habituated wolves near a northern work camp killed a young Canadian worker who had gone for a walk by himself away from camp.

So, enjoy the very special sound of wolves in the outdoors and the rare glimpse of the animals themselves, but act respectfully and sensibly. In the unlikely event that you encounter wolves that appear to be aggressive and/or unafraid of you, try

Cow and calf moose freshly killed by a pack of eight wolves. From swelling on one of the cow's legs, it was apparent that it had taken two or three days to perish after its initial wounding. Nature is not always pretty.

to dissuade them from approaching too close (100 metres may be close enough) by making yourself appear as large as possible, making lots of noise, and if necessary, throwing rocks or tree branches at them. Retreat slowly without turning your back, and keep children close to you. General advice about keeping a clean campsite in order to avoid bear problems also applies to wolves and other predators.

ECHINOCOCCOSIS

A potentially serious but less obvious problem with canids is with their feces. When you come across canid scat in the bush, give it a wide berth and especially do not touch, kick or disturb it in any way. When a canid eats a prey animal that is infected with hydatid cysts (the larval stage of the echinococcus parasite) it may ingest larvae which later develop into adult tapeworms and produce eggs that are passed with the feces. For example, where wolf scat gets kicked when a hiker walks by it, eggs can become airborne in huge numbers and be involuntarily ingested by humans or animals through inhalation or from unknowing contact via the lips. The gestation period before symptoms appear in humans could be a decade or more and the results could be serious. There are several forms of echinococcosis, which can variously affect the liver, lungs and, in a small percentage of cases, the brain. In some cases, surgery can be an effective treatment, but often the cysts are inoperable and the only recourse is chemotherapy. This is another reason to keep control of your dog in the backcountry, since if it should become infected without your knowledge by eating infected carrion or picking up echinococcus eggs in some way, it could later deposit eggs in your house or yard and potentially infect you or your children. Young children especially could be vulnerable, as they love to play on the floor or outside in the dirt, and symptoms might not show up until they are in their teens or older. It's also another reason to think twice about drinking untreated groundwater in the outdoors.

REALITY CHECK: On a wolf-caribou-moose telemetry survey I was invited to fly along on in early 2010, we landed to check out a radio-collared wolf pack that had killed a moose cow and calf in the Rocky Mountains north of Prince George, BC. As we snowshoed up the slope from the helicopter to the kill site, the pilot carelessly kicked at some fresh wolf scat. The biologist we were with, a highly experienced and normally easygoing individual, got quite animated as he explained the hydatid risk. Previously, I had thought that the risk of hydatid infection was through eating infected wild meat, whereas the reality is much more insidious. Once again, after decades of bush experience, I had learned something new. It's interesting how things often come in twos and threes, as a few days later I heard a visiting speaker at the University of Northern British Columbia describe the same phenomenon in the context of Canadian wolves transplanted to the US and their interaction with local wildlife and nearby human populations.

WOLVERINES

Despite their relatively small size, wolverines have one of the most fearsome reputations of all Canadian wild animals, and they are capable of killing prey as large as a woodland caribou. However, the chance of even seeing one, much less encountering one, is exceedingly rare.

REALITY CHECK: In over 30 years of exploring the backcountry of north central BC, I have only seen two wolverines. One was a fine but distant sighting in an alpine meadow (the usual scenario), but the other was an incredible face-to-face encounter, just two metres apart. We watched each other for more than half a minute before the animal scurried quietly away through the scrub subalpine bush, completely belying its terrifying reputation.

If you meet a wolverine, enjoy the moment, but be sensible and don't give it any sense of being cornered. The strength of its jaws is second only to that of the African hyena for an animal of its size, and there is no doubt that it could be a deadly foe if threatened.

COYOTES

Coyotes, long thought to be a danger to domestic animals, pets and in some cases small children, have recently been elevated as a threat to people, following two attacks on Canada's east coast. In October 2009 a young woman was attacked and killed by coyotes while walking in Cape Breton Highlands National Park. When I was there nine months later, Parks Canada had erected coyote warning signs. And with good reason, for soon after we left, a teenage girl was attacked and injured by coyotes while camping in the same park. The advice being given is not unlike that for other predatory animals:

- Keep human food and grey water away from coyotes to avoid habituation to people.
- Don't hike alone, and make sure that children are accompanied by an adult.
- If you are camping, sleep inside, not outside, your tent (this is especially good advice in bear country as well).

- If you see a coyote, watch it carefully to assess its behaviour, and do not approach it.
- If the coyote approaches you or is close, keep your distance but do not flee or turn your back. Stay together and retreat slowly. Make yourself appear large and make lots of noise to try and scare it away, and identify possible escape routes.
- If you are attacked, continue to make lots of noise, throw stones and fight back with whatever is at hand.

PORCUPINES

Porcupines are more of a nuisance than a danger, unless you are unwise enough to make physical contact and get quills thrust into your skin. Or unknowingly have your vehicle's brake lines get chewed through while parked in the backcountry.

If you have a dog with you, keep it under tight control around porcupines, as you do not want to have to deal with a mouthful of quills, especially in the backcountry when you are far from veterinary help. This is a fairly common occurrence, however, and having a small pair of pliers with you may enable you to alleviate the dog's anguish until you get home. Despite the sometimes comical appearance of a dog with a face full of quills, it's not a laughing matter, and some dogs die from the aftereffects of their porcupine encounters, even after veterinary care.

Porcupines eat plywood, perhaps attracted by the animal blood that is sometimes used in the glue. Apart from the damage they cause, this tendency has resulted in more than one sleepless night for me when porcupines were making a terrible racket as they attacked backcountry cabins I was using. During the daytime they may take refuge in outbuildings, so be careful when entering a woodshed that you don't corner a porcupine in a confined space. And be especially careful when using an outhouse, as porcupines have been known to take refuge under the toilet hole! A friend once had two porcupines take up residence under a single-seat outhouse at his backcountry lodge. The frame-and-plywood structure stood high on log cribbing because of the deep winter snowpack, so after a difficult eviction my friend tried creosoting the logs as a countermeasure. Bad mistake, as the porcupines were further attracted by the creosote. The best defence is chicken wire or metal sheathing.

Although I have personally never had a problem, many people, when leaving a vehicle parked overnight in the backcountry wrap chicken wire all around it to prevent porcupines from chewing tires and brake lines. You do not want to be stuck in the backcountry with no brakes, as has happened to at least one person I know. Another possible preventive measure is to keep the vehicle well washed underneath to minimize possible attractants such as salt, oil or fuel.

And speaking of fuel, the need to store stoves and fuel as well as food well away from tents and out of the reach of wildlife was demonstrated to me one night by the actions of a rogue porcupine:

REALITY CHECK: This final, quirky note of caution about wildlife concerns a porcupine that tried to make off with my gas stove at midnight during an eight-day trek in northern BC. Twice I had to leave the tent to rescue the stove and chase the porcupine up a tree before I was finally able to scare it away. This incident alerted me to the need to take similar precautions with caching stoves and fuel in the outdoors as with food. This story involved only a porcupine, but it could as easily have been a grizzly bear.

NATIVE PLANTS

EDIBLE AND POISONOUS PLANTS

Many native plants are edible and/or have medicinal value. Others, such as Indian hellebore (*Veratrum viride*), mountain monkshood (*Aconitum delphiniifolium*), water hemlock (*Cicuta douglasii*) and many others are deadly poisonous. Unless you are very knowledgeable in identifying edible plants or you happen to be amid unmistakable patches of ripe blueberries or huckleberries or you are many weeks away from any help, gathering wild foods should probably be a low priority for you in a survival situation. Remember that you can survive for several weeks without food if you are not moving around much and if you can conserve your energy reserves. However, if you have to be active, and/or are having problems keeping warm, you may need to eat sooner. If you are interested in learning more about edible wild plants, there are many good books and other resources available. For British Columbia, two excellent general texts are MacKinnon and Pojar's *Plants of Northern British Columbia* and Parish's *Plants of Southern Interior British Columbia*, plus the related *Plants of the Pacific Northwest Coast*. All three books are worth owning, as there are many overlaps, regardless of where you live in the province. Even better, find someone in your area who is very knowledgeable about edible plants and take a field workshop from them.

PLANT METABOLITES

Many plants create chemicals, as by-products of their metabolic systems, that are often associated with deterring large and small animals from harming or devouring them. These secondary metabolites, as they are called, exist in very large numbers, along with associated fungi, and are of increasing interest to science. There are believed to be hundreds of thousands of secondary metabolites in the world, of which only a few thousand are yet known (a good reason for conserving plant biodiversity). Despite many established and potential benefits as medicines, secondary metabolites can also cause harm in cases of indiscriminate exposure. Well-known examples are stinging nettle and poison ivy, but there is a lesser-known problem plant in Canada: the cow parsnip (*Heracleum lanatum*) can cause a severe skin reaction when bruised or crushed and its secondary metabolites come into contact with exposed skin in sunlight (photo effect). The reaction affects a deeper layer of skin, which is damaged or killed if exposed to ultraviolet light within a few days of exposure to the plant, resulting in severe blistering.

A similar hazard exists with a related plant, the giant hogweed (*Heracleum mantegazzianum*), which was introduced into western Canada from Europe only a few decades ago and has become quite newsworthy.

Regarding hazards posed by plant metabolites, wear long pants and long-sleeved clothing, especially when bushwhacking, and try not to bruise or damage the vegetation you are travelling through.

FUNGAL LUNG INFECTIONS

A lesser-known disease risk to otherwise healthy users of the outdoors has been gaining prominence in recent years in parts of Canada and the US. There are three main types. Blastomycosis is an infection arising from *Blastomyces dermatitidis*, a fungus found in acidic soil throughout much of central Canada. Histoplasmosis is an infection caused by the fungus *Histoplasma capsulatum*, found in dusty areas of Alberta in bird, chicken and bat droppings. And *Cryptococcus gattii*, a very rare tropical fungus, appeared on Vancouver Island in 1999 and has since spread to parts of the mainland. This latter infection is acquired by inhaling spores and can be very difficult to diagnose in the early stages, as it is easily mistaken for other lung diseases such as pneumonia, cancer and tuberculosis. As a result, effective treatment can be delayed until the fungus spreads to other parts of the body such as the skin, where it becomes easier to recognize. There isn't much you can do to avoid this risk in the outdoors other than trying to avoid inhaling dust or spores, and general awareness of possible risks should you have symptoms.

If you are in the deserts of the US southwest, be aware of a common hazard there known as valley fever, or coccidioidomycosis. It too is caused by fungi in the soil that can become airborne and be breathed into the lungs, causing fever, chest pain, coughing and other symptoms. Most people who inhale valley fever fungi have few problems, but pregnant women and people with weakened immune systems can develop a serious or even fatal illness from valley fever.

The spines of the fearsome devil's club plagued early explorers and contemporary bushwhackers alike, yet First Nations recognize its many traditional medicinal values.

AFTER SOMETHING HAS HAPPENED

ASSESS THE SITUATION – PRIORITY ACTION APPROACH

Despite your best efforts of preparation and prevention, something unexpected has happened to you or your party in the outdoors and you must now deal with it. The first (normal) reaction, especially if you are alone, is likely to be shock, disbelief and fear, even a rising sense of panic if you are caught in a circumstance that has life-threatening implications. Or anxiety could simply arise from work or other commitments you may have for the next day or from people at home worrying about you or initiating some kind of emergency response that could be embarrassing. These reasons alone may be enough to cause you to push on dangerously when all you really need to do is stop and wait for morning.

- The first consideration in assessing a situation is to determine whether everyone is accounted for and whether anyone is in immediate danger, and if so, to take urgent steps to minimize that exposure. Assessing the situation will help you select the most effective action – it can be as short as taking a few seconds to scan the scene while walking toward it.
- Deal first with any medical, first aid or urgent rescue requirements, such as re-covering someone from an avalanche or a water or rockfall.
- The initial first aid assessment and response starts with the ABCs of airway, breathing, circulation, cervical spine and major bleeding or other trauma.
- Use a triage approach to set priorities if there is more than one victim. Determine how many people have been hurt and how they have been hurt.
- Follow this with a more complete first aid assessment; utilize the group's first aid supplies; comfort the casualties and make them secure, warm and dry while starting any treatment. If they are conscious and responsive, ensure that you have obtained their consent to help them, and start documenting vital signs and actions taken. If the injuries you have to deal with are severe, it is essential to maintain calm and problem solve to choose the best and safest actions under the circumstances.
- Injuries that are not immediately life-threatening may still require medical attention within a few hours. Examples include minor amputations; hard-to-close wounds that are long, deep or over joints; wounds with particular risk

of infection such as those resulting from bites and embedded objects or dirt; wounds to critical sites such as face, hands or feet; and wounds where there is a risk of destroyed flesh.

- Once immediate threats and urgent first aid have been taken care of, pause and thoroughly assess the situation and think through the problem presented and options available. Don't rush into action unless the situation is immediately life-threatening. Avoid doing anything that will compound the situation and/or cause added danger to others in the party.

- Assess the equipment the group is carrying, as well as any natural materials at hand that could be used for making splints, building a fire or constructing a stretcher or a shelter if needed. Review what skills the group has and how those can be applied to the situation. Are there any other health concerns among the party? How strong are the participants in the event an evacuation of an injured person is required? Keep in mind that circumstances can change, so continuously reassess the situation, think through "what if" scenarios and look for more options.

- Typical choices you will be faced with are to continue with the trip; abort the trip and return the way you came; stay put; or evacuate an injured member of your party. Consider any decision to continue on with the trip very carefully, as even a minor injury could become problematic later on. Conventional survival advice is to stay put, particularly with a downed aircraft or stuck vehicle, and especially if you have left a good travel or flight plan so that you have a good chance of being found. However, you should assess your situation carefully, and if you do decide to walk out or send someone for help, do so early enough while you still have food and energy reserves. Some key issues to address are: How long do you think will you be able to survive with the resources you have? Do you know where and how far you will have to go, and do you think you can make it? Have you stayed close to your planned itinerary or travel route, and how long do you think it will take for a search to get started? Depending on circumstances, there may not be a clear right or wrong answers to these questions, but consider that people in a survival situation can underestimate how long they can survive and overestimate how far they can travel. Whatever you decide – and ultimately it may come down to luck – try to stay positive and do everything possible to survive.

- Other things to consider are the availability of shelter; remaining hours of daylight; weather; visibility; terrain; distance to travel (forward or back); possibility of getting lost; dangers en route, such as creek crossings; group size, group strength, participant skills, group dynamics and combined equipment;

means of communication, both within the group if you need to split up and with the outside world; the time you are expected back and what sort of itinerary you filed.

<hr />

REALITY CHECK: In March 2011, 56-year-old Rita Chrétien and her husband, Albert, were driving from their home in Penticton, BC, to Las Vegas, detouring through some back roads in a remoter part of Nevada when, possibly misled by their GPS, their vehicle became mired in mud and stuck. There was a stream nearby for drinking water, plus they had some trail mix and candy with them in the vehicle. There they waited, faced with the very difficult decision whether to stay or go. After three days Albert left to try and walk out to find help, and as of the time of writing this section several months later he has not been found. Rita stayed with the vehicle, where she did everything right to survive and was found alive seven weeks later by recreational ATV riders.

A few weeks earlier, in mid-February, 68-year-old Jerry McDonald became snowed in with his pickup truck on a back road in Oregon. According to his diary, he survived an amazing 60 days before dying of starvation and hypothermia. His remains were found in his sleeping bag two weeks later by a forest service crew. Incredibly, Jerry made the decision to stay with his vehicle even though he was only three miles from the nearest town. In these parallel, concurrent situations, both Rita and Jerry survived for weeks in a stuck vehicle, and in the end Rita was lucky to be found in time, while Jerry was not. In either case, a satellite phone or an inexpensive Spot device or a PLB would likely have quickly resolved these tragic situations. (See chapter 20 on communications, beginning at p. 125.)

<hr />

- If you develop an evacuation plan and decide to act on it, the best situation will be if the injured person is able to walk, perhaps aided by one or two people and possibly with someone carrying their gear. If it is necessary to carry somebody out, be aware that this can be an extremely arduous undertaking even for a good-sized group, so consider the following: How far do you have to go? What is the strength of your party? What is the nature of the terrain? What are the injuries? Do you need technical aid such as ropes and rigging? Does your casualty have a suspected spinal injury such that he should only be moved fully immobilized by qualified people? Does advanced hypothermia pose a risk of death if you decide to move the casualty? If in doubt, and if there is sufficient time and the opportunity to do so, call or send for specialized help. If you are in the midst of an extended multi-day trip, you may have a particularly difficult situation to problem-solve unless you have the means, such as a satellite phone, to call for help.

- If somebody is too badly injured to travel and you decide to send someone for help, ideally they should not go alone and there should be at least one person to stay behind with the injured. If there are only two of you in the party, you will have a difficult judgment call to make as to whether the uninjured person goes for help or stays and waits for rescue, depending on the severity of injuries, remaining daylight and the likelihood of a quick rescue. This is another good reason to have groups of at least three or four people.

- If you have a radio or satellite phone with you and decide to request a helicopter, and if it is getting late in the day (or even past late morning or noon in some locales), you may have to wait until next morning for the helicopter to arrive, taking into consideration the time required to assess the information you provided, assemble people and gear, dispatch, flying time there and back and limits of operation (daylight). If you are able to procure a helicopter evacuation, you may need to clear a suitable landing space and you will need to secure any loose items. If you are in communication with authorities but decide to self-rescue, it might still be a good idea to ask for backup. When the helicopter arrives, always approach it from the front, well clear of tail rotors and in full view of the pilot. Stay very low, especially if the ground is not quite level or there is snow that the machine could settle or tip into or if there is a possibility of strong wind gusts that could deflect rotor blades low to the ground.

OTHER POSSIBLE ACTIONS

… in rough order of priority:

- Ensure that everyone has warm, dry clothing and/or protection from inclement weather.
- Procure drinking water if your supply is low.
- Find your way out if you are lost and if you have a reasonable expectation of being able to do so safely. Note that the imperative to do this will depend on whether you left a clear itinerary or not. If you did and you stay put, it will give searchers the best chance of finding you quickly the next day.
- Find or build shelter, preferably sited either for warmth or for least cold and near water.
- Build a fire for warmth and psychological comfort, but beware of starting a forest fire. If you are wet, building a fire to dry off would be higher, possibly first, on this priority list. Otherwise, it will probably not be your first priority.

- Prepare for travel or evacuation the next day if that is your decided course of action.
- Prepare to signal rescuers if the opportunity arises.
- If possible, procure food, but generally only if you expect to be in a survival situation for a very long period (more than a few days) and if you know what's safe and what isn't, and only if you don't spend more energy getting food than you obtain from consuming it. Food will help in several ways: psychologically, energy-wise and to help ward off hypothermia through increased metabolism.
- Be prepared to improvise in any way you can, **and don't give up!**

REALITY CHECK: On Saturday, October 17, 2009, four climbers were ascending a passage known as The Corkscrew as they prepared to exit Fang Cave in Evanoff Provincial Park in north central British Columbia. Suddenly, a large rock to which a rope anchor had been attached came loose and crushed a member of the party. John, who was pinned by the rock and initially not breathing, survived this calamity through the dedicated efforts of a lot of people and a series of very lucky circumstances. The first critical success factor was that he was with able companions who acted promptly and effectively to resuscitate and stabilize him and initiate rescue efforts. Second, by considerable good fortune there was a separate party of four cavers nearby who quickly became part of the rescue effort (ordinarily a very unlikely circumstance in this remote cave). Third, they had a satellite phone and were able to reach a control centre in Texas from the cave's middle entrance and trigger an immediate rescue response via the RCMP in British Columbia. Fourth, a rapid response had key people from the local search and rescue and cave rescue groups, with critically needed medical supplies and rescue gear, fly 100 kilometres to land in the subalpine meadows above the cave just barely before nightfall. Fifth, BC's provincial cave rescue coordinator just happened to be teaching a rescue course that afternoon in the nearby city of Quesnel, and he quickly joined the operation along with others from his course. Sixth, after the cave had been rigged and the victim extracted, some 50 volunteers, who had driven to the scene and hiked up the mountain in the dark, lowered the stretcher down the mountain through the night, pushing themselves to the limit. Seventh, military search and rescue technicians from the Comox air base on Vancouver Island were able to parachute to the base of the mountain in the middle of the night by the light of flares. Knowledge of what they would likely be facing had caused first responders to request military support early on in the operation. Climbing up to reach the descending rescue party, the SAR technicians bought their expertise and essential supplies, including more oxygen, intravenous drip and large heating pads, at a critical time. Eighth, a military Cormorant helicopter with night-flying capability was able to pick up the stretcher from a staging point on the lower slopes in the early hours. It was the second one to try, after the first had to turn back for mechanical reasons. And ninth, but definitely not least, John's own knowledge and fortitude enabled him to assist his rescuers when he was able.

The late George Evanoff descending into the middle entrance of Fang Cave during one of the first explorations in the early 1980s.

Many lessons were learned by the combined rescue parties during this operation, and like the crew of Apollo 13 and their NASA supports, it was ultimately one of their finest hours, snatching success from what had earlier seemed like sure disaster. A combination of providential circumstances, availability of key resources and the skill, determination and endurance of rescuers brought about a happy ending. Three local search and rescue groups, local cavers, BC Cave Rescue, RCMP, BC Ambulance, 442 Squadron (three military aircraft plus several civilian helicopters) and others were involved in the rescue. For John, the end of the rescue operation just marked the beginning of his long journey of recovery from the critical injuries he had received, but within six months he was back climbing again. First responders had not expected him to make it through the night; that he did was a combination of good luck and everyone involved pulling out all the stops and not giving up.[15]

A helicopter is often the best way to evacuate an injured person from the backcountry, but depending on weather, communications and when the accident happened, you may have to wait at least one night for pickup.

EMERGENCY SHELTERS

After a problem occurs and you have decided to stay put for a while, finding shelter is one of your highest priorities after first aid. With know-how, shelter can be relatively easy to come by in the Canadian outdoors, especially in wooded areas or where there is good snowpack. As with most things related to outdoor safety, though, practice is important when it comes to finding or building shelter. I recommend that you take a survival course (it can be a fun thing to do), and/or practise shelter-building with someone who has experience doing it. Following are some basic points about survival shelters.

BUSH SHELTER

HOW MUCH DAYLIGHT IS LEFT?

The amount of daylight you have will determine how much effort you will be able to put into finding a suitable spot and constructing your shelter.

FIND A GOOD SPOT:

- Avoid, as much as possible, exposure to wind, rain and snowfall.
- If possible, locate the shelter near water and fuel and in a place where your fire will not start a wildfire. The need for fire is probably less important than shelter and water unless you are wet and need to dry out. Fire, though, will provide a huge psychological boost during the night and give you something to occupy your mind as you tend it.
- Try to find some reasonably level ground. Even on a slope you likely won't have to go too far to find something.
- If you are near a large water body, try to place your shelter at least five metres or so above the water to avoid being exposed to the cooling and wetting effects of morning mists.
- Utilize natural shelter materials and any forest cover around you.
- Consider locating the shelter in a breeze if biting insects are likely to be a problem.
- Consider katabatic winds caused by cold (dense) air descending downslope. I once set up my tent in what I thought was a nice sheltered gully, out of the strong breeze that was whipping across a surrounding plateau. Unfortunately, as evening came on, the breeze died on the plateau and an icy wind started blasting down the gully from glaciated Mount Edziza above – a perfect example of a katabatic wind and where not to camp.

- Similarly, avoid sheltered hollows, because cold air may pool there overnight. I have measured a temperature difference of more than 10°c in such a depression (−50°c), compared to a place just 30 metres upslope (−39°c).
- Consider any sun exposure and the angle of the sun relative to your shelter. Sun is generally unwelcome during the heat of a summer day, but is more welcome in winter and in the morning and evening at any time of year.

VENTILATION AND CARBON MONOXIDE

Be very careful with ventilation if your shelter is a confined space such as with a tight tent, tarp or snow shelter, especially if a cooking stove or fire is to be employed. Carbon monoxide is an insidious and deadly gas, as related in the tragic *Reality Check* in the Snow Trench section at p. 182.

OTHER CONSIDERATIONS

For the first night, you should probably spend no more than about half an hour looking for a site. You don't want to use up too much energy at this stage or move very far from your position, which hopefully is on a route that somebody knows about. If you are going to be there for more than one night, you will have plenty of time the next day to either relocate or improve your shelter. For the first night the shelter should be as small (for warmth) and as easy to build as possible. Make it as waterproof as possible (this is where a thin sheet of plastic is invaluable) and gather lots of material such as green boughs to provide good ground insulation. Try making your shelter small like an animal den; and don't get too fancy for the first night. In heavy timber, look for natural shelters under deadfalls or the roots of old trees, perhaps using sheets of bark for added roofing material.

If you have a piece of plastic, a type of shelter I have built and used successfully on several occasions is constructed as follows. Find a long pole and set one end into the ground and the other in a tree notch at breast height. Then lay your plastic and/or green boughs as shingles over this sloping ridgepole. If you are still there the next day, you might try upgrading to a classic lean-to, which works well in conjunction with a fire to direct heat into the shelter.

REALITY CHECK: The most comfortable two nights I have ever spent outdoors were in a lean-to shelter on a two-day survival course taught by British Columbia's Provincial Emergency Program. I had a foot-thick bed of green boughs and a fire that burned all night – it was better than a high-quality tent and sleeping bag.

For firewood, use a small, folding pruning saw from your emergency kit to collect a few good-sized dry snags perhaps three or four metres long, and save energy by feeding their ends into the fire over time instead of cutting them up. Focus on staying dry and warm, and if you cannot make it out safely on your own, improve your rescuers' chances of finding you by staying on your stated route. Busying yourself about camp will be psychologically helpful, as long as it is not done at the expense of too much energy loss. As you set your priorities, remember that you can go several minutes without air, several days without water and several weeks without food. Over time, however, the lack of food will slowly deplete your metabolic energy resources, which will affect your ability to stay warm.

SNOW SHELTER

Snow is one of the best insulators in the natural world, a characteristic that has allowed humans to migrate over time from the warm climate of Africa to Arctic regions. There are many types of snow shelters that are suitable to various conditions and are discussed below.

SNOW BLOCK SHELTER

In Arctic tundra regions with open country and wind-packed snow, the well-known snow-block shelter, or igloo, was and still is commonly used for survival and for living out on the land. Building a traditional igloo, however, requires considerable skill and practice, so a survival situation is not the best time to learn how to do this. Elsewhere in Canada, you will generally be at or below treeline, where there are easier alternatives to consider, also discussed below. However, if you plan to live, work or travel in Canada's Arctic, learn how to build an igloo from the people who live there – it is a skill worth acquiring.

A more general and easier type of snow-block construction is a wall or series of walls to create windbreaks for tents and gear when camped in an exposed place such as on a glacier.

SNOW CAVE

A snow cave requires a good depth (at least two-and-a-half to three metres) of reasonably consolidated, cold, dry snow, preferably on a slope in order to facilitate the removal of snow and the escape of cold air downslope. The ideal situation, if you can find one, is a good-sized snowdrift – this, by its nature, will have well-consolidated snow that should provide good structural strength. A roomy, two-person snow cave takes several hours to excavate (four hours for the ones I have built) but will serve you well for several days. You will almost certainly get wet doing this, so have a change of clothes, and if you are below treeline, build a good-sized fire away from the snow cave to dry out when you have finished.

After excavating a low entrance passage, hollow out a chamber, with a double sleeping platform across the back of the cave or single platforms on either side of the entrance passage. It helps enormously if there are two people involved: one working inside the slowly enlarging chamber, moving snow into the entrance passage, and the other on the outside, clearing the excavated snow from the entrance. In the unlikely event your partially built snow cave collapses, having a person on the outside is also a good safety measure.

If you are snowshoeing or skiing in the backcountry, it is a good idea for each person to carry a small snow shovel for this eventuality. This is a multi-purpose item, being essential safety equipment when travelling in avalanche terrain, plus it makes snow shelter construction a lot easier. If you don't have a shovel, you can use a snowshoe for excavating, and if you don't have that, you may have to improvise.

The sleeping platforms should be elevated above the level of the entrance to allow cold air to settle out. Use a ski pole or something similar to poke a ventilation shaft in the roof of the chamber and leave the pole in place so that you can use it to keep the shaft clear during a snowstorm. Lay down a good layer of insulating material on the sleeping platforms using closed-cell foam pads if you have them and/or green boughs; and close the entrance with a block of snow or your pack. Where the snowpack is deep enough for a snow cave in temperate latitudes, the ground temperature is never far below freezing. Therefore, if you excavate the snow cave down close to the ground, the inside temperature should be ideal from the standpoint of optimal warmth without getting wet from condensation or melting snow. If you have reasonable winter clothing and/or a sleeping bag, you should be able to maintain a comfortable body temperature inside the cave. Alternatively, if you lack a good sleeping bag and there are two or more of you, huddling together may keep you warm.

The late George Evanoff shows the author how to build a deluxe snow cave.

SNOW HOLE

If you don't have much daylight left and/or you can't deal with getting some clothes wet, a quick survival hole can be excavated into the side of a snowdrift or the "well" that develops around the base of some trees later in the snow season. The hole should not be much larger than you are and the base should be lined with green boughs or other insulating material. Then, wearing whatever clothes you need for the night, wriggle into the hole, feet first, with your head – protected with a warm toque – at the entrance. It won't be very comfortable, but it shouldn't take you more than 15 to 30 minutes to make it and you will be surprisingly warm inside.

SNOW TRENCH

A quick but possibly less effective survival shelter is to dig a shallow, one- or two-person trench in the snow, line it with green boughs or other insulating material and cover it with branches, skis, snowshoes and/or snow blocks. A disadvantage of this type of shelter is that cold air, having no way to flow out, may collect in the trench. More serious concerns are the risk of collapse, and keeping the shelter well ventilated in a storm to avoid possible suffocation. The idea of lying in a trench in the snow may not be very appealing, but in the absence of other shelter opportunities or a warming fire, it will likely be better than being out in the open, especially on an exposed plateau or snowfield.

REALITY CHECK: In January 2007, two young but experienced backcountry skiers died in a snow trench shelter on the Wapta Icefield in the Canadian Rockies north of Lake Louise. Seeking refuge on the high, exposed, flat icefield, they excavated a snow trench, which they covered with a tarp, skis and possibly snow blocks. They cooked in the shelter, from which it may have been difficult to vent fumes from the stove. Sometime during the night they died from what was thought to be a combination of carbon monoxide poisoning and the collapse of the shelter. The heat from the stove was likely a contributing factor in glazing the inside of the shelter and possibly weakening the overlying snow, leading to the collapse. The carbon monoxide poisoning may also have hindered or incapacitated their efforts to escape. There are specific pointers from this tragic story, to be aware of the dangers of snow shelter ventilation and collapse and of cooking in confined spaces. This story also emphasizes that experience, caution and doing it by the book – they had a training manual diagram of a trench shelter with them – are not guarantees of safety.[16]

FIRE AND SNOW

Fires are obviously not compatible with snow shelters, but another option (especially in shallow snowpack) is to simply sleep outside in front of a good-sized fire if you have the means to make one and the fuel to keep it going all night. Ideally this is done in conjunction with a lean-to type of shelter, but it can also be as simple as lying on the ground or on a platform carved out of the snowpack in front of the fire. This will not work in deep snowpack, as the fire will gradually melt its way down through the snow, but you can slow this process for a few hours by building the fire on a bed of good-sized green logs.

There are a couple of things to watch out for in choosing a fire for warmth in snowy conditions. Beware of overhanging, snow-laden tree branches that may drop their loosened load of snow, possibly extinguishing the fire and wetting you, with potentially serious consequences.

REALITY CHECK: Don't do what I did once and melt the soles of your boots after falling asleep with your feet close to the survival camp fire! Not everyone has had the distinction of being portrayed in a cartoon, but that doubtful honour fell to me after I wrote about the incident in a local newspaper, and the paper's cartoonist drew a remarkably lifelike portrayal of my dilemma from his imagination.

Another winter camping technique was described to me by a First Nations man who grew up in the mountain backcountry of Ilgachuz, north of Anahim Lake in British Columbia. He told me he would build a fire to heat lava rocks that were plentiful in the area. Any rocks would work, provided they did not contain moisture (avoid river rocks) that might cause them to explode. While the lava rocks were heating in the fire, he would excavate a depression in the ground underneath a tree for shelter, place the hot rocks in the hole and cover them first with the excavated dirt and then with a thick layer of green boughs. Lying on the boughs and covering himself with a blanket, he told me that he would sleep through the night as warm as if he were in a heated house. Some kind of digging tool such as a forestry worker's pulaski is needed for excavating the frozen ground.

POWDER SNOW SHELTER, OR QUINZHEE

This type of shelter works well in cold, dry snow, even in a shallow snowpack. Like a snow cave it takes about four hours to build. First, using shovels or snowshoes or some other improvised means, pile a large mound of snow about two metres high and three metres wide at the base. Periodically, as each layer of snow is shovelled onto the pile, tamp it down lightly. When the pile has been completed, finish it off by shaping it like a hemisphere (for maximum strength) and then walk away and leave it for about an hour to set. This is the same principle as a snowplow leaving a berm across the entrance to your driveway – if you get to it right away it's easy to shovel clear, but an hour or two later it has set firm. Use the time to organize your gear, gather green boughs for ground insulation or firewood for a nearby fire (not close to the shelter, obviously). After the snow pile has set, hollow it out in much the same manner as the snow cave described above. Leave a shell thickness of 20 to 30 centimetres – you will know when it's about right because it will transmit light through to the interior of the shelter. An alternative method that would also work in low light is to insert 30-centimetre-long sticks in the snow mound before excavating it. The inside tips of the sticks will indicate where to stop shovelling when digging out the shelter. When the quinzhee is finished, pull out the sticks to create some additional air holes. Again, have a raised platform of snow inside the shelter to sleep on and to allow cold air to flow away. A single candle will provide ample interior light and will slightly glaze the inside of the dome to add strength and ensure that any droplets of condensation or meltwater flow to the ground around the inside edge of the structure and not on you.

REALITY CHECK: Beware of making a quinzhee in heavy, wet snow, as it could collapse on you. This happened to a backcountry skier I know, but luckily his partner was there to dig him out.

One small powder-snow shelter I built in a shallow snowpack at −15°c lasted for about a week. When I visited it a few days later, it was so strong that I was able to stand on the by now only 15-centimetre-thick roof (although I wouldn't recommend trying this when it is newly made). A powder snow shelter might make a good option in cold open country such as the prairies or during an early-winter cold snap when there isn't much snow on the ground yet.

A shelter should provide protection from the elements and proximity to drinking water – and a view that might provide a psychological boost.

WINTER SURVIVAL

Winter is a time when the woods are quiet and the detritus of the landscape is periodically renewed with a pristine blanket of snow that refreshes, displays interesting animal signs that aren't as evident in summertime, and provides new backcountry recreational opportunities such as skiing, snowshoeing, snowboarding, ice climbing and snowmobiling. In fact, winter is one of the best times to be outdoors. A good part of what is needed to survive outside in winter has already been covered in preceding sections: preparedness, equipment, hypothermia and shelters. If you are reasonably equipped, have left a clear itinerary with a trusted source and have the skills and the means to build a good shelter, you should be fine. There are advantages to winter travel versus summer: you are less likely to encounter wetting rainfall, annoying bugs and bears; and the absence of cleared trails becomes less of an impediment to travel, as the snowpack deepens and covers brush and deadfall. You are more likely to be able to follow your own tracks back out; and if you do find yourself in trouble, and you are familiar with some of the classic winter survival stories listed in Appendix A, at p. 253, you will know that you too can survive.

REALITY CHECK: It is very easy for vital equipment to disappear in the snowpack, especially during a snowstorm. So when you stop for a break or are camped in the snow, make sure your camp and equipment are well organized or you may find yourself returning in the summer to look for lost equipment, as I have.

WINTER CLOTHING AND EQUIPMENT

As well as items already suggested for all-season use, take along extra clothing, especially extra gloves in case you get the first pair wet or lose one. More than one climber has suffered from severe frostbite after losing a glove to the wind or to gravity on a mountain ridge. If you have a spare pair of wool socks, they can also double as spare mitts. Insulated winter boots are preferred over regular hiking boots, and your clothing should include warm headwear, long underwear and gaiters to keep the snow out of your boots. A rain- and wind-resistant breathable shell is essential in winter in order to avoid getting wet from within while exercising. Sunglasses (wrap-around and/or with side shades) will help prevent snowblindness, especially in the spring months at higher elevations when there is still plenty of snow but the sunlight is getting intense. Dress in layers and take the time to stop and take off or put on layers frequently as circumstances dictate in order to stay dry and warm. Not getting wet from sweating is of paramount importance in winter.

WINTER DRIVING

Service and winterize your vehicle by late fall, including brakes, tires, engine oil, cooling system, windshield and wipers, lights (functional and properly aimed), exhaust (no carbon monoxide leaks), battery and terminals, hoses, belts and wiring. Put good winter tires on all four wheels, even if it is a two-wheel-drive vehicle, with studs and/or chains if required for steep mountain roads. All-season radial tires are not sufficient for most winter driving in Canada, and not having good winter tires may invalidate your insurance in case of an accident. If you are going to own your vehicle for more than a few years, I have found that it is cost-effective to buy a spare set of inexpensive steel wheel rims so that the winter tires can be kept permanently mounted and you can change them yourself. It requires a bit of work but should pay for itself in one or two years. A side benefit of this is that if you are going off-pavement for any distance in the summer, you can easily throw one or two of your winter wheels in the trunk for extra spares.

Winter comes early to the Banff–Jasper Icefields Parkway.

EQUIPMENT TO KEEP IN YOUR CAR IN WINTER

- Spare windshield washer antifreeze.
- Windshield scraper and snow brush. Take the time to properly clear all of the windows of your vehicle of snow, ice and frost before driving. Also, be kind to those who are driving behind you and brush the snow off the roof of your vehicle rather than leave it to the slipstream.
- Spare tire. Check its pressure and make sure you have a serviceable jack and wheel-bolt lock if required.
- Small shovel. Strength, not weight, is what is important, since this tool stays with the vehicle. Although standard advice to drivers is to stay with your vehicle if caught in a winter storm, the shovel could also serve for building a snow shelter off to the side of the road if you are stranded. If you have some survival training and know how to do it, a snow shelter may be warmer than staying in the vehicle, with less risk of being trapped or suffocating during severe drifting. But make sure you build the shelter well clear of snowplows, and leave a note in the vehicle saying what you've done.
- Jumper cables.
- Toolkit.
- Tow rope, hand winch, come-along or jack-all. Traction pads or even pieces of old carpets could also be handy for getting your vehicle moving.
- Methyl hydrate, for use in freeing frozen gas lines and door locks. It can also be used as a fire starter and for fuelling an improvised stove such as a toilet roll placed in a tin can. An alcohol stove can also be used to warm a badly frozen engine compartment in extremely cold conditions in an emergency, by putting a blanket over the hood and placing the alcohol stove on the ground underneath the engine. Be careful not to overdo this and cause a fire or damage to the engine block. I have known more than one person to have extricated themselves in this manner in −40°c conditions in north central British Columbia, although such temperatures are becoming less common with climate change.
- Warm blanket (s) and/or sleeping bag (s), especially if you are undertaking a long trip on northern winter roads.
- Flashlight and spare batteries.
- Signal aids such as road flares, reflective triangles, red-coloured cones.
- Matches and candles.
- Hand saw, axe and possibly even a power saw if you are travelling off-highway where you could find your way out blocked by a fallen tree.
- Winter clothing and footwear – don't undertake an out of town winter drive

dressed for the city, even if you are going directly from a building in one town to a building in another.

REALITY CHECK: Many years ago when I was working in downtown Toronto, during one winter lunchtime I took a long trip across town using an ingenious combination of underground malls, connecting passageways and the subway. It was an uncommonly cold (for Toronto) –15°c day, with typical wind and humidity from Lake Ontario making it far worse. I was dressed for the office – dress shirt, not even a jacket – I didn't need anything more, since in this paragon of northern civilization I didn't need to go outside. Alas, when I had achieved my purpose and was ready to head back, I learned that the subway system had been shut down due to a rare bomb threat, and of course there were no cabs. Not exactly life-threatening, but in my zeal to get back to work I was faced with several kilometres of stark winter reality. In different circumstances, say, driving a back road in winter, a mistake like this could be vastly more costly than the discomfort I suffered that day.

- Emergency food and drink.
- Vehicle first aid kit.
- Communications: cell phone (if in a coverage area), radio, satellite phone, Spot or PLB.

BEFORE YOU HEAD OUT

- Check road conditions and weather forecasts along your intended route.
- Let people at both your origin and your destination know when you are leaving and your expected arrival time.
- Top up your gas tank as opportunities arise.
- Practise safe driving and good separation from other vehicles, especially snow-plows. Remember, accidents are seldom accidental. There is almost always some contributing human factor that is attributable to complacency or an attitude that "it won't happen to me."

REALITY CHECK: A couple decided on the spur of the moment to take their newly acquired vehicle out for an early-winter test drive, leaving their winter clothing and survival gear in their other vehicle. Kilometres off the beaten track, they got stuck with nightfall approaching and were faced with a lightly clad, long walk to safety. They were fortunate to be spotted after walking for a few hours; others in similar circumstances have not been so lucky.

Slow down and drive according to conditions, especially at the beginning of the winter season with the arrival of the first frosts and snow. Avoid unnecessary driving during winter storms, especially out of town. Consider taking a winter driving course if you are new to snow and ice. Learn how to avoid, and if necessary steer out of, skids; and never give up trying to correct a skid if you do get into one. And of course, always wear your seatbelt.

REALITY CHECK: A few months after obtaining my first industrial first aid ticket, I was the first person to arrive on the scene of a two-car head-on collision that had just occurred on a bend of an icy highway in November, about 45 minutes from the nearest town. I had been driving off-highway and as I turned onto the pavement I saw a single vehicle stationary in the middle of the road with some objects appearing to be innocuously scattered about. I didn't see the second vehicle in the ditch until I had parked my car and walked over to the scene. The strange calm of the situation utterly belied what had taken place. Of the seven occupants of the two vehicles, three died, including a child; two were critically injured; and two, who were wearing seatbelts, walked away with minor injuries. The driver of the vehicle in the ditch had been ejected and was lying on the highway, dead with catastrophic head injuries. From what I could see, every seat in both vehicles was survivable had seatbelts been worn. This was before airbags came into general use, and there could have been no more graphic demonstration of the value of seatbelts. The accident occurred at around 11 a.m. on Remembrance Day and the first RCMP officer to arrive on the scene an hour later had been called right out of the parade still wearing his ceremonial red serge.

Some further recollections of this event:

• During the hour on the scene before the first emergency responders arrived, and for about a half-hour afterward while I continued to help with CPR in one of the ambulances, I recall that I acted calmly and professionally as I had been trained. Just minutes after I was discharged from further responsibility, however, the shock hit me and I drove the 60 kilometres back to town shaken, at half the posted speed limit. We have within us the ability to function appropriately in a life and death situation in circumstances that we would otherwise find horrific and debilitating.

- Not everything may be as it seems in times of crisis. One man assisted me for half an hour without revealing, until later asked by an ambulance paramedic, that he was a doctor. Perhaps he felt that things were going as well as they could and saw no reason to assume control of the scene. The vehicle on the highway as viewed from the front appeared to have only two occupants. In reality they were the back seat passengers who had been wearing seatbelts; both the driver and the right-front passenger had been thrust out of sight under the dash. Similarly, the child in the other vehicle was out of sight beneath the front passenger seat. Coincidentally I had seen a training film on just this circumstance, and it looked shockingly familiar to see the real thing. One of the first police officers to arrive on the scene ordered us to stop CPR compressions after doing a cursory check and announcing there was a pulse. The power of the uniform was such that both the (doctor) and I paused to reassess, before agreeing that there was no pulse and resuming the CPR.

- The 90 minutes I spent attending the casualties was timeless while it was happening, yet paradoxically seemed compressed afterward. This is another coping strategy of the human mind.

- It often seems to be the case that when you take a first aid course, you will soon find yourself called upon to use it; so keep that in mind as you go through the practice drills.

- In the life and death situation we suddenly found ourselves in, one thing that stood out was the willingness of almost everyone who came on the scene to help in any way they could. Some people needed someone to take charge and tell them what to do, and they unhesitatingly responded to the best of their abilities. Others walked in, saw a need or a gap and immediately went to work without being asked.

- I've always thought that a basic first aid course with a simulated vehicle accident scene should be a prerequisite of obtaining (and perhaps even renewing) a driver's licence. Others aren't so sure, wondering if unskilled intervention with severe-trauma accident victims might, overall, do more harm than good. What do you think?

REALITY CHECK: In the early 1980s I was a passenger in the rear seat of a rented car, returning home from a spring day of hiking at Mount Robson. I was sharing the back seat with a very large Great Dane dog that was jealously guarding his three-quarters of the seat. Approaching the curved high bridge over West Twin Creek, west of McBride in British Columbia's Robson Valley, our driver lost control on icy frost heaves on the curved bridge approach. He was a technically good driver from New York, but was travelling way too fast both for the posted speed limit and for the conditions, 80 m.p.h. (129 km/h) he said afterward. He fought the slide masterfully to the end, but the combination of frost heaves, ice and the curve was ultimately too much. We spun out at high speed and I closed my eyes and tried to relax my whole body for what was coming. By amazingly good fortune we didn't hit any oncoming traffic; we didn't run out of ice and take a high-speed roll sideways on dry pavement; and after doing a full 360-degree rotation, we slammed sideways into a huge snow bank left by an unusually heavy-snow winter, just above the long drop into the West Twin Gorge. As we resumed our journey in the now battered but still driveable vehicle, it was ten minutes before anyone spoke, the first question being to ask whether we were going east or west.

It is not sufficient for a driver to be technically competent – he or she must also drive according to the rules of the road, the speed limit and most importantly the comfort level of others in the vehicle and others on the road. There's nobody I would rather be riding with than a technically good driver once we're in trouble, but I'd sooner ride with someone who is also less likely to get into trouble in the first place!

Lastly, and this applies to driving at any time: stop driving if you are fatigued – pull over and take a break; and avoid driving while under the influence of alcohol or drugs.

WILDLIFE IN WINTER

You have much less risk of encountering a bear during wintertime, because most of them are asleep. However, neither black bears nor grizzlies are full hibernators, and unless they are females with cubs, some have been known to be active during all but the most severe winter months, especially when there is plentiful food around, such as moose. There are historical reports of male grizzly bears hunting moose for ten months of the year in the northern Rockies; and it is worth noting that the winter climate was much more severe then than it is today.[17]

REALITY CHECK: In over 30 winters of tramping around the mountains of north central British Columbia on skis and snowshoes, I have yet to see fresh bear sign between mid-November and mid-March. However, I have regularly encountered grizzly tracks in the spring mountain snowpack; and one of the book's reviewers told me he has seen grizzly tracks in the snow in late November and early December. He noted that two of his acquaintances were stalked by a grizzly for an hour in January on a popular mountain trail in a local provincial park.

REALITY CHECK: I have sometimes wondered about the risk of disturbing a bear's den by inadvertently skiing or snowshoeing over the top of it. This happened to two forestry surveyors in January 2007 when they unknowingly disturbed and were attacked by a grizzly while working on the east slope of the Rockies.

If you do see bear tracks in the winter or spring snowpack, they should give you warning of the bear's presence and the opportunity to turn around and go somewhere else. Overall, though, if you are overly concerned about encountering bears in the outdoors, winter is a good time to travel and camp in the backcountry.

With fresh snowfall, we knew these grizzly bear tracks had been made within the past hour.

TRAVEL ON WINTER ICE

Before the advent of railways and highways, travel on frozen lakes and rivers was a preferred way of getting around in the north in winter. It was always risky and is certainly no less so today with our warmer climate. Ice conditions vary with temperatures and snowfall. Heavy snow early in the season can insulate the ice before it has a chance to thicken. Springs in lakes that are fed by the water table; moving water at lake inflows and outflows; and narrows or pinch points in a lake – all these things can weaken the ice. Even if the ice is strong enough to support you, there may be surface or subsurface water that can freeze to skis or snowshoes and render travel difficult or result in wet and frostbitten feet. Weakness in the ice may be indicated by the sunny side of a lake, by darkness in the ice caused by water seepage, and by rocks or logs at or near the surface absorbing solar radiation and weakening the surrounding ice. A child's small feet may exert more pressure per unit of surface area than an adult's, possibly putting them at greater risk. Tracks of animals may provide clues as to whether the ice is likely to be safe or not. You can distribute your weight by using skis or snowshoes, but try to ensure you can release the bindings quickly underwater if the ice fails. Have the hip belt on your pack undone, and when practical keep your thumbs under your shoulder straps so that you can throw off your pack and significantly reduce your weight in an instant if you should break through. A probe or a ski pole can be used to test the thickness of the ice ahead by the sound that the tip makes as it strikes the ice. And carrying small ice picks may provide the means to grab the ice and pull yourself out should you fall through. See the *Reality Check* at p. 9 about Fred Van der Post's experience falling through the ice of a remote northern lake.

Be prepared for weak ice when walking, snowshoeing or skiing on frozen lakes or rivers.

AVALANCHE

In a general book on outdoor safety, it is impossible to do more than skim the complex field of avalanches. But I will introduce some key points and urge you, if you are active in the winter, spring and early summer in hilly or mountainous terrain, to take a recreational avalanche course and practise what you learn (see Appendix C for resources, beginning at p. 261). Since the first edition of this book was published in 2007, there have been two seasons of high avalanche death rates in Canada's mountains, mainly among riders of high-powered snowmobiles. Self-propelled recreationists aren't immune, either: in 2003 seven members of a party of 14 youths on a school ski outing were killed in an avalanche in Rogers Pass, an incident that caused Parks Canada to introduce new standards of custodial care for leading youth groups in the national parks in winter. But according to a 2010 report by David Ebner in *The Globe and Mail*, citing data from the Canadian Avalanche Centre, snowmobile deaths surpassed backcountry skiing deaths as a result of avalanches in the winter of 2007/08 and have continued rising since.

RECREATIONAL AVALANCHE COURSE

Apart from its obvious safety value, an avalanche course is an interesting and satisfying experience that will increase your appreciation of the winter outdoors. Most recreational avalanche courses are offered in December and January, at the start of the winter recreational season; and they fill up fast, so book early. It might make a timely Christmas present for the backcountry skier, snowshoer, snowboarder or snowmobiler in your life.

EQUIPMENT

If you are travelling in potential avalanche terrain, every member of your party should carry a snow shovel (which can double for campsite or snow shelter construction), a collapsible probe and an avalanche transceiver with good (not rechargeable) batteries. Some of the latest avalanche transceivers (sometimes known as avalanche beacons) have multiple antennas and sophisticated computing capabilities that can simultaneously locate several buried victims.

Your transceiver, probe and shovel will do you no good if you are the only one who has them and if it is you who is buried, so every member of your party should be similarly equipped. At least one person, and preferably several or all members of your party, should have at least some recreational avalanche safety training. Take time before the trip to practise a transceiver search if any of the participants have not done so for a while. One of my acquaintances, while heading up a local mountaineering club, encouraged members to attend a transceiver search practice session at the start of each season, emphasizing that his personal policy was that he would not ski with anyone who had not taken the time to practise. Good advice indeed, since it does not matter how proficient you are if you are the one who is buried – your survival depends on the equipment, skill and practice of your companions.

Different models of avalanche transceiver have different battery life, and battery life on TRANSMIT equals available search time. Battery life may also be much reduced in cold temperatures, either in snow burial or when exposed to the elements in search mode, as a first responder discovered in an avalanche accident on the Burnie Glacier near Smithers in early 2011. So, find out what battery life you can expect from your avalanche transceiver, change your batteries often and **never use rechargeables** in this safety-critical equipment. You can always reuse batteries that still have 70 per cent life left in something less critical such as a headlamp or camera.

Make sure your equipment meets current standards and upgrade it as necessary. In May 2011 the Alpine Club of Canada announced a new avalanche transceiver policy whereby participants in all of the club's mountaineering, skiing and ice climbing trips, camps and courses in avalanche terrain are required to use a modern, digital, multi-antenna transceiver as recommended by the Canadian Avalanche Centre. Analog and single-antenna transceivers are no longer acceptable to the club. Members were also advised to note the manufacturer's recommendations for the expected useful service life of avalanche transceivers and were encouraged to upgrade to digital, three-antenna models. The bulletin reminded members that the "usefulness of any transceiver depends on the familiarity of the user with the transceiver" and that "regular practice throughout the season is strongly recommended."

At the start of the trip, check to make sure each person's transceiver is on transmit. This is easily done by having each member of the party walk past one person, usually the trip leader, whose transceiver is switched to receive, and then switching the last device to transmit after this check has been done.

Immediately after an avalanche has occurred, survivors who will be conducting the search for buried companions should switch their transceivers from TRANSMIT to RECEIVE so that they can conduct the beacon search and/or not confuse the search with their beacon's signal if they are on probe, shovel or other duty.

AVALANCHE FORECASTS AND REPORTS

Before the trip, check the avalanche danger level in your area on the Canadian Avalanche Centre (CAC) website, avalanche.ca, as well as recent and forecast weather

This size 4 avalanche triggered by a cornice collapse killed a dog and almost took the lives of two backcountry skiers.[18]

and route information. Develop trip goals and a trip plan. The CAC website lists five colour-coded avalanche danger ratings (low, moderate, considerable, high and extreme) along with avalanche probabilities, triggers and recommended actions to take while in the backcountry. Most people heed the "high" and "extreme" ratings and stay out of avalanche terrain while they are in effect. Consequently, and although experience and good judgment are important in avalanche terrain at all times, it is often during the period when the "considerable" category is in effect that these skills become most essential, because that's when most people are out in the backcountry.

In March 2010 the federal government announced a new avalanche warning system. Developed by Parks Canada, it has communication and forecasting components and targets three levels of awareness: little, basic and advanced knowledge. It uses essentially the same five-level system as before, but with a new forecasting system that helps amateurs avoid having to second-guess what the professionals are saying. It will be part of a North America-wide standard and will be compatible with the European system, using similar numbers, symbols and colour-coding. It provides information on avalanche sizes, likelihood of avalanches occurring and recommended actions if they do. It also helps forecasters explain the risks more clearly. The CAC website also has a tool that lets you compare the avalanche danger rating with the avalanche terrain rating ("simple," "challenging" or "complex," with examples for popular areas) to get an idea of the frequency and likelihood of accidents occurring.

IN THE FIELD

En route, use the skills you have acquired on an avalanche course and take the time to assess the likely stability of the snowpack. If in doubt, turn back or find a safer route. If it is absolutely necessary to cross a risky slope, expose only one member of your party at a time, loosen the straps of your pack so that you can quickly shed it if you are caught in an avalanche, and ensure you are wearing your mitts and toque in case you are buried. Learn about snow packs, effects of slopes, wind loading and wind slab, soft slab, terrain traps, snow metamorphism (how snow crystals and the snowpack change over time), cornice danger, wet snow slides in the spring, route finding, digging snow pits and how to conduct an avalanche search and rescue if necessary. A Jasper National Park alpine safety specialist once proposed a series of questions to help simplify the often difficult transfer of knowledge from classroom theory to the practicalities of the field: Are you in avalanche terrain or threatened by avalanche terrain? Is the snowpack stable? If it goes, how much will go and where will it go? And can you live with the consequences?[19]

What route-finding considerations might there be in this beautiful north-facing bowl?

AVALANCHE SEARCH AND RESCUE

This is one area of outdoor safety where minutes count and self-help is absolutely essential. Unless a buried victim is fortunate to be caught in an air pocket and hasn't succumbed to hypothermia or the trauma of being twisted around and thrown into a tree or a rock, the chances of a live recovery diminish rapidly within the first 15 to 30 minutes, due to suffocation. When you practise finding an avalanche transceiver that has been buried (transmitting) in the snow, aim to locate it and dig it out in five minutes. By the time a professional rescue team can be alerted and transported to the scene, it will almost certainly only be to conduct a body recovery and accident investigation. If you have to conduct a search and rescue following an avalanche, be alert to the possibility of a second avalanche coming down, perhaps from a side slope or gully that has been weakened by the first release. This is especially important to those who are searching the debris field of the first avalanche, because their transceivers will be switched to RECEIVE instead of TRANSMIT. Some newer-model transceivers will automatically switch back to TRANSMIT after a period of time in case a searcher is later buried by another avalanche. Expose only as many people as you have to, and post at least one member of your party as an avalanche guard or safety person to watch the other searchers and warn them of further instability from above. The safety person can

Controlled release of a cornice with explosives triggers a large avalanche during an avalanche course in BC's northern Rockies.

check everyone at the search site to make sure their transceivers are on RECEIVE, and may also assess the skills of new arrivals. As a searcher, be ready to switch your transceiver back to TRANSMIT if another avalanche is released toward you.

REALITY CHECK: In extreme conditions it may be necessary for the authorities to first stabilize a slope with explosives before allowing searchers onto an avalanche scene. This was the case at Raven Lake, east of Prince George, in 1995 after two young people died.

WHAT IF YOU ARE LOST?

Finding yourself lost or off-route in the outdoors can invoke feelings of fear, no matter how experienced you are. The questions therefore become: What should you do to control the inevitable fear? How do you stop it from escalating into panic (which can be deadly)? And how do you work toward solving the problem?

First, stop and assess the situation and get a firm grip on any surging sensation of panic. If you are in immediate danger – for example, if you have stumbled into very steep terrain while descending a mountain off your original route or you find yourself struggling in a swamp – first try to get out of harm's way, perhaps by backtracking upslope to more secure ground.

Second, assess whether you can safely retrace your steps to a familiar location. Do you remember the route? Can you backtrack with confidence using your map, compass, GPS or other means such as following the sign that you left in vegetation or snow as you were coming in? Did you take strategic GPS waypoints and/or compass bearings on your way in that you can now use? Can you navigate safely by another route using your map, compass and GPS? For example, on most of the highway-accessed trails on the south side of the Rocky Mountain Trench in north central British Columbia, bushwhacking in a northerly direction by compass will cause you to hit the highway, albeit after a few kilometres of rough travel. Keep in mind that severe bushwhacking at perhaps one kilometre an hour can seem never-ending (even frightening), requiring good self-control, patience and careful attention to direction of travel and injury avoidance. Furthermore, being with someone who is significantly slower than you are can cause added stress on the party, as you are forced to hold back. If you are alone and you panic or injure yourself amid nearly impenetrable vegetation, gullies, hidden holes, rock bands, swamps, creeks or fallen trees, it will be much harder if not impossible for a later search party to find you, especially if you are substantially off route. Assuming you are not alone, other members of your party should be able to continue on and raise the alarm. Incidentally, this is another benefit of having a GPS in order to provide rescuers with the pinpoint the location of an injured person.

Third, can you see where you are going in mist and/or thick bush? If not, proceed with extreme caution to avoid terrain traps such as crevices, potholes and sudden drop-offs such as are found in the popular north shore mountains near Vancouver. If you decide to travel or even just move around to try and spot

It's easy to get disoriented and separated from a group in the mountain mist.

something familiar-looking, you should flag, GPS and/or mark your route in some way so that you can return to your present position and avoid compounding your situation. Ask yourself: Is there sufficient daylight to get out today? Do you have the strength to continue? What is the weather like? How bad are the biting insects? Are you alone or with others? Do you have the means to call for help? Did you leave an itinerary and have you stuck reasonably close to it? If the answer to the last question is yes, and if you are in doubt about finding your way out, you are probably better off staying put and not risking compounding a later search. Remember that a reasonable amount of self-reliance in the backcountry is important and help should not be expected or summoned frivolously if you do have the means to help yourself. Things may look different in the morning and you may be able to find your way out or follow some other course of action.

Fourth, assess your clothing, equipment, food and water, and your group dynamics if you are not alone. If you decide to stay put, look for a sheltered spot nearby, preferably close to water – see chapter 25 on emergency shelters, p. 178. Prepare yourself mentally and physically to spend one or two nights out. Construct a basic shelter; collect firewood and build a fire if it is feasible and safe to do so, and especially if you need to dry out; reassess the situation in the morning; ready any signalling devices; and keep busy while also conserving your energy.

Last, remember the Stop, Think, Observe and Plan slogan sometimes used in the military and other outdoor training programs.

Reflect on your own experiences. If you have spent any amount of time in the outdoors, you are likely to have had some. How did you feel? What did you do? What would you do differently? How can you learn from your past experiences?

WHAT IF SOMEBODY ELSE IS LOST?

You are the leader of a group and someone has gone missing. Perhaps they fell behind or hurried ahead to try and catch a faster-moving subgroup or they took a toilet break in the bushes without telling anyone. Or perhaps you are travelling with just one other person and have become separated – it is easy to do.

REALITY CHECK: Coming down a well-defined mountain trail late in the day, I found myself ahead of my wife. I stepped a few metres off the trail to wait, in a nice patch of sunlit moss with a view down into a wild-looking gully. Unbeknownst to me, Judy was closer behind me than I thought and she went sailing past a couple of minutes later without either of us seeing the other. The upshot was that after waiting for ten minutes and getting concerned, I hiked most of the way back up the mountain looking for her, while she, having reached the parking lot, backtracked looking for me. Neither of us could imagine what could have happened to the other and we were both within minutes of flagging down a vehicle on the highway and raising what would have been an embarrassing false alarm.

Something like this, embarrassing on a day hike, could be quite serious in a multi-day backcountry trek. It is important to have clear understandings within a group about staying together; letting someone know if you have to stop; staying put if you get separated; and having some clearly defined meeting or camping places in case, despite your best efforts, you do get separated. Obviously it helps in this situation if everyone has their own map and compass and knows how to use them. Carrying a compass in the outdoors and seeking opportunities to practise with it along the way adds to the enjoyment and skill-building aspect of a backcountry trip. Making copies of relevant parts of maps available to all members of a group (with your intended route marked) is an excellent practice on a multi-day trip. If you don't have your own copy of the route map, ask to see the leader's copy often so that you remain familiar with the map and where you are.

However, let us suppose that despite all your preparations and best efforts, somebody has gone missing from your party. What should you do? (Consider pausing here to answer the question from your own experience before reading on.)

First, assess the situation. What was the last-seen point? What are the skills and experience of the missing person? What preplans were made or instructions given for this eventuality? What are the group's size, experience, equipment and strengths? What skills are available in the group; for example, someone may have first aid training while another has search and rescue experience. How can you deploy your resources to locate the missing person, while at the same time protecting the scene (preserving any sign or scent that may be important in the event of a later formal search) and without compounding the problem by sending people off in all directions and potentially losing other members of the party. One obvious first step is to backtrack to the last-seen point, periodically shouting or blowing a whistle, making sure you allow silence in between noise-making in order to hear a possible response. If necessary, consider sending the less experienced members of the group back, making sure that somebody among them knows the way and is competent to lead. You could give instructions to them to notify the police if they haven't heard from you by a prearranged time, perhaps later that evening. Start documenting – names, locations, events, actions taken, times. Then, with your selected search team, make a rapid search of the area around the last-seen point,

The group should discuss contingency plans at the start of an off-trail bushwhacking trip in the event somebody gets separated, as later happened on this trip.

taking care to look for any human sign in the vegetation, soil, snow. After assessing the situation, decide how long to wait before escalating it into an official search. As a rule of thumb, don't wait too long after you have exhausted the obvious options, and almost certainly do not wait past nightfall. Then, send or go for outside help. You may wish to have a small group camp overnight near the last-seen point (especially if the missing person is a child), making periodic loud noises. If safe to do so, maintain a good-sized fire while you wait for search and rescue people to arrive on the scene.

INDUSTRIAL-ROAD SAFETY

Much of Canada's backcountry is accessible only by unpaved industrial roads used for logging, mining, oil and gas exploration and extraction. Safety on these roads is a huge issue, both for industrial users who may be working long hours and who are under financial pressure to get as many trips in as they can, and for recreational drivers who may be unfamiliar with the rules of the industrial road and who may lack two-way radios on the relevant frequencies.

HAZARDS

Some of the hazards faced are narrow roads; loose gravel surfaces that can catch a wheel and take you off the road; obscuring dust raised by other traffic; potholes, washboard and other poor road conditions resulting from heavy industrial use and/or sporadic maintenance; winter ice or blowing snow; soft surfaces during spring break up; narrow, one-lane bridges; steep hills; tight corners; wildlife on the road; and other drivers not following the rules of the road. Those rules include staying on the right side of the road; slowing down for oncoming traffic and when passing parked vehicles or road maintenance vehicles; driving according to the speed limit and the prevailing conditions; using pullouts when necessary to avoid loaded traffic; calling out kilometre markers on the radio; and using headlights at all times. With long work days and the pressure to get the job done, complacency and the "it won't happen to me" attitude discussed earlier can be serious issues and these basic rules are sometimes forgotten. As well, there may be a temptation to use the ability to communicate location and direction via radio as a substitute for driving according to the conditions of the road in sight, or even, in worst-case scenarios, to gain an edge on oncoming traffic instead of working cooperatively to avoid problems.

Perhaps the main hazard is meeting oncoming industrial traffic, especially those with long loads that sometimes require the full width of the road in order to negotiate corners. For these reasons, most industrial haul roads, and certainly those in my home province of British Columbia, require the use of two-way radios during hauling periods, with a protocol for calling out your type of vehicle, your status as loaded or empty and your location every two kilometres or so. The roads are generally marked with kilometre signs, and radio calls should state which kilometre marker you are passing and your direction of travel. For example, "up" means you are heading in, with kilometre numbers increasing; "down" means you are heading back out to the highway, with kilometre numbers decreasing.

These roads are also usually far from any services, so you must be self-sufficient for fuel and basic repairs or for removing deadfall from little-used back roads after a windstorm. Beware of roads that have been deactivated (typically by digging drainage ditches across the road and/or removing culverts and bridges), trenched with shallow water bars, washouts, and winter roads that are unsuitable or outright impossible for summer driving because they have no firm base.

REALITY CHECK: In British Columbia, after an extensive period of public consultation, the Ministry of Forests, Lands and Natural Resource Operations (the ministry's name as of August 2011 – it has changed several times in recent years, as the government has repeatedly restructured its resource ministries; the name may be different again when you read this) is introducing revised radio procedures for BC's extensive network of forest service roads. (The government is also considering a new Resource Roads Act in the next year or two that may have further implications.) Standardized radio calling procedures were introduced in May 2010, with standardized channels and signs beginning to be introduced in May 2011. Remember, though, making other drivers aware of your position and direction of travel by radio is no substitute for driving according to road conditions and visibility. To quote the ministry's website: "Drive Defensively – Expect the Unexpected."

REALITY CHECK: A forestry worker was driving his pickup truck back to town on an industrial road in BC's interior. He was using the radio to call out kilometre markers, as was the driver of a larger truck approaching from the opposite direction. They were aware of each other's approximate positions as they sped toward a one-lane bridge, each of them thinking they would clear the bridge before the other. They met at the bridge, with catastrophic results. The point of the radio protocol is cooperation for maximum safety, not competition to get there first.

WHAT SHOULD YOU DO?

- Keep to the speed limit. Stay within your and your passengers' comfort zone for the conditions, especially on loose gravel or winter snow and ice.
- Keep well to the right, especially on curves; pull over to allow loaded trucks or faster traffic such as empty logging trucks to pass.
- Do not stop or park on an active haul road except at a pullout or other place where there is good visibility and it is safe for others to pass.
- Only pass another vehicle going the same way when signalled that it is safe to do so.
- Be alert for poor road conditions, including loose gravel, potholes, washboard, water bars and road deactivations. Be especially alert when approaching bridges and negotiating corners, especially at night and/or in stormy conditions.
- Carry flares or other hazard warnings in case of breakdown.

The occupants of this SUV were lucky that one of them was able to get out and flag down the author's vehicle on a remote stretch of highway in northern BC after the driver fell asleep at the wheel. Every year, someone goes missing after their vehicle leaves the road and the wreck is not visible from the road. There have been some phenomenal survival stories of people trapped for days without water or food. As with a backcountry trip, leave a good itinerary when driving off-highway or in sparsely populated areas.

Would you have spotted these exit tracks if you weren't looking for them, or bothered to check them out if you were?

- On ice, slick roads or loose gravel, avoid using your brakes too much; slow down at crests of hills, use low gear on steep downhill stretches, pump your brakes if necessary and steer into skids.
- If you are a passenger, it is unreasonable for you to have to sit white-knuckled, stressed or scared as your driver matches his or her skills with an unpaved and/ or icy road. This is something I have been on the receiving end of too often and that I have heard about from others too many times. Don't be reluctant to voice your feelings and demand that your driver slow down. Regardless of whether the driver feels his or her skills are up to the challenge, as a passenger you have a right not to be put to undue stress or risk. It is not worth spending the rest of your life as a paraplegic (or worse) for the sake of your driver's ego, some hard feelings or saving 15 or 30 minutes on the road, because those are the stark trade-offs.
- Check into local regulations for use of radios and radio frequencies on active haul roads. If you have no radio and you feel you must still travel, one option is to make an arrangement to follow a radio-equipped vehicle, although it won't be much fun (or particularly healthy for your vehicle) if you are enveloped in a dust plume for long periods.

DOWNED AIRCRAFT

THE CHALLENGE OF SPOTTING A CRASH SITE

If you have not been involved in an air search, as either an airborne spotter or a subject on the ground, it may be hard to understand how difficult it is to spot a person or even a downed plane from the air. To appreciate this, it helps to understand the human side of an air search. First, it is intrinsically hard to spot a small, stationary target on the ground from a fast-moving aircraft, and a crash site can easily blend into snow, rocks, vegetation and trees. Search aircraft usually have at least two spotters on board in addition to the pilot, with one spotter on either side of the plane. Spotters are trained to follow a scan pattern with their eyes and to look for anything that appears unnatural, such as a linear or angular feature where an aircraft may have crashed through the forest canopy or left a piece of wing or fuselage in sight. Spotters' frame of reference is the ground, which makes them more prone to motion sickness than the pilot, and after half an hour of concentrated scanning, it is easy to miss something. For these reasons, military search and rescue aircraft usually have at least two teams of spotters on board, who trade places frequently; and even these experienced people can occasionally become nauseous in bumpy, low-level, circuitous flying. Civilian light aircraft, by comparison, sometimes make up the majority of search aircraft, and with fewer opportunities to trade places, spotters may be looking for two or three hours without a break. In this situation, it is easy to miss something at a critical moment. So, if you are a subject of an air search, you must do everything possible to make yourself and the crash site highly visible from the air.

REALITY CHECK: Soon after joining the Prince George Search & Rescue Group and taking a basic spotter course, I flew on an armed forces Buffalo aircraft looking for a downed plane in the Rocky Mountains northeast of this north central BC city. It was not until the third day of the search that the bad weather that had contributed to the accident finally lifted in the prime search area and we were able to look there. Right away, the crew of our sister Buffalo spotted the crash site on the side of the Ice Mountain glacier, north of Herrick Creek. We immediately diverted from the Walker Creek area we had been searching and flew over the crash site just 15 minutes later. This was mainly to provide practice for our crew and spotters. To my rookie eyes, all I could see at first was a discoloration on the ice – it was not something I would have recognized as a crash site if it had not been pointed out to me.

HELP YOURSELF AND THE SEARCHERS

If you are using a small aircraft, perhaps to access a favourite place in the backcountry or for business travel to a job site, there are some things you can do to make your experience safer.

- Dress for the season and for the countryside you will be flying over. Even if you are just commuting from one town and office building to another (as I occasionally used to do by helicopter when I worked for a forestry company), you could be forced down in the bush and have to spend a night or two out.
- Don't assume that the pilot will be able to help you after a crash; you may end up in better shape than he or she is. Therefore, ask about the aircraft's survival kit, emergency locator transmitter (ELT) and any other safety procedures before you take off. Learn where any spare ELTs are stowed and how to turn them on manually if they do not activate automatically. Bush pilots should include this information in a preflight briefing, but if they don't, ask. As well, take along a small pack with your own personal survival gear and extra clothing for one or two nights out.
- If, during the flight, you become aware that the pilot is deviating significantly from the flight plan, ask whether he has notified anyone by radio about the change. If your aircraft is forced down, the flight plan will become the basis for the ensuing search, just as with an itinerary for a backcountry trek.
- Ensure that any hazardous substances (yours or other people's) such as bear spray, bear bangers and fuel, are stored outside the passenger cabin, such as in an outboard storage compartment of a helicopter or in the float of a floatplane. Most pilots are sticky about transportation of hazardous goods; but again, if the pilot doesn't insist on safe stowage, you should.
- If you are forced down and have survived the crash, your best chance is almost always to stay at the crash site, especially if your ELT is functioning as designed. Although there have been exceptions, the odds of finding a downed aircraft are much better than locating a person on foot. If after many days you become convinced that the search has been called off or that you are very unlikely ever to be spotted, it may become necessary to consider another course of action. Then, timing becomes important as you weigh the possible onset or end of winter, snowfall, food supply and your energy. The books by Helen Klaben and Nando Parrado listed in Appendix A, at p. 254 and p. 256 respectively, recount two examples

211

where moving from the crash site did save lives. However, those were extreme cases. It is almost always better to remain at the crash site, which, it should be noted, the individuals in those two stories did for many weeks before attempting to walk out.

- If you are flying in a seaplane or floatplane, ask about exiting the aircraft if it capsizes and sinks. Many people have died in floatplanes in Canada in otherwise survivable crashes when the aircraft they were riding in flipped and sank on landing and they couldn't get out. As a result, there have been recommendations for improved safety doors on floatplanes. Transport Canada, in its passenger guide to seaplanes, suggests asking the pilot if you can practise opening the exits prior to engine start-up. The guide has tips on underwater egress, noting that in water accidents floatplanes often end up inverted. These tips include not inflating your personal flotation device (required on seaplanes according to Transport Canada's website, though this is unclear in some news reports of floatplane accidents) until you are clear of the aircraft; releasing your seatbelt only when ready to move in order to lessen unintended effects of your natural buoyancy; noting the location of the nearest exits in relation to your right or left knee as an aid to orientation when you are possibly upside down (take note of this when you

Be prepared when flying in the backcountry, especially in winter.

board the aircraft); and moving toward the exit hand over hand, keeping at least one hand on some part of the aircraft at all times. Transport Canada publishes several aircraft passenger safety bulletins.[20]

REALITY CHECK: Since the first edition of this book, there have been several more floatplane accidents in Canada where passengers may have survived the initial impact of a crash on water but drowned when they could not get out of the aircraft. It is a double tragedy to survive the trauma of a crash and then die trapped, and it is time Canada mandated floatplane door design and crew training to improve chances of underwater egress. Some floatplane companies, responding to the publicity of these events, have taken the initiative to retrofit their aircraft and/or provide their pilots with specialized training in underwater escape.

When dropped off in the field by a helicopter or floatplane, it's good practice to leave a survival kit at the landing site in the event that weather or equipment failure prevents a pickup later in the day.

PREPARING FOR AN EXTENDED OUTDOOR TRIP

GENERAL PLANNING AND EQUIPMENT

Planning for a major backcountry trek typically starts months in advance. This begins in one of two ways: select a destination and then choose a well-matched group for the undertaking; or pick a well-matched group and then mutually agree on an area of interest. Either way, the emphasis should be on the compatibility of the participants relative to the goals. Each person's fitness, experience and interest should be appropriate for the objective, and they should be able to get along with each other and be willing to put group interests first. The degree of compatibility required will vary, depending on the undertaking. For a trek that involves travelling and moving camp every day in a remote area, a high level of compatibility is needed. In that situation, the group usually has to stay together, and nobody should have to get too frustrated with a pace that's either too slow or too fast or a travelling day that's too long or too short for their liking. On the other hand, a trip that operates out of a base camp day-to-day will be more forgiving, as there is room for flexibility by breaking up into subgroups of various strengths and interests. For example, some participants might like to get up early and try for a hard objective, while others may prefer a more leisurely start and an easier hike, or simply to take a day off and remain in camp.

The other initial tasks are to shortlist possible destinations and obtain maps; choose an objective; investigate access logistics; and (I recommend this) research the wildlife, vegetation, geology, anthropology and history of the area in order to get the most out of the time spent there. Some backcountry trips can be accessed by vehicle, but those to untrammelled places are more likely to require helicopters, packhorses or fixed-wing aircraft. Depending on the situation (the nearest base and a suitable body of water to land on) a floatplane usually offers a cost-effective way to get to out-of-the-way places in Canada's hinterland. An air charter is best booked a few weeks or months ahead, and most bush-flying outfits I have dealt with accepted a telephone booking followed by payment at time of flight. A good policy is to withhold part of your payment until you have been picked up. A friend once lost some base camp equipment that was too heavy to move very far when the charter company arbitrarily changed the agreed pickup location.

A few weeks before departure, check your equipment. Do you need to replace any major items such as sleeping bag, tent, backpack, boots or stove? It is important to try out any new equipment well before a big trip in order to become familiar with it, to make any necessary adjustments, and especially to break in new footwear if you will be doing a lot of walking. By doing this you will lessen the likelihood of nasty surprises on the trip, and you will be much more likely to have a pleasant experience rather than a miserable one. There are quality outdoor stores in most cities, as well as mail order options; and it pays to buy good-quality gear. Of prime importance is to have a robust, weatherproof tent and warm, dry sleeping bags to give you security at night – don't compromise on this just to save a kilogram or two of pack weight, although there are some quality lightweight options available today. If you've thus got nighttime covered, you can generally put up with whatever the weather throws at you during the daytime.

If you are just starting out and don't have much equipment, and like most people you are on a budget, buy one major item each year and consider starting with shorter (weekend) trips with a local club where you might be able to share or borrow some gear. It doesn't take too many years before you are both mentally and physically ready and well-equipped for a longer trip. The other key trip preparation item is food planning and preparation. I have found that home-dried food is the best way to eat well and pack light. Because the drying process can be lengthy, it's best to get that done a few weeks before you leave. See the next section for more information. Store-bought food should be repackaged to be robust and odourless. Many people use heavy-duty zippered plastic food bags, preferably double-bagged. Get rid of such things as dried-food boxes, but remember to clip any preparation instructions and keep them in the zippered bag with the food.

About a week before departure, assemble all your food and equipment, test stoves, calculate how much fuel you will need, and put fresh batteries in headlamps, GPS devices, radios, phones, cameras and other gadgets. Develop a checklist and refine it from trip to trip with lessons learned, things to take or not to take, types and quantities of food that worked well and those that didn't. For a first-time trip, consult other experienced members of the party (hopefully you aren't all novices) and read a book on the subject – the one you're now reading is a good start. As technology improves and gear becomes lighter, more new gadgets get invented all the time, and if you are not careful your overall carry-weight will be heavier. So be selective, look for items that have essential or multiple uses, and consider opportunities for shared equipment. Everyone should have personal items such as a toothbrush, sleeping bag, bear spray and a compass, but there can be many shared items such as tents, tarp, cooking gear, food, water filter, GPS and satellite phone.

FOOD PLANNING AND PREPARATION FOR THE OUTDOORS

An essential part of a successful wilderness backpacking trip is good, nutritious food that is light to pack and easy to prepare. One can consider fancy recipes (or luxuries such as baking bread in a reflector oven) when weight isn't as much of a problem, such as on a canoe trip, but if you have to carry it on your back, my advice is to keep it simple. Aim for menus that are satisfying and easy to prepare in one pot, in 15 minutes or less, in the rain, by people who are tired and hungry. A key concern in bear country is to take food that is nearly odourless before it is unpackaged and cooked; therefore, good as it is, you might want to leave the salami at home.

BREAKFAST

Breakfast should be high in carbohydrates and have good staying power for the day's activities. Whole oat flakes, multi-grain cereals, granola, dried fruit, and skim milk powder with some water, tea or coffee all work well. Granola mix and water can be used for rainy mornings when you don't feel like cooking.

SNACKS

Trail mix (nuts, dried fruit and candy-coated chocolate that doesn't melt on a hot day) along with some home-dried fruit provide good, fast energy and morale-boosting snacks for mid-morning and mid-afternoon breaks.

LUNCH

On a day trip, lunch can be a fairly weighty affair of sandwiches or bagels and real fruit. On a one- or two-week trek, though, all that would be too much weight to carry. An alternative that has worked well for me is to use crisp-bread style crackers as a base on which to put cream cheese or peanut butter and jam and chase it with home-dried fruit and a handful of trail mix. Unless there are medical reasons to the contrary, avoid low-fat foods, since on a backcountry diet of mostly dried food, you will need all the fat per unit of food weight you can get. Cured meats are delicious in the outdoors, but in recent years I have avoided them because of the preservatives that are used in most commercially cured products, not to mention the risk of the strong odour attracting unwanted dinner guests.

SUPPER

A good way to start supper is a generous helping of soup made from a good-quality package of dried soup mix. It will provide much-needed electrolytes (salt) and liquid and is a good psychological and communal bridge while waiting for dinner to cook. The main course should be filling and is the best opportunity of the day to consume the protein part of your diet. A dish that I have found works well is homemade chili – precooked extra-lean ground beef with onions, red peppers, garlic, spices and tomato sauce, dried for 12 hours in a food dehydrator and packaged in doubled, heavy-duty zippered plastic food bags. It has kept well on the trail for me for at least two weeks, and rehydrating and cooking can take as little as 15 minutes. It can be served with freshly cooked pasta and home-dried rehydrated vegetables.

Dessert can be as easy as a few pieces of a chocolate bar to sweeten the meal. An alternative dessert, and a nice group supplement after a hard day, is to bake a premixed bannock in a small frying pan and top it with jam or freshly picked berries. The frying pan is an extra utensil to carry, but it doesn't add much to the individual if it is considered to be group equipment. It can also double for making pancakes in order to vary your breakfasts.

As well as the meal, it is essential that you consume lots of water and/or other non-caffeinated beverages such as herbal tea throughout the evening in order to rehydrate. The human body does not have a good autonomic thirst response, and you will generally need more fluid than you think you do. A better way to find out if you are getting enough to drink is the mountaineer's trick of monitoring the colour of your urine, which should be reasonably clear. The downside of drinking adequately in the evening is that you will likely have to get up at least once during the night, but this is worthwhile in order to maintain a sense of well-being and fitness in the backcountry. A bonus of your nighttime excursion is that you will experience the raw nighttime landscape around you, lit by local stars and the Milky Way as you rarely see them in the glaring city. If you wear eyeglasses, put them on and allow a few minutes for them to defog before you exit the tent at 2 a.m., so you can fully appreciate the starry spectacle.

Should you cook individually or as a group? What may work best is to break the group into cooking units of two to four people, each with a portable stove. You can always combine the end result into a smorgasbord if you wish. You can take turns preparing breakfasts and dinners for your cooking group and take individual snacks and lunches.

FOOD DEHYDRATING

A dehydrator can be used to dry a wide range of foods. The results are tastier, probably more nutritious and have fewer preservatives than if you bought commercially dried foods. Staples like pasta, rice, lentils, beans and milk powder can be taken just as they come from the store; just repackage them into meal-sized portions according to your needs. As well as the precooked ground-beef chili sauce already mentioned, you can use the dehydrator to home dry a large quantity of fruit, including apples, peeled and sliced a quarter-inch thick, mangos, kiwis, strawberries, bananas and oranges as well as canned goods such as sliced pineapples. Canned baked beans, removed from the can at home and easily dried, rehydrate quickly to supplement any meal. The same applies to most vegetables, either lightly cooked or the frozen variety. These foods can be dried, packaged and stored in the deep-freeze well before the trip. Experiment with different foods and try them at home. For example, I have learned to avoid dehydrating cooked chicken, because it takes a long time to rehydrate and is still tough to eat.

A trip like this, remote and off-trail in the northern Rockies, requires serious planning.

OUTDOOR LEADERSHIP

THE LEADER

This final chapter provides a comprehensive checklist of what might be expected of you as the leader of an outdoor trip and what you might in turn expect as a participant. As a member of an outdoor trip, you cannot blindly assume that the leader is always right; you have to take some responsibility for your own and others' safety and well-being while supporting the leader. Leadership and the group dynamic go together and both are fundamentally important, especially if your outdoor trip becomes a matter of survival for someone.

Informally organized groups of perhaps two to five reasonably matched peers can sometimes operate by consensus decision making, without having a formal leader. Larger groups and/or those with a wider range of skills and experience, or groups engaged in expeditionary types of trips, will generally have a leader whether or not the role and the individual are formally recognized as such within the group. Some clubs use the concept of a trip coordinator in order to lessen their perceived liability, but this does not obviate the need for a leader or diminish the leader's responsibilities and liability, regardless of what you choose to call that individual. In the absence of a designated person in charge, the leader of an outdoor activity can be anyone who, by virtue of their knowledge and experience, either naturally steps into the role or is presumed (later, by a court of law, for example) to be leading the group.

It is equally important to provide opportunities for leadership development, mentoring and review. And leaders must be ready and able to make command decisions in the event of a sudden emergency or disagreement, and at all other times to work cooperatively using good group-management skills.

STANDARDS AND PROCEDURES

Good-quality standards and procedures, along with leadership, good communication and teamwork, are essential ingredients of safety with group activities in the outdoors just as they are with safety-critical systems. The gold standard is found in aviation and aerospace, with their preflight and in-flight checklists and procedures.

REALITY CHECK: An example of a breakdown of procedures, with tragic consequences, occurred in 1970 when Air Canada Flight 621 crashed after an aborted landing. The DC-8-63 was a top-of-the-line aircraft about to touch down at Toronto International Airport on a routine flight from Montreal to Los Angeles, in good weather, on a quiet Sunday morning with 109 people aboard. The plane was commanded and piloted by one of the company's most experienced captains.

The captain and first officer had flown together a number of times, and, like other DC-8 flight crews in the company, they had an ongoing discussion about the safest time at which to arm the aircraft's ground spoilers. The captain distrusted the standard operating procedure for the DC-8-63 to arm them early in the approach, fearing it could lead to premature accidental deployment, whereas the first officer preferred to follow the standard procedure. Ground spoilers are slats on the back of the wings that flip up on landing to kill lift on that part of the wing, thus making sure the aircraft stays down and putting weight on the wheels to ensure effective braking.

The issue with the DC-8-63 was that its ground spoilers had to be armed manually before they could be deployed, whereas with many other aircraft types, wheel spin-up on contact with the ground was required for arming the spoilers. Because of the captain's concerns, he and the first officer on AC621 had devised a compromise whereby each officer had a slightly different procedure depending on who was piloting the aircraft, neither procedure being the company's standard one. An added complication in their arrangement was that arming and deploying the spoilers was done by the co-pilot using the pilot's preferred procedure, which meant that they were both involved in procedures that alternated from one landing to the next depending on who was flying the plane. The first officer, when he had the helm, elected to have the spoilers armed when flaring-out over the runway just before touching down; the captain preferred to have them armed and deployed in a single action immediately after landing. In each instance, it was the other person who had to actually move the lever, which, according to the board of inquiry report,[21] also had a design defect "... in that it was possible, by a single movement of the actuating lever, to cause the ground spoilers of this aircraft to be deployed while it was in flight with its undercarriage down, thereby destroying a major portion of the lift on the wings."

The final ingredient in this recipe for disaster was introduced on the morning of Sunday July 5, 1970, when the captain, who was piloting the aircraft, was later heard on the cockpit voice recorder saying, "All right, give them to me on the flare. I've given up. I'm tired of fighting it." He had suddenly acquiesced to the first officer's way of doing it. However, the first officer, used to both arming *and* deploying the spoilers on the captain's command *after* touchdown, then accidentally armed *and* deployed the spoilers on the flare, 60 feet above the runway, causing the plane to sink rapidly and hit the ground hard enough to lose an engine and rupture a fuel tank, which shortly afterwards ignited. Meanwhile, the captain reacted in a fraction of a second, before the plane hit the ground, to apply full power, thereby deactivating the spoilers and taking the plane up again for a go-around. This "by the book" action prevented a more serious impact but fatally committed the aircraft to going up. Had they been following standard procedures and had they accidentally deployed the spoilers in the air earlier in the approach, there would have been more time for recovery. The plane flew on for 2 minutes and 58 seconds before a series of explosions and the loss of parts of a wing brought it down in a field north of the airport, killing all 100 passengers plus the cabin crew of six and the flight crew of three.

A year after this incident, I was invited onto the flight deck of a DC-8 during a tour of a Toronto hangar, where I was shown one result of the inquiry, a tiny sticker near the ground spoiler lever advising the flight crew not to activate while airborne. I was struck by several things in this scenario: the magnitude of the disaster; the sequence of small events that had led to the loss of a nearly new plane under the command of a top pilot on an idyllic morning with good flying conditions; the lengthy enquiry that ensued; and the symbolism of this tiny sticker. The board of inquiry report revealed many other contributing factors to the crash concerning aircraft design, instruction manuals, pilot training and maintenance of standard operating procedures in the cockpit, but ultimately it came down to a potentially hazardous situation becoming critically dangerous by the introduction of non-standard and varying procedures compounded by a last minute ad hoc change and the design of the actuating lever. The tragic irony of this story is that the captain's concern with a "what if" scenario (usually not a bad thing to do in a survival or safety-critical situation, and validated, in a sense, by what happened) ultimately led to its coming to fruition.

Like the *Reality Check* in the section earlier on checking out and back in (see p. 60), adopting an ad hoc procedure and especially making last-minute changes to it can be fraught with risk. The case of Flight 621 also illustrates how a series of small events can quickly lead to disaster. Relating this to outdoors trips, leaders should stick with sponsoring organizations' standard operating procedures unless there are compelling reasons to deviate from them, and should watch out for small things going wrong that could lead to something big. Keep thinking through "what if" scenarios and alternative responses, without becoming too obsessed by them or ignoring the possible consequences of your own mitigating actions.

LEADING A TRIP

One person can easily keep track of from three to six people, depending on the activity and circumstances. A larger ratio of leaders to group members is advisable when leading children in the outdoors. Beyond this, it may be necessary to count heads from time to time and designate one or more assistants. The leader and his or her assistants should carefully monitor each participant as to their equipment, knowledge, preparedness and progress before and during the journey, and ensure that the experience is enjoyable and interesting for all. The leader must discourage anyone from participating who is unlikely to be able to do so safely; and conversely, having accepted someone, the leader must ensure that the activity is conducted according to the pace and abilities of the weakest and/or least experienced member of the group. Real life will challenge the orderly, textbook approach to outdoor leadership detailed below, as illustrated by the following *Reality Check*. And when things don't go according to script, the leader must respond by following a disciplined approach and doing his or her best to be safe while being both reasonable and flexible in the circumstances.

REALITY CHECK: The official opening of three new mountain trails had been widely publicized, creating uncertainty as to who would show up or what issues would arise to challenge hiking leaders. After the ribbon-cutting, three hikes were offered and I was asked to lead a ridgewalk. This was to be a one-way trip entailing 15 kilometres of distance and an elevation gain of 1,300 metres, including some light bushwhacking and steep sections.

It was a beautiful fall day, which meant the turnout was good. The scene at the trailhead was chaotic, and from a leader's perspective, daunting. There were 70 people milling about, many of whom were unknown to me. I had earlier thought that perhaps 12 or 15 people would participate on the cross-over hike I was to lead, but I had already signed up more than 25 and gone through a pretrip briefing before we had even left town. The first issue of the day had arisen when I reluctantly turned down one person who did not have adequate footwear for the terrain. She was keen to participate, however, and sped back home to pick up her boots after I agreed to wait for her and her friends at the trailhead.

At the trailhead, there was added turmoil as several people switched to other hikes and new people joined ours. I reluctantly turned down a couple with a young child. They too were keen to participate and assured me they had done harder trips as a family, but I was not comfortable as the leader with what they proposed for a group hike of this nature. Saying no to someone is one of the hardest things a trip leader has to do. I also said no to an individual who I knew was an accomplished outdoorsman but who had brought along a large dog. The club, under which auspices I was to lead the trip, had a policy against dogs on group trips.

Then, in the midst of the confusion, I found myself being pressured to get under way so that one of the other groups could also leave without having our two parties commingle on the first, common part of our routes. Resisting this wasn't easy, but I took the time to do a full roll call in order to be sure who we had on the trip and to reconcile some missing waivers.

At last we were ready. It had taken about 20 minutes, which wasn't too bad under the circumstances, and the party of young ladies had caught up with us by then. We now had a total of 26 people and had designated a leader, two assistant leaders and a first aid person. The group proved to be well matched with respect to pace, and because of this the ratio of leaders to participants worked well. However, the day's challenges weren't over yet.

A few minutes down the trail, the man I had previously turned away because of the child caught up with us and asked if he could join our group, saying that

It was important to systematically follow trailhead procedures during the turmoil of this trip.

his partner and child would do one of the easier hikes. That seemed reasonable to me, until a few minutes later he passed me again going the other way, intending (I understood him to say) to return and walk with his family for a while and perhaps catch up with us later. As he sped off, I was not at all happy with the situation. Because of the nature of the trip (one-way, with some bushwhacking) it was important that we stay together as a group. It was also unclear to me, on reflection, whether or not this fellow had even signed a waiver. I radioed my concerns back to the trailhead (an example of the usefulness of the small GMRS and FRS radios) and we resolved that he would remain with his family on their hike and would do the ridgewalk on some later occasion.

An hour later, as we were getting high into subalpine terrain and as I was moving among the group, I noticed that two young people ahead of me were wearing low-cut footwear similar to what I had rejected earlier. If I had realized this back in town, or even at the trailhead with the other trip options available, I would have turned them down also, but because of the confusion and large number of people at the trailhead, and the pressure to get going, I had not been able to do a complete visual check of everyone's footwear. This far into the trip, however, it was too late to do anything about it short of aborting the hike, which would likely have been overkill. So I made a judgment call to continue, cautioning them to be careful on the steep descent late in the day when they would be tiring.

The next surprise came partway across the ridge when I became aware that the man with the large dog was making the trip on his own anyway and was keeping a respectful distance from our group. Hiking club rules notwithstanding, the most hospitable (and safest) thing to do in the circumstances was to invite him to join us when he caught up to us at a snack break.

Before resuming hiking, I used the opportunity to do a head count. This is not as simple a task as it might seem, with 26 (now 27) people continually moving around, some of them behind trees or in the bush. After several false starts, to my consternation I counted 29 people! Having too many people perhaps isn't as bad as having too few (we had a couple of spares, as the joke goes), but it became important to know exactly who we had on the trip, both for head counts along the route and for check-in purposes at the end. Much as I disliked the "back at school" feeling, there was no recourse but to do another full roll call. This caused somebody to volunteer that another couple was hiking with us unofficially, and caused me to reflect on the joys of leadership. While this latest quirk may not seem like a bad thing, the effect of having a false head count could have been serious if we had left one or two other people behind without realizing we were missing somebody.

Doing a head count and then a roll call was not easy with 29 people wandering in and out of the bush!

Despite the trials of a large group in what was essentially an off-trail hike, it was a great day!

That was the last surprise of the day. Nobody suffered sprained ankles on the descent because of inadequate footwear; we didn't meet a bear for the dog to chase; and we did account for 29 satisfied people and one dog at the end of the day. It was a great hike, made easy for the leader by fine weather, a well-matched group, great assistants and with nobody going missing or getting injured. But it did illustrate the challenges that are inevitable with a group of this size and why it is far better to have groups that are, at most, half this number.

Because outdoor leadership is a two-way relationship, this section is relevant whether you are a trip leader or a participant in a trip. In the latter case, the following may help you to understand, support and if necessary query the role of the leader. All of the things I have discussed here about safety for individual outdoor activities are even more important when you are in a leadership role. If you are taking children into the backcountry, for example, make sure you have the necessary skills and knowledge of the area you are going to, and remember that the standard of care expected of you is much higher when dealing with minors than it is for adults. With children, a low ratio of one adult supervisor to every one to four children (depending on circumstances, individuals involved and ages) is desirable. The consent form and/or liability waiver that a minor and/or their parent or guardian has signed may not hold up nearly as well as a liability waiver signed by an adult.

REALITY CHECK: As a general personal rule, when my children were small I did not take them into areas of the backcountry that I had not previously been to myself, so that I always had a pretty good idea of what we were getting into.

LEADERSHIP ATTRIBUTES

If you cultivate the following attributes, you are likely to be more successful as a leader:

- Be willing to assume responsibility for others and ensure that your own outdoor skills, fitness and equipment are relevant to the trip you are leading.
- Be a listener, team builder, consensus builder, and when necessary a decision maker. Communication, good and bad, among the members of a group is often a factor in outdoor incidents, so make every effort to foster and maintain a climate of open communication. That way, if somebody has a concern or is developing a problem, you are more likely to know about it sooner. When you are briefing or addressing the group before and during the trip, make sure your message is understood. Throughout the trip, listen to and observe participants and ensure that your own body language supports rather than belies what you are saying.
- Before the trip, know the area you are going to and its hazards. Know the participants and any medical conditions they may have; ensure they are properly equipped; and brief them before you leave town and again at the trailhead. Try to ensure balance in the group, and emphasize team-building and buddy systems while in the backcountry. Mundane but no less important responsibilities

will include familiarity with forms and procedures such as sign-in sheets and liability waivers; appointing, identifying and briefing assistant(s) and first aid person(s); and coordinating transportation.

- In the field, you must manage pace and rest stops. Well-managed pacing is one of the hardest challenges of outdoor leadership. See the section on pace and rest stops, at p. 237.
- Take opportunities to learn about participants, and look for both informal teaching moments and formal interpretive opportunities. Be sensitive to the likelihood that some participants are more knowledgeable and experienced than you are. Where possible, utilize and leverage that knowledge, especially if a problem develops. Verbalize your decision making during the trip as a way of developing others.
- It is reasonable to "stretch" people a bit, but not (except in cases of emergency or with bad weather, darkness or other potential problems approaching) to "push" them. It may sometimes be a fine line to find this sweet spot, but the ability to do so is one mark of an experienced leader.
- Be prepared for problems such as conflict between participants, injury, medical problem, a missing person and sending a person back. Remember to keep a written log of any problems that arise and actions taken.
- After the trip, you may have a trip report and/or incident report to complete, if only for your own records. You may need to retrieve loaned-out equipment, pass along a leader's kit and group first aid kit to the next trip leader, and de-brief through feedback and/or self-appraisal. Take a moment to ask for feedback from the group before they disperse.

LEADING VOLUNTEER OUTDOOR ACTIVITIES

This section discusses the responsibilities, opportunities and pitfalls involved in leading an outdoor trip of day-long or overnight duration. A longer trip requires additional skills and experience. Although written from my perspective as a hiking trip leader, the list can be adapted to other types of groups and outdoor activities. Again, if you are not a trip leader, the following will illustrate the standard of leadership that you as a participant have a right to expect with respect to outdoor safety, as well as the leader's expectations of you.

PREPARATION
BEFORE THE TRIP

- Do the research about the trip, including transportation and accommodation logistics. Learn about the abilities of prospective participants and consider how the range of abilities suits the particular trip. Plan to take only as many people as you can safely lead. Consider past experiences on this or similar trips, and communicate your expectations to participants. Don't just assume competence for difficult, technical or longer-duration trips; ask for details and if necessary a résumé (common practice for technical or expeditionary types of trips).

- If the trip is in any way technical or other than an easy hike, it is far better to ask prospective participants contact you ahead of time rather than publicly announce a meeting place and time where you will have no control over who shows up.
- Research weather and other conditions (snowfall, river crossings etc.) and monitor conditions as the date approaches.
- Consider the many good online resources now available for maps, including the National Topographic System maps from Natural Resources Canada (a web search on either of these two terms will get you there), provincial maps, commercial map sites, 3D topographical views on Google Earth, and the many trail and club websites. If going off trail, plan how you will navigate using map, compass and GPS and discuss it with the group. Make a few map photocopies and distribute them. If you are a member of a group and you don't have your own map, ask to see the leader's often. If you get separated from the group or you are a survivor after a group mishap, yours and others' safety may depend on your knowing where you are.
- Plan to take some common extra equipment that people will inevitably need, and divide the weight among the group. Such items may include spare mitts, toques, sweaters and AA and AAA batteries for showstopper items such as avalanche beacons.
- Develop and practise good leadership attributes.
- For the most part, these should not be autocratic, although there will be times when decisions must be made on behalf of the group. Depending on the urgency of a situation, take the time to get input from others about group actions and problem solving, and where practical, use consensus decision making. Aim to develop good judgment, listening and problem-solving skills, but be prepared to take charge and make decisions for the group when circumstances demand. Discuss your ongoing decision-making rationale with the group along the way.
- As leader, you should have the outdoor skills and experience appropriate to the particular situation you are leading. Seek opportunities to develop new leaders so that the club or group does not always have to rely on existing ones. It may be appropriate for a less experienced person to lead a group, provided he or she has taken some leadership training and is backed up and mentored by an experienced leader.

- Identify and use the range of skills available within the group. Provide development opportunities for interested but less experienced members, for example, by asking them to act as assistant leaders; and look for learning and growth opportunities for everyone in the group, including you as leader.
- Consider liability.
- Practise due diligence – for example, by holding an annual leadership training and review seminar for members of a club or group that regularly go into the outdoors together. This should include, as a minimum, a review of procedures; a discussion of the upcoming trip schedule and specific issues to watch out for; one or more specific classroom training topics; and a practice field trip to give potential new leaders an opportunity to try out their skills with simulated problems. Ideally these sessions should be open to all interested members of the club as a way of attracting prospective new leaders and developing others' knowledge of what to expect from a leader.
- Take liability waivers seriously. They can work, and we'll talk more about that later.
- Liability could arise in situations where a leader's peers might agree that there was a serious error in judgment or gross negligence: for example, sending somebody back alone after they have decided they do not wish to continue, or leading a group into a hazardous situation such as onto a snowfield or glacier without the knowledge, skills, preparation or resources that are considered best practices for such a circumstance. Crevasse rescue, for example, requires specialized equipment, skills and practice.

ENSURE BASIC OUTDOOR SKILLS, KNOWLEDGE AND FITNESS

- Everybody in the group should have general outdoor skills and fitness adequate to the trip. The group should include adequate leadership and first aid skills, and there should be current knowledge of the area being visited (for example, access roads, trails, creek crossings and hazardous parts of the route), preferably by the leader.
- The leader's fitness must be adequate to the trip. The leader does not have to be the strongest member of the group (although in some instances this may be desirable), but should be at least as fit as the average participant so as to not physically lose touch with the others.
- In a survival situation or the aftermath of an accident, the leader should strive to keep healthy in order to be able to help others under their care. As an example,

this is not likely the best time for a leader to give their rations to a weaker member of the group unless it is a matter of life and death. This is akin to first donning your own oxygen mask on an aircraft before assisting others.

ESSENTIAL EQUIPMENT

- Map, compass and group first aid kit.
- Increasingly, with the availability of new technology, and depending on the nature of the trip, a communications device is becoming more essential. (See chapter 20 on Communications, beginning at p. 125, for options.)
- Adequate clothing, raingear, footwear, food and water carried by all participants, keeping in mind the possibility of an unplanned overnighter.
- Sign-in sheet, logbook and pen to record details of any incidents.
- Any specialized safety equipment such as a helmet and ice axe for borderline mountaineering situations or avalanche gear (transceiver, shovel and collapsible probe) for winter mountain travel. Again, this is an area where standards and expectations are changing. For example, helmets are beginning to be used in backcountry skiing (read your insurance policy carefully).

AT THE MEETING PLACE

Get there early so that you are set up and prepared before others start to arrive. Don't allow yourself to be rushed or flustered by a large crowd; delegate assistance as needed; and take this part of the trip seriously as an essential part of leadership and due diligence. When everyone has signed in, give a pretrip briefing that highlights safety issues and encourages people to speak up if and when they become uncomfortable or have questions about something.

SIGN-IN SHEET

- Be the first to fill out the sign-in list as an example of what is required of others.
- Verify numbers by head count at the meeting place and again at the trailhead. Add people to the sign-in and waiver lists who, by prior arrangement, have joined en route or at the trailhead. Periodically verify numbers and participants during the trip. This is a simple task if there are only a few people, but can be very challenging if there are, say, more than 15 or 20. In the latter case, there may be opportunities to split the group, and in any event you will almost certainly need assistance to keep track of that many people.
- Ensure that everyone has completed the required sign-in sheet fields legibly. Cross check against waivers as necessary according to your own group's procedures.

- Take the sign-in sheet from the clipboard and carry it with you on the trip. If you don't have a separate logbook, use the back of the sign-in sheet to record details of any trip incident. Your insurance company may have their own requirements in this regard. If you split the group, make sure both you and the other leader has a list of people in the splinter group. Assign a two-way radio to each leader if you have them available.

LIABILITY WAIVER

- Ensure that everyone has read, understood and signed a current waiver. A well-written (and well-understood) waiver will inform participants of inherent risks, help demonstrate due diligence by thinking through what might happen, and provide a degree of legal protection to trip leaders, assistants, coordinators, the club and its executive. Waivers should be dated and signed above a clearly printed name, and should be dated and witnessed by the trip leader or other officer of the club, preferably not by a friend or relative of the person signing.
- Depending on your group's particular procedures and the dictates of their insurance policy, you may require that a waiver be signed for every trip or only once per season. Regardless, ensure that each person takes the time to read the waiver carefully before signing. If necessary, ask them to step aside to do this in order to avoid holding up others or subjecting the signer to what may later be interpreted as undue pressure. Benefits of having every participant sign a waiver for every trip ensures that everyone has in fact signed a waiver and not just saying they have. Also, because trips differ, this approach encourages participants to think about the risks they are assuming in the context of the particular trip they are signing up for. Also, if a person has signed several waivers in a season, a later argument that they didn't understand what they were signing will be less credible.
- Waivers should be signed before leaving the in-town meeting place, in order to avoid any implied duress. If waivers are not presented until everyone is gathered at the trailhead, it will be more difficult for someone who is uncomfortable with signing to back out. This could create a problem in the case of someone meeting you at the trailhead, so make sure ahead of time that they understand they will have to sign the waiver there.
- A waiver for a minor must also be signed by a parent or guardian, but be aware of the limitations on a parent or guardian being able to sign away a minor's rights. Depending on the age and experience of a minor, as well other possible circumstances, a court of law might hold that no one can sign away a child's rights. However, the waiver still has value in demonstrating a level of due diligence and understanding of risks. You will need to exercise extra care to keep

track of minors (they could be 18 years old, strong and adventuresome – in other words, hard to keep track of) and make sure their experience is a safe and positive one. It might not be too strong a statement to say that this one trip could help shape a person's entire life at an impressionable age vis-à-vis the activity being undertaken.

- In the case of a minor living away from home (such as a student) whose parent or legal guardian has to co-sign the waiver, or possibly for someone meeting you at the trailhead, post your waiver on your website so that participants can download it ahead of time and if necessary fax a signed copy to you.

ENSURE PARTICIPANTS ARE ADEQUATELY EQUIPPED AND FIT

- General things to look out for at the meeting place are clothing, footwear, backpack, other essential gear for the particular trip and general appearance of fitness and health. Footwear that provides good ankle support is essential if the trip entails steep and rugged mountain terrain. Low-cut walking shoes are just not adequate for this scenario, no matter how confident the individual is that they have strong ankles. Note that not everyone agrees with this philosophy, some holding that it might be better to use light footwear in order to develop strong limbs, but my advice is that while this might be alright for individuals doing their own thing, a group or group leader has the right to set expectations and standards for the well-being of the group as a whole.
- Consider the risk to the individual and ensuing impact to the group if someone is inadequately equipped or not as fit as others. Be reasonable in this assessment, since everyone has to start somewhere, but do consider the possibility that someone may not be able to complete the trip or may seriously impair the pace and objectives of everyone else. Perhaps there will be opportunities to split the group into separate parts with differing objectives, but if there are warning indications, explore this at the meeting place rather than in the field. The group or subgroups must be reasonably balanced for the objectives, and once committed they must be prepared to accept the pace of the slowest.
- If, after your initial inspection, you have any doubts, discuss these with the individual(s) privately and if necessary with the group as a whole in the pretrip briefing before you leave the meeting place.

MEDICAL OR OTHER SPECIAL CIRCUMSTANCES

- During the pretrip briefing (or preferably sooner if you are doing prescreening in the days or weeks before the trip) ask participants to advise the leader of any medical conditions or critical medications. This can be kept confidential from the group at large, but the first aid person and assistant(s) should also be briefed.

- Any emergency medicines are the responsibility of the individual who needs them. That person is also responsible for administering or delegating the administration of such medicine in the event that they need it during the trip. Unless acting under the direction of a physician (there might be one in the group) or the patient, it is beyond the practice scope of a first aid person to prescribe or administer medications. This may become critically important if the person requiring the medication is unable to recognize that they need it or is unable to help him or herself. An example might be a type-1 diabetic requiring urgent treatment for exercise-induced hypoglycemia. A good way to manage for this eventuality is for a susceptible individual to have a knowledgeable companion accompany them on the trip.

APPOINT ASSISTANT(S)

- Appoint at least one assistant leader. Either you or your assistant should be at or near the front of the group. This is usually the leader, since in my view you cannot influence decisions being made en route if you are at the back, although in some circumstances, by mutual consent, it could be the assistant at the front. The other person acts as a sweep at or near the tail end to ensure that nobody gets left behind. You may need more assistant leaders to lead a faster or slower splinter group. A good rule of thumb is to have an assistant if the group has more than six participants. The sweep should be an able and trustworthy individual who doesn't mind being at the end of the line. Consider changing the sweep occasionally so as not to burden one person throughout the trip. For example, the tail end may be the appropriate place for the leader during the final stages of the return trip.
- Even if you, as trip leader, have a current first aid certification, find out if someone else is qualified and willing to assume that role. This spreads the burden of responsibility and helps to develop other people. Ideally, the designated first aid person will agree to carry the group first aid kit. If they don't wish to take on that added weight, the leader will usually end up carrying it. Having delegated the role of first aid attendant, that person is then in charge of any first aid incident that may arise, unless they voluntarily relinquish that responsibility or are deemed to be acting incompetently. If there is more than one person with first aid skills, most attendants will naturally utilize the resources available to them in the patient's best interests. The same principle applies to group leadership if problems arise and there are more experienced people than yourself present. Use your resources well.
- Having selected your assistants, make them known to the group. Use this as a development opportunity for prospective new leaders. In other words, don't always appoint the experienced people – they'll still be there as a resource or as someone to hand over to in the event you find yourself in a tight spot.

ORGANIZE CAR POOLING

- This is a task that can readily be delegated to someone else at the meeting place while you are busy with your other responsibilities. Every seat must be equipped with functioning seatbelts and any other mandatory safety equipment.
- In your pretrip briefing, advise everyone what the cost-sharing expectations are, though you might recommend that the actual transactions take place at the end of the trip in order to avoid the implication of a "fare." I have heard people ask what the "fare" is for a particular trip; this is the wrong way to think of it. Costs should reasonably reflect vehicle wear and tear, not just fuel, especially if you are going off highway and especially if there is an imbalance between those who take vehicles and those who do not. It is reasonable to expect people to take turns bringing their vehicles on group trips so that the burden does not always fall to the same people. Some prefer to drive, however, and will take their vehicles regardless, while others may always show up without a vehicle. Usually it works out.

PETS

Will you allow pets (usually dogs) along on your trip?

The two dogs on this mountain hike in Alberta's Kananaskis Country were leashed most of the time and well controlled.

- Dogs are great to have with you on a hike, and most owners probably would question why they would even have a dog if they couldn't take it with them on walks. That said, dogs can be a nuisance to others in a group, especially if there is more than one pet along. Not everyone likes to have dogs underfoot, walking on ski tracks, begging food during rest breaks, chasing wildlife (which is illegal) and fighting with each other. Dogs can be a disturbance and a hazard to wildlife and can reduce your chances of seeing any. They can also be a danger to you or others if they chase a bear and bring it back to you. For these reasons many outdoor clubs have learned from experience that it is best to restrict pets on club activities, or at least to insist that they be kept leashed at all times.
- On the other hand, allowing adequately controlled dogs to come along can add to the enjoyment of a trip and, if properly handled, even to the safety of it. Allowing dogs may attract participants who would otherwise not feel able to come without their pets. Ultimately it is each club or group's decision whether and how to allow pets. One approach, if there are a sufficient number of people interested, is to designate certain trips as "pet friendly," with guidelines for such matters as on or off leash, wildlife encounters and managing pet excrement on trails and in other environmentally sensitive areas.

AT THE TRAILHEAD

You have arrived at the trailhead, where perhaps you have met additional participants who found it more convenient to meet you there rather than at the original meeting place. It usually takes people about 10 to 15 minutes to get organized at this stage, securing vehicles, putting on boots, sorting out gear, perhaps finding a convenient bush for a preemptive pee. And it is another opportunity for a pretrip briefing.

NEW PARTICIPANTS

- Get any new participants who have joined you at the trailhead signed in and get their waivers signed. If you have agreed to meet someone at the trailhead, you will have advised them ahead of time that they will be required to sign a waiver and what the expectations of the trip are, so that there are no unpleasant surprises awaiting them or implied duress to participate.
- Cover off any essentials with the new arrivals that they missed in the in-town briefing.

BRIEF YOUR ASSISTANTS

- Brief your assistant leaders, sweeps and first aid persons – agree on each person's roles and responsibilities. If you have small two-way FRS or GMRS radios with you (see chapter 20 on Communications, beginning at p. 125), distribute them among your assistants and yourself, making sure all devices are tuned to the same frequency, and get each person to test them. If you are using two-way radios, recognize the line-of-sight limitations of UHF radio waves. Units that have the longest range are likely to give better performance, but terrain, trees and weather will still limit usefulness.

- Ideally, the first aid person will have a current first aid ticket, with a wilderness designation preferred. For commercial undertakings, this may be a requirement of the operating permit and/or insurance, with an 80-hour wilderness first aid course being the standard. Both the first aid person and the trip leader should monitor anyone who appears to be developing problems and keep each other apprised of any concerns.

Then, let your assistants do their assigned jobs.

FINAL BRIEFING OF THE GROUP

- Review the trip objectives and expected timelines and advise what planned rest stops and places for regrouping can be expected. Stress safety and encourage people to speak up if they become uncomfortable about something.
- Check specialized equipment such as avalanche beacons, helmets etc.
- Discuss the need to keep together and the option of splitting into faster and slower groups. Splitting may be feasible where there is a clear destination with a return via the same route on a well-marked trail, provided it can be done safely. If it's an exploratory or bushwhacking trip, however, or you'll be returning by a different route, then the group should stay together. One way to balance a group that has disparate speeds and fitness is to prearrange places for periodic rest stops and regrouping, but although this may be suitable for easier sections of the route, on demanding or hazardous sections each group and splinter group should stay together and be small enough for the leader(s) to manage safely. See following section on pace and rest stops.
- Explain participants' responsibilities to the group to not get separated. If they need to step off the trail or take an unscheduled break for any reason, they should let someone know. Encourage people to use a buddy system. If necessary, you may have to suggest to someone who continually goes off by himself that he is not welcome to join a future trip that you are leading if he persists in that behaviour.
- Pay attention to novices and minors, and ask others in the group to take some time during the day to socialize with newcomers and resist the temptation to form familiar cliques.
- Advise people what they should do if they find themselves lost or separated from

the group. In most circumstances this means staying put for at least 24 hours in order to optimize the search time.

- Review again with the group who your assistants are, and make a final pretrip head count.

ON THE TRAIL
PACE AND REST STOPS

- Encourage a good pace that is also not too demanding for the slower members. It is the slowest member of a group or subgroup who determines the pace. Ensure that whoever is in front keeps a reasonable rein on the faster members of the group in accordance with what has been agreed. Most professional guides set a pace that is slow but steady, allowing participants, whose fitness levels should already have been estimated as being reasonably compatible, to continue all day and achieve the objective. An inexperienced leader may either set too fast a pace at the start or allow someone else to do so. This risks fragmenting the group and wearing slower people out too soon. That can be bad news for a club, causing potential new members to walk away and perhaps complain about their experience to the community at large, and it is definitely bad news for the activity, as people are turned off who might otherwise have become engaged.
- Plan to stop 10 to 15 minutes into the trip (possibly sooner if ascending steep ground) to allow people to do the inevitable relayering. Keep it short, as some may have started light and may get cold standing around. Better, make it clear before starting out what you are going to do so that everyone starts warm.
- Allow sufficient rest stops, but keep them reasonably short so as not to impede the day's main objectives. A longer lunch break can be taken. Rest stops are a good equalizer and provide socializing, team building and interpretive opportunities.
- Match pace to breathing, so that participants can hike all day with short breaks.
- If the pace is being well managed, rest stops should not routinely be required for the purpose of recuperating from exhaustion, a dangerous and injury-prone state that should be avoided.
- Discuss with participants before the trip what the frequency and duration of rest stops will be so that they can plan to utilize them efficiently for such purposes as clothing or gear adjustments, snacks and toilet breaks. Keep ad hoc breaks short to avoid delaying and frustrating other members of the group and to keep energy levels up. One model that seems to work well is to take a five-minute break every half-hour or hour. If you break for too long and too often you lose energy and momentum.
- Recognize that there are situations when a fast pace is important: for example,

to reach an objective the group has deemed desirable; to cross a suspect slope; or to escape from bad weather or approaching darkness.

- If the group is not well matched, you may find yourself in situations where the fastest member is completing their five-minute break just as the slowest person catches up. This can be terribly frustrating for the former and demoralizing for the latter. Ways to avoid this are to start with a balanced group and to have the person near the front help moderate the pace. Stronger members should be encouraged not to go charging off ahead, although this can be hard to manage on an established, familiar trail and many of us been guilty of it at one time or another.

- In situations where balancing the needs of faster and slower members of the group entails splitting the group, ensure that each component has an able subleader.

HYDRATION

Monitor hydration, especially in the winter and/or in drier climates. It's easy to lose a litre of fluid to respiration, perspiration and evaporation before a thirst response kicks in. This isn't just a matter of comfort, since many accidents and fatalities in the backcountry may have dehydration as an underlying cause due to the effect on mental ability. An accident may be attributed to a trip or a fall but could be more deeply rooted in dehydration.

POSITIONING OF THE LEADER AND ASSISTANTS

- Your options are to be at the front, at the back or somewhere in between, depending on circumstances. But regardless of your exact position, you should stay close to the group; there is no excuse for the leader to wander off on his or her own, except perhaps in cases of dire emergency. Yet, bizarrely, I have heard of several such instances in recent years, including one strange case where a trip leader on a multi-day backpacking trip went on ahead of his group and ended up camping by himself a kilometre away from the others.

- As the leader, you may wish to range up and down in order to maintain contact with all segments of the group, but you should be in control of the route at decision points such as trail intersections or divergences, unclear sections or hazardous places, or have delegated that responsibility to a trusted assistant with whom you have already determined decision-making criteria. Personally, I think the leader should be near the front, as I've seen too many occasions where this was not the case and less than ideal things resulted.

REALITY CHECK: On a week-long backpacking trip in a remote, off-trail mountainous area, a group had become spread out on some steep, difficult bushwhacking where the only discernible trails (at times more like tunnels in the thick alpine bush) were those made by grizzly bears. The leader, who had by far the best route-finding experience and intuition in such country, was near the back, checking on the slower members of the party — also essential in the circumstances. Those in front were strong, enthusiastic mountaineers, hard to contain and not as experienced at this kind of bushwhacking, and several times they struck out to take us unnecessarily through some of the worst tangle imaginable where forward progress with heavy packs almost came to a standstill for the weaker members of the party. At other times, parts of the group lost contact as factions tried different routes — potentially dangerous in the circumstances. When the leader resumed his position at the front, progress was much improved and the group stayed together.

It's crucial when bushwhacking that the group stay together and that only one person (leader or designate) do the route finding.

Good group management is essential when snowshoeing in the mountains.

- On a hazardous part of a route, the group or subgroup should be small enough that the leader can stay in touch with every participant. Prior to starting a difficult or hazardous section (for example, a place where someone could dislodge loose rock onto other members of the party) the leader should stop and explain the nature of the hazard about to be encountered, the need to be vigilant and any special procedures to be followed.
- The leader's sweep and any other assistants should know the specific plans.
- If you are bushwhacking or exploring off trail, the designated route finder should be in front and able to focus on the trail without distraction. He or she should not have to worry about or second-guess people who are scouting for better routes, getting ahead or outflanking him. The responsibilities of everyone else in this situation, unless specifically asked to do otherwise, are to stay together and to stay behind the route finder. While someone who is heading off at a tangent in an off-trail situation may think they can safely stay in touch, not hinder the group and possibly find a better way, the reality is that they will pressure the leader to miss cues, not think things through thoroughly, be reluctant to take the time to stop and consult his map, compass or GPS and be pulled in directions he or she might not otherwise have chosen. The leader will not always pick the best route through a particular spot (there are usually several options and it is often easier to see better-looking choices from behind), but the overall route will be better if one experienced individual is given the space to do the route finding.

REALITY CHECK: On several occasions (in both thick forest and in dense mountain mist) I have been a member of a group that has gone badly and unnecessarily astray when two or more people were simultaneously vying to navigate.

CHANGE IN LEADERSHIP

- As in first aid, someone can offer advice or assistance to a leader or even offer to assume the leadership if they feel they are better skilled to deal with a particular problem or situation that has arisen. An example might be where someone has local knowledge and is asked or offers to guide part of the route. Except in cases of gross negligence or incompetence, the leader does not have to waive the leadership role, but he or she should always consider the best interests of the group in deciding whether or not to accept an offer of help.
- If a change in leadership or assistants is agreed, ensure that everyone in the party

is apprised of it so that there is no confusion as to who is leading, and likewise when leadership reverts to the original leader. Otherwise, the original leader retains overall responsibility for the group's well-being.

SPLITTING THE GROUP

- This is often an attractive choice if the group is too large for the situation or for one person to handle, or if there is significant disparity in fitness and/or desire to reach a particular objective. For example, a splinter group may enjoy a slower pace and the opportunity to spend a pleasant hour or two sitting in the sun by an idyllic alpine lake, while others may wish to make a push for the ridge or summit above. Alternatively, it may be necessary to break into smaller groups for safety reasons such as avoiding human-triggered rockfall hazards. Again, having small two-way radios will allow the separate groups to communicate their status, plans and any problems.
- If you do split the group, ensure that someone does not accidentally get caught between two subgroups and separated from both of them. This is easy to do and is a common occurrence on group hikes of more than a dozen people.

REALITY CHECK: On a local mountain trail, a member of the hiking party who was unfamiliar with the route got tired of being in a slower group and tried but failed to catch the faster party. He ended up wandering around lost and alone in a subalpine forest frequented by grizzly bears.

LEARN ABOUT PARTICIPANTS

- Use the opportunity to observe and get to know people, especially prospective or newly joined members of a club, and deal with any special problems, concerns or questions they may have.
- Take advantage of any special knowledge or skills that could be useful or informative for others in the party.

REALITY CHECK: Most leaders, if they are open to it, learn something new on every trip they lead.

USE INFORMAL TEACHING AND INTERPRETIVE OPPORTUNITIES

Some examples might be:

- Clothing, equipment, pace, breath control, minimizing energy output.

- Natural and cultural history along the way.
- Ethics concerning such things as trail etiquette, garbage, fires, human waste, cutting firewood.

PROBLEM SITUATIONS

- The leader must be prepared to take charge and act quickly in an emergency. If there is time, seek input from the group; but if consensus is not obvious or time does not permit, the leader may have to make a decision for the group.
- If there is an incident, document what has happened, with times, names, descriptions of events and notes of actions taken. Such notes may be valuable later during a search or may possibly be called upon as evidence in a subsequent coroner's inquest or court case. Even if a particular trip is incident-free, such record-keeping may prove useful later. For example, should the same club or organization someday experience, say, a fatality, a coroner may come looking for documentation from previous trips to get an idea of how seriously you and the club have taken your responsibilities.
- Practise similar note-taking diligence in administering first aid.

SENDING A PERSON BACK

- In what circumstances might someone wish or have to go back? Some factors might be pace, fitness, injury, illness or simple disinclination to continue. Are there any alternatives, such as splitting the group or changing the group objectives?
- How many people should you send back with the person who is returning, and do they have knowledge and skills adequate to the situation? Should you abort the entire trip and turn the whole group back? This may be necessary if you have a serious injury, medical problem or other unexpected situation to deal with, such as an obdurate member of the party who will not agree to an essential course of action.
- When should you not allow a person to go back? The main circumstance would be if the group has already passed the point of safe return and it is easier to go on.

REALITY CHECK: Once, as a trip leader, I was faced with a problem posed by the guardian of two children (preteen boys) when the latter declined to continue only a few minutes after the start of a hike. I had prescreened them in town and the boys appeared keen and well-equipped. Based on a recent comparable hike they said they had done, they were up to the demands of the trip. The reality on the trail proved to be quite different, but the real problem, it turned out, was not the children. The guardian was unwilling to abort her trip, insisting that the boys were old enough to return unaccompanied and wait for several hours at the vehicles. An extraordinary circumstance like this is grounds to cancel the entire trip and turn everyone back. Having driven two hours to get to the trailhead, some may choose to go on regardless, but having refused your directions as leader, they would do so on their own and would no longer be part of an organized trip. Fortunately, a situation like this is very rare – but it can happen, so be prepared for it. As the famous mountain guide Conrad Kain once said: "[The guide] should know when and how to show authority and, when the situation demands it, should be able to give a good scolding to whomsoever [sic] deserves it!" (See note about Kain's classic book, in Appendix A at p. 257.)

CONFLICT

Conflict within groups is sometimes unavoidable – it seems to be part of human nature. The question becomes how best to deal with it in the circumstance and whether the situation can be turned into positive energy for the group. Conflict resolution is the subject of entire training courses and there are many techniques that can be tried. Here are a few tips I have found helpful:

- First, identify or clarify the problem and try to get past the emotions.
- Listen respectfully, verify through feedback and then state your own views.
- Find any areas of agreement and identify the areas of disagreement that remain.
- Define the problem in terms of individual and group needs, and brainstorm possible solutions.
- Choose a solution that best meets the needs of all parties to the dispute.
- If a conflict between individuals threatens the safety or unity of the group, the leader must act quickly to stem the disagreement and get the group out of any immediate danger before attempting to resolve the dispute.

REALITY CHECK: Amid a dispute between two members of a hiking party about the safety of a route vis-à-vis the danger of rockfall, another member of the party was narrowly missed by a falling rock. The objective danger was compounded by an open and heated disagreement within the group and by the lack of clear leadership at that stage of the climb.

On this scramble in Alberta, the leader acted quickly to stem a dispute that had broken out early in the trip between two participants.

Conflict can also arise between your group and others you encounter on the trail or in the backcountry, for example, due to conflicting types of activities such as between motorized and non-motorized recreational users. Again, the best approach is to get past the emotions, and if the parties are willing, to use the opportunity to discuss respective interests, values, impacts and sharing. If a satisfactory outcome is not possible in the field, avoid confrontation and consider following up the incident later with relevant parties.

INJURY OR MEDICAL EMERGENCY

The first aid person and the trip leader should:

- Assess the scene, ensure there is no further immediate danger, and if necessary take steps to mitigate such danger. If there are multiple casualties, follow a triage approach in order to determine immediate priorities and efficiently assign resources.
- Follow a priority action approach to ensure that the casualty has a clear airway with no cervical spine problems, is breathing and has good circulation and no major bleeding or other trauma. Apply any immediate responses or treatment that may be required, such as clearing an airway, dealing with major bleeding or immobilizing a person with a suspected spinal injury.

- After the priorities have been taken care of, do a secondary and more detailed examination. Write down a history of what happened, along with a list of signs, symptoms and treatments.
- If necessary, treat the patient for hypothermia or shock; make him or her comfortable and do what is necessary to keep him warm and dry.
- Make the decision to stay put, travel and/or send for help.

LOST PERSON

- Review the chapter dealing with what to do if you have lost somebody, at p. 203.
- Determine the last-seen point and gather all other known information.
- Determine how to utilize your resources without compounding the problem by destroying sign that might later be valuable to trained searchers or to tracking dogs, or risking losing other members of your group. You may wish to send some of the group back with instructions on when and how to raise the alarm, and commit others to an immediate search. If you have lost someone in an avalanche, boating accident or other situation where urgent action is required, your immediate response may offer that person their best or only chance of survival. In this situation the priority should be on self-help within your group.
- Conduct a hasty search and watch carefully for any sign left by the missing person. Allow silence between shouts and whistles in order to hear possible responses.
- Make a missing person report to the police as soon as is reasonable in the circumstances, but probably no later than by the evening in order to allow a proper search operation to be organized for early the next day.
- Document what has happened.

AFTER THE TRIP

- Complete a trip report and file it with the sign-in sheet, waivers and incident log according to your group's or club's procedures. Even where no incident has taken place, these documents should be kept for several years. They can be a useful training and historical resource, and in the event of a future incident they can be very helpful in establishing a due diligence defence. For example, if a person claims in a lawsuit that they didn't understand the waiver they signed, the presentation of evidence showing that they'd signed several such waivers on previous occasions should refute that argument.
- Do a round-robin debriefing to seek feedback from others, and conduct a self-appraisal. What have you learned and how will you do it differently the next time?
- Pass on the leader's kit, if you have one, to the next event coordinator or as required.

EPILOGUE

SCENARIO

As I was working on revisions to this second edition, a student in a technical college class where I was a guest lecturer asked me how I would deal with a scenario involving a team member on a multi-day trip sustaining a severe wound with bleeding and where the only available cell phone was not working due to a low battery or being out of range. There could be any number of survival situations one could envisage, but I thought this one would serve as a nice wrap-up scenario.

Before reading on, consider what you've already learned and what you would do in this situation.

RESPONSE

I will assume that one or more people in the group has taken some level of first aid training before going on the trip, and should therefore be able to stem the major bleeding and stabilize the victim. If they can't stem the bleeding, then this will quickly become an entirely different scenario, possibly involving a more herculean response and a less certain outcome. Severe bleeding suggests that the patient will not be able to be moved very far, except by a trained and equipped rescue team. But it is likely, and perhaps imperative, that the patient can be moved a short distance to a safer and/or more sheltered position after the injured parts have been treated and immobilized to prevent further injury. It is not likely that a small, untrained group will be able to carry the injured person very far unless he or she is partly ambulatory.

In the epic rescue from Fang Cave in November 2009, recounted in the *Reality Check* at p.175, the responders numbered 50 trained search and rescue and cave rescue volunteers, aided by four search and rescue technicians who parachuted to the scene in the middle of the night, and still it took them many hours to move the critically injured patient halfway down the mountain to where he could be picked up by the helicopter. It is a lot harder than most people think to carry a person off a mountain or even out of the bush, although adrenaline can work wonders in the short term.

I wouldn't be too concerned about the smell of blood attracting animals (a concern of the student posing this scenario), especially in the short term and where there are several people in the party. It might conceivably become an issue if the injured person is (left) alone or with only one other person, but it's unlikely to be the main concern in this scenario. It might be possible, if there is water nearby, to clean up some of the blood, taking care not to expose wounds to further infection from untreated water. Building a fire may help if it is feasible and safe to do so, and boiling water on either a stove or a fire might be useful for cleaning wounds.

There are several recommendations arising from this scenario:

- Ensure there is no immediate danger to other members of the party.
- Provide first aid, dealing first with the priority action approach of airway, breathing, circulation, cervical spine and bleeding; then stabilize and make the patient comfortable, warm, dry and reassured.
- Assess the situation, the state of others in the group and the combined resources.
- Get help, which, since the communications device is not working, means that somebody (preferably two if there is at least one person who can stay with the patient) goes for help as soon as it is safe to travel.

Hopefully, the hiking party will include someone who has first aid training and will also have left a good itinerary with a trusted contact who will notify authorities should the party become overdue.

Remember, there are no guarantees – just do your best, stay positive, keep thinking through "what ifs" and alternative actions, and don't give up as long as there is life. Above all, go out and enjoy the outdoors. If you respect the environment as you explore the backcountry, the planet will likely be better off for it, and you will almost certainly live a longer, healthier and more fulfilling life. Why venture into the outdoors? Look no further than these closing images:

Online References: Where I have referred to websites in the text, I have mostly avoided giving actual web addresses, since they are liable to change and are, in any case, easy to search for using relevant keywords.

ACKNOWLEDGEMENTS

I would like to recognize all of the individuals and organizations that I have been associated with in connection with the outdoors over the last 40 years, ever since my first overnight hike in Ontario's Algonquin Provincial Park in May 1970 when I shivered, tentless, in a cheap sleeping bag under a starry and frosty night on the rocky shore of Provoking Lake. They are too many to mention individually by name, but I learned, with them, to enjoy my time in the outdoors as fully and as safely as possible, and I have had many fantastic outdoor adventures and experiences in the process. In 1978 I moved to north central British Columbia, where I began to broaden my outdoor horizons with hiking and ski-touring groups and by joining a volunteer search and rescue group. In the 1990s I branched out from organized group trips and undertook a number of mountain treks in remote parts of British Columbia with just one or two companions. These helped me to expand my horizons and to build my confidence in the outdoors.

I wish to thank those who helped review and suggest changes to the first edition of this book, *Outdoor Safety and Survival in British Columbia's Backcountry*, and to those, especially at Rocky Mountain Books – publisher Don Gorman, editor Joe Wilderson and art director Chyla Cardinal – who helped bring this second edition to a wider readership.

I make no pretense to being an expert in the outdoors; indeed, as the title of my previous book suggests, there may not be such a person. Nor do I claim to be technically proficient in any particular aspect of the outdoors beyond putting one foot in front of the other and trying to be comfortable with my surroundings. I have simply taken the opportunity as a writer to share what I have learned in four decades of outdoor experiences and the consequent safety awareness that I have developed.

— Mike Nash
August 2011

APPENDIX A: LESSONS OF HISTORY, AN ANNOTATED LIST OF CLASSIC READING

I have gained a sense of what the human spirit is capable of from reading some of the greatest adventure and survival stories ever published. An added bonus is that for the most part, they are also wonderful reads. So, here is my recommended reading list, arranged by title rather than by author.

Annapurna, by Maurice Herzog. New York: Dutton, 1952, and later editions. A postwar classic that inspired many subsequent 20th-century mountaineers, Annapurna is the account of the first ascent of an 8,000-metre peak and of a frostbitten descent and later retreat through monsoon floods.

Arabian Sands, by Wilfred Thesiger. New York: Dutton, 1959, and later editions. One man's extraordinary explorations of Saudi Arabia's Empty Quarter during the period 1945 to 1950.

Bartlett: The Great Canadian Explorer, by Harold Horwood; Garden City, NY: Doubleday, 1977. The biography of Newfoundland's Captain Robert Bartlett, considered to be the greatest ice navigator of the 20th century. As well as Bartlett's considerable Arctic achievements on the east coast of North America and his key role in north polar expeditions, the book has an account of the loss of HMCS *Karluk* in the Arctic icepack in 1913–14 and the year-long survival story that ensued. Although Bartlett may have made some errors of judgment during this epic, his achievements were later described by maritime historian Thomas Appleton as "the finest example of leadership in the maritime history of Canada." Other books have been written about the *Karluk*, including one by Bartlett himself and one by a member of his crew, William Laird McKinlay.

The Climb: Tragic Ambitions on Everest, by Anatoli Boukreev and G. Weston DeWalt. New York: St. Martins Press, 1997, and *Into Thin Air*, by Jon Krakauer. New York: Villard, 1997. Two very different accounts and perspectives of the tragic events on Mount Everest in 1996 and of the heroic rescue efforts and survival stories of those involved. I heard both Boukreev and Krakauer speak at the 1997

International Mountain Book Festival in Banff, less than two months before Boukreev, considered by many to be the strongest mountaineer in the world at the time, died in an avalanche on Annapurna on Christmas Day 1997.

Endurance: Shackleton's Incredible Voyage, by Alfred Lansing. New York: McGraw Hill, 1959, and later editions. This story has been retold in many other books and films in recent years and may be the greatest self-help survival story of all time. It is certainly the finest account of exemplary leadership that I have come across. It is set in the Antarctic region from 1914 to 1916.

Escape from Lucania: An Epic Story of Survival, by David Roberts. New York: Simon & Schuster, 2002. The riveting account of Brad Washburn and Bob Bates's 1937 epic first ascents and subsequent survival trek through the mountainous wilds of the Yukon after being abandoned on a glacier without their intended companions or the chance of a pickup.

Fatal Passage: The Untold Story of John Rae, the Arctic Adventurer Who Discovered the Fate of Franklin, by Ken McGoogan. Toronto: HarperCollins Canada, 2001. In this award-winning book, John Rae emerges as one of the most competent all-around outdoorsmen of all time. Of interest, McGoogan later told the counterpoint story in *Lady Franklin's Revenge: A True Story of Ambition, Obsession and the Remaking of Arctic History* (Toronto: HarperCollins Canada, 2005), an account of a remarkable 19th-century woman.

The Forgotten Explorer: Samuel Prescott Fay's 1914 Expedition to the Northern Rockies, by Samuel Prescott Fay, edited by Charles Helm and Mike Murtha. Calgary: Rocky Mountain Books, 2009. During a five-month period in 1914, Samuel Prescott Fay, with outfitter Fred Brewster and three other men, travelled through the largely unexplored territory of the northern Rocky Mountains between Jasper and the Peace River. As far as is known, this was the first party to make a continuous south to north traverse, travelling against the grain of the land on a route so arduous that it has never been duplicated.

Guardians of the Peaks: Mountain Rescue in the Canadian Rockies and Columbia Mountains, by Kathy Calvert and Dale Portman. Calgary: Rocky Mountain Books, 2006. This compelling history of the first 50 years of mountain rescue in Canada provides many gripping stories of courage and improvisation that provide knowledge, inspiration and more than a few warning flags to those who would venture into the mountain backcountry.

Hey, I'm Alive, by Helen Klaben. New York: Scholastic Book Services, 1964. The amazing 49-day survival story of bush pilot Ralph Flores and his passenger, Helen

Klaben, who were stranded with injuries and almost no food after a midwinter plane crash in northwestern British Columbia.

Highest Duty: My Search for What Really Matters, by Captain Chesley "Sully" Sullenberger with Jeffrey Zaslow. New York: HarperCollins, 2009. The inspirational story of one man's life preparing for the successful ditching of US Airways Flight 1549 in the Hudson River in January 2009.

Into the Wild, by Jon Krakauer. New York: Villard, 1996. The gripping account of what went wrong for one individual in 1992; later made into a major motion picture.

Into Thin Air, by Jon Krakauer. See *The Climb*, above.

The Last Blue Mountain: The True and Moving Story of the Ill-starred Expedition against Mount Haramosh, by Ralph Barker with foreword by Sir John Hunt. Garden City, NY: Doubleday, 1959. Another of the great survival stories, this is the account of the 1957 Oxford University expedition to 7,397-metre Mount Haramosh in Kashmir's Karakoram Range. Minutes from retreating safely from their final high point, a triumphant reconnaissance instantly turned into a nightmarish disaster when two members of the final party of four decided to go another 100 feet for a slightly better view and were swept away by an avalanche into a nearly inaccessible snow bowl. Having miraculously survived the 1,000-foot fall but losing some of their gear, a three-day rescue epic began that stretched human will and endurance to the limit and beyond as it ultimately took the lives of one of the fallen and one of the rescuers. In a cruel twist of fate, the two who had originally fallen escaped from the bowl and the two rescuers fell in. Were it not for a single lost crampon partway through the rescue, all would likely have survived. The principle hero of this expedition, Tony Streather, had earlier distinguished himself in the rescue efforts on the ill-fated American K2 attempt in 1953, and had succeeded in reaching the top of Kangchenjunga in 1955. Of related interest with respect to Streather's K2 role is *K2 The Savage Mountain: The Classic True Story of Disaster and Survival on the World's Second-Highest Mountain,* by Charles Houston and Robert Bates. New York: McGraw-Hill Book Company, 1954.

Measure of the Earth: The Enlightenment Expedition That Reshaped Our World, by Larrie D. Ferreiro. New York: Basic Books, 2011. This is the wonderful story of the world's first scientific expedition, the 1735 Geodesic Mission to the Equator. It was as much an epic story of exploration, adventure, mountaineering, survival and endurance as it was of its prime mission to determine the shape of the earth by measuring the distance of one degree of latitude, adjusted for sea level, at the equator.

To accomplish this, expedition members spent ten years accurately surveying by triangulation over 200 miles along the spine of the high Andes, sometimes spending weeks at a time on 4,600-metre and higher peaks waiting for brief survey shots in some of the worst weather to be found anywhere. In order to achieve their goals, they had to overcome many and varied obstacles where human ingenuity and perseverance were essential factors in their eventual success.

Minus 148°: The Winter Ascent of Mt. McKinley, by Art Davidson. New York: Norton, 1969. The account of surviving a week-long storm in an ice cave near the summit of what is now called Mount Denali immediately after the first winter ascent. This was considered by some to be the coldest place on earth because of its combination of high altitude and high latitude.

Miracle in the Andes: 72 Days on the Mountain and My Long Trek Home, by Nando Parrado with Vince Rause. New York: Crown Publishers, 2006. A compelling contemporary account by a survivor of the October 1972 crash of a plane carrying a Uruguayan rugby team in the Andes. The 1973 bestseller *Alive* documented this tragedy and ensuing survival epic in detail, while Nando Parrado's 2006 account allows the reader to nearly live the events through his words, emotions and spirit. Parrado finally decided to write the book with the help of ghostwriter Vince Rause after realizing that his story was everyone's story – one of emotion, despair and overcoming. This is among the most forthright and spiritually rich survival stories I have read and I highly recommend it.

Nanda Devi, by Eric Shipton, with foreword by Hugh Ruttledge. London: Hodder & Stoughton 1936. *The Ascent of Nanda Devi,* by H.W. Tilman, with foreword by T.G. Longstaff. Cambridge University Press, 1937. Shipton and Tillman were two of the leading explorers and climbers in the 1920s and 1930s. Their respective accounts of first penetrating the Nanda Devi Sanctuary and then successfully achieving the summit are classics of human achievement. These two books, along with other material, were combined into a single, great-value paperback publication, *Nanda Devi: Exploration and Ascent.* Seattle: Mountaineers Books, 1999.

The North-West Passage by Land: Being the Narrative of an Expedition from the Atlantic to the Pacific, by Viscount Milton and Walter Butler Cheadle. Toronto: Prospero Books, 2001. First published 1865 by Cassell, Petter & Galpin, London. Full text available by searching book title at archive.org. See especially chapters xiv and xv describing the party's 1863 travails journeying from Tête Jaune Cache south toward Fort Kamloops in British Columbia. This section has wonderful descriptions of the primordial forests they fought their way through in the mountain valleys, some remnants of which still exist in the Rocky Mountain Trench of north central BC today.

Over the Edge: Death in Grand Canyon: Gripping Accounts of All Known Fatal Mishaps in the Most Famous of The World's Seven Natural Wonders, by Michael P. Ghiglieri and Thomas M. Myers. Flagstaff, Ariz.: Puma Press, 2001. Despite its colourful title, this is a detailed, thoughtful and at times entertaining account by a biologist/river guide and a physician of the many things that can and do go wrong in this famous desert canyon.

Shackleton's Forgotten Expedition: The Voyage of the Nimrod, by Beau Riffenburgh. New York: Bloomsbury Publishing, 2004. An account of the British Imperial Antarctic Expedition, otherwise known as the Nimrod Expedition, of 1908 to 1909. Led by Ernest Shackleton, it was the first to find the route onto the Antarctic Plateau via the Beardmore Glacier, to come within 97 nautical miles of the South Pole. Like Shackleton's later Endurance adventure, this is another incredible story of survival of Shackleton's entire crew against enormous odds, highlighted by Shackleton's most courageous decision to turn back when he could certainly have reached the South Pole, but, like Scott later, at the certain cost of the lives of himself and his South Pole party on the return.

Touching the Void, by Joe Simpson. New York: Harper & Row, 1988. The account of one man's incredible will to survive and the mental and physical tortures that he went through as he struggled, alone, to climb out of a deep ice crevasse and dragged himself for days across a glacier and through rock debris. He had fallen into the crevasse with an already badly broken leg after his partner was forced to cut the rope on which he was suspended while descending from the first ascent of 6,400-metre Siula Grande in the Peruvian Andes. In 2003 a documentary-style film of the same title was released, directed by Kevin Macdonald.

Where the Clouds Can Go, by Conrad Kain, with forewords by J. Monroe Thorington, Hans Gmoser and Pat Morrow. New York: The American Alpine Club, 1935. In 2009 a new edition was published by Rocky Mountain Books to mark the 100th anniversary of Kain's arrival in Canada. Conrad Kain, best known for his 1913 first ascent of Mount Robson, was considered by some to be the greatest mountain guide in the world in the early 20th century and perhaps of all time. A poorly educated man from Austria, he was not shy about voicing his self-learned philosophies of life and the mountains, and he was well known for his love of nature and for lingering to enjoy a fine view or a sunset. Despite his stunning record of safe ascents on three continents, he had no time for competitiveness in mountaineering. He articulated his principles of leadership thus: "First [the guide] should never show fear. Second, he should be courteous to all and always give special attention to the weakest member in the party. Third, he should be witty and able to make up a white lie if necessary, on short notice, and tell it in a convincing manner. Fourth, he should know when and how to show authority, and when the situation demands it, should be able to give a good scolding to whomsoever [sic] deserves it!"

Will To Live: Dispatches from the Edge of Survival, by Les Stroud (Survivorman). Toronto: Harper Collins Canada, 2010. A cross-section of compelling real-life survival stories compiled and analyzed by Stroud and ghost writer Michael Vlessides.

A NOTE ON ACCESSIBILITY

Many of these books are early classics that have been reissued by modern-day publishers. Early editions and out of print books can usually be obtained at reasonable prices from online used or out of print booksellers. Lending sources include public libraries and university or college libraries; their interlibrary loan services can obtain almost anything for you, and often you can reserve the book or ebook by simply logging on to your local library's computer from home.

APPENDIX B: COMMONLY USED KNOTS

This is a reference list of common knots, noting where they can be useful. New media is a fun way to learn how to tie knots. Just search online for the knot you are interested in and look for animated graphics or YouTube or other videos on knot tying.

bowline. This is perhaps the most useful knot to know for its simplicity and security. If you only learn one knot, make it this one. It is used to make a secure loop that does not jam and is easy to tie and untie after being under load.

bowline on a bight. This is a variation of a bowline and is used to tie a secure loop into the middle of a rope or line. It has similar advantages to the bowline.

clove hitch. Used for tying something (for example, a boat or a horse) to a post, a tree or to another rope. It is easy to adjust and untie; it jams well; but it is not entirely secure. It is useful as a temporary knot, for example, for tie-downs.

figure eight. This is one of the strongest knots and is commonly used by climbers to tie into a rope. It is easy to inspect and is also used as a safety stopper at the end of a rope. It can be made more secure with an additional backup knot such as a double fisherman's knot.

fisherman's knot. Also known as the half grapevine knot, the fisherman's knot is used to tie the ends of two ropes of equal thickness together, for example, as an alternative to the figure eight for tying into a climbing harness or to make a sling loop. It is not as secure as a double fisherman's knot, but it can be used in conjunction with a backup knot and is itself useful as a backup knot.

fisherman's knot (double). The double fisherman's knot, or grapevine knot, is an excellent knot for securely tying rope ends together, either to join two ropes or to make a sling loop. It is commonly used in climbing and is very secure as long as sufficient rope is left on the loose ends. A triple version of this knot provides even greater security.

grapevine. See **fisherman's knot** and **fisherman's knot (double)**.

half hitch. A single half hitch knot is by itself insecure and is sometimes used as backup knot. A double half hitch is much more secure and is simple to tie.

mooring knot. The mooring hitch is commonly used to tie a boat to a dock. It is secure under tension, but is easily released by pulling on the loose end. This is a temporary knot that you should not leave unattended for very long.

overhand knot. This is the simplest of all knots. By itself it is insecure and is commonly used as a backup or stopper knot on a rope.

prusik. A friction knot that is commonly used in climbing a rope as a sliding, ratcheting knot connecting a sling to the main rope. It can also be used in connection with a pulley to haul an injured climber. There are several variations of the prusik.

reef knot. See **square knot**.

ring bend knot. See **water knot**.

sheetbend. Easy to learn and fast to tie, the sheetbend knot is used to join two ropes or lines of different thickness together and for net-making. It is used for boating, but is not secure enough for climbing use. The double sheetbend is a stronger method of joining ropes of different thicknesses together, but is still not entirely secure.

square knot. Otherwise known as the reef knot, the square knot is the easiest and most commonly used knot for tying two ropes together; but it is not a secure or permanent knot and its use should be limited to non-critical situations. It can both jam and untie with movement.

water knot. Sometimes known as the ring bend knot, the water knot is an overhand knot that is commonly used to tie the ends of flat webbing together to make slings and loops as in climbing. It is strong and simple to tie and is the strongest knot commonly used to tie webbing.

APPENDIX C: SOURCES AND RESOURCES

BOOKS, ARTICLES, WEBSITES

Archer, Laurel. *Northern British Columbia Canoe Trips*. 2 vols. Calgary: Rocky Mountain Books, 2008, 2010.

Association for Mineral Exploration British Columbia Safety Committee. *Safety Guidelines for Mineral Exploration in Western Canada*. 4th ed. Vancouver: AMEBC, 2006. This publication is particularly relevant to the occupational use of the outdoors and is one of the best and most compact safety resources I have come across. It has gone through many revisions over several decades and is packed with sound, down-to-earth information and advice.

Banfield, A.W. Frank, et al. The *Mammals of Canada*. Toronto: University of Toronto Press, 1974.

Barlee, Gwen, and Jim Wilson. "Lyme disease in BC: more needs to be done." *The Vancouver Sun*, April 11, 2011, A11.

Bartlett, Robert Abram, and Ralph Tracy Hale. *The Last Voyage of the Karluk, Flagship of Vilhjalmar Stefansson's Canadian Arctic Expedition of 1913–1916; As Related by Her Master, Robert A. Bartlett, and Here Set Down by R.T. Hale*. Toronto: McClelland, Goodchild & Stewart, 1916. Full text available at archive.org (accessed Oct. 25, 2011).

Boudreau, Jack. *Crazy Man's Creek*. Prince George, BC: Caitlin Press, 1998.

Canadian Avalanche Centre, www.avalanche.ca.

Canadian Red Cross, "Drownings and other water-related injuries in Canada: 10 Years of Research. Module 2," (April 2006).

Daffern, Tony. *Backcountry Avalanche Safety: Skiers, Climbers, Boarders and Snowshoers*. Calgary: Rocky Mountain Books, 2009.

Deutsch, David. *The Beginning of Infinity: Explanations that Transform the World*. New York: Viking, 2011.

Ebner, David. "Avalanche safety targets snowmobilers." *The Globe and Mail*, Dec. 6, 2010, A5.

"Fang Cave Rescue, The." Regional and Provincial Cave Rescue Coordinators' Reports. *BC Caver* 23, no. 3 (Fall 2009): 18–25.

Gibson, Hugh F., Commissioner. "Report of Board of Inquiry into Accident at Toronto International Airport, Malton, Ontario, to Air Canada DC8 CF-TIW Aircraft on July 5, 1970." Ottawa: Information Canada, 1971. See also Wikipedia, "Air Canada Flight 621," http://is.gd/MJeija (accessed Oct. 25, 2011).

Giesbrecht, Gordon, and James Wilkerson. *Hypothermia, Frostbite and other Cold Injuries: Prevention, Survival, Rescue and Treatment*. 2nd ed. Seattle: Mountaineers Books, 2006.

Giles, Wayne, and Barbara Robertson, eds. *Canoeing and Kayaking BC's Central Interior: A Guidebook*. Prince George: BC: Northwest Brigade Paddling Club, 2002.

Gonzales, Laurence. *Deep Survival: Who Lives, Who Dies, and Why: True Stories of Miraculous Endurance and Sudden Death*. New York: W.W. Norton & Co., 2003.

Grubbs, Bruce. *Desert Sense: Camping, Hiking & Biking in Hot, Dry Climates*. Seattle: Mountaineers Books, 2004.

Hamilton, Gordon. "Death rate drops as BC loggers embrace safe practices on the job." *Vancouver Sun*, April 23, 2011, D3.

Herrero, Stephen. *Bear Attacks: Their Causes and Avoidance.* Toronto: McClelland & Stewart, 2003.

———. "Fatal attacks by American black bear on people 1900–2009." *Journal of Wildlife Management* 75, no. 3 (April 2011): 596–603. Abstract available at http://is.gd/tk6rE9 (accessed Oct. 25, 2011).

Heuer, Karsten. *Being Caribou: Five Months On Foot with an Arctic Herd.* New York: Walker, 2007.

Homer-Dixon, Thomas. *The Ingenuity Gap.* New York: Knopf, 2000.

Ishikawa, Toru, et al. "Wayfinding with a GPS-based mobile navigation system: A comparison with maps and direct experience." *Journal of Environmental Psychology* 28, no. 1 (March 2008): 74–82. Abstract available at http://is.gd/k7YNJr (accessed Oct. 25, 2011).

Kearney, Jack. *Tracking: A Blueprint for Learning How.* El Cajon, Calif.: Pathways Press, 1978.
The essential methods of man-tracking developed by the US Border Patrol and widely adapted for search and rescue.

Kerley, Jeff. "Safe and Dry: Winter Cruising on the BC Coast." *BC Forest Professional* (January/February 2011): 14–15. Full text (PDF) available at http://is.gd/g6dUpC (accessed Oct. 25, 2011).

Kjellström, Björn. *Be Expert with Map and Compass.* Hoboken, NJ: Wiley, 2010.

Letham, Lawrence, and Alex Letham. *GPS Made Easy: Using Global Positioning Systems in the Outdoors.* Calgary: Rocky Mountain Books, 2008.

MacKinnon, Andy, and Jim Pojar. *Plants of Northern British Columbia.* Edmonton: Lone Pine Publishing, 1992.

———. *Plants of the Pacific Northwest Coast.* Rev. ed. Vancouver: Lone Pine Publishing, 2004.

McKinlay, William Laird. *Karluk: The Great Untold Story of Arctic Exploration.* New York: St. Martin's Press, 1976.

Merry, Wayne, and St. John Ambulance Ontario Council. *St. John Ambulance Official Wilderness First Aid Guide.* Toronto: McClelland & Stewart, 1994.

Middleton, Laura E., et al. "Activity Energy Expenditure and Incident Cognitive Impairment in Older Adults." *Archives of Internal Medicine* 171, no. 14 (July 25, 2011): 1251–1257. Full text (PDF) available at http://archinte.ama-assn.org/cgi/reprint/171/14/1251 (accessed Oct. 24, 2011).

Nash, Mike. *Exploring Prince George: A Guide to North Central BC Outdoors.* Calgary: Rocky Mountain Books, 2004, reprinted 2007.

———. *The Mountain Knows No Expert: George Evanoff, Outdoorsman and Contemporary Hero.* Toronto: Dundurn Press, 2009.

Nieman, David C., et al. "Upper respiratory tract infection is reduced in physically fit and active adults." *British Journal of Sports Medicine* (Nov. 1, 2010). Abstract available at http://is.gd/WS2csB (accessed Oct. 25, 2011).

Parish, Roberta, et al. *Plants of Southern Interior British Columbia.* Vancouver: Lone Pine Publishing, 1996.

Powter, Geoff. "Death on the Wapta." *explore magazine* (June 2007): 59.

Pretorius, Thea, et al. "Thermal effects of whole head submersion in cold water on non-shivering humans." *Journal of Applied Physiology* 101, no. 2 (August 2006): 669–675. Full text available at http://jap.physiology.org/content/101/2/669.full (accessed Oct. 25, 2011).

Ralston, Aron. *Between a Rock and a Hard Place.* New York: Atria Books, 2004.

Rennicke, Jeff. "Trapped! The Mike Turner Story." *Backpacker Magazine* (June 2002). Full text available at http://is.gd/o3l7ec (accessed Oct. 25, 2011).

Schooler, Lynn. *Walking Home: A Traveler in the Alaskan Wilderness.* New York: Bloomsbury, 2010.

Sherwood, Ben. *The Survivor's Club: The Secrets and Science that Could Save Your Life.* New York: Grand Central Publishing, 2009.
What determines who survives and who doesn't? What appears to count are the will to live and a positive mental attitude combined with a realistic assessment of the situation and a sense of optimism. We are hard-wired to respond rapidly to short-term crises, but we are perhaps less adapted to longer-term stressful situations.

Steele, Peter. *Backcountry Medical Guide.* 2nd ed. Seattle: Mountaineers Books, 1999.

Toft, Murray. "Willi Pfisterer: Deconstructing avalanche decision-making." *Alpine Club of Canada Gazette* 21, no. 3 (Fall 2006): 16–17.

Transport Canada bulletins:
"A Safety Guide for Aircraft Charter Passengers," TP 7087
"Helicopter Passenger Safety Guide," TP 4263
"Seaplane/Floatplane: A Passenger's Guide," TP 12365
Full text of each bulletin available at http://is.gd/lEw7ib (accessed Oct. 25, 2011).

COURSES, SEMINARS, VIDEOS

Avalanche courses, recreational, with at least a one-day field component, typically offered in December and January. The Canadian Avalanche Centre has an online avalanche course designed for first responders, at http://is.gd/nJWpDB.

Bear safety seminars: typically available in the spring and early summer.

Bear safety video: *Staying Safe in Bear Country: A Behavioral-Based Approach to Reducing Risk.* Atlin, BC: Wild Eye Productions, in association with AV Action Yukon Ltd. and Safety in Bear Country Society (n.d.). VHS, DVD, 50 min. Purchase information, synopsis outline and complete script (both PDF) available at www.bearsmart.com/video/206.

Canoe and kayak courses; swift water rescue training.

First aid courses are available from a variety of sources. Typical offerings are a half-day cardiopulmonary resuscitation (CPR) course; one-day emergency first aid; two-day standard first aid; five- or ten-day wilderness first aid (a ten-day, or 80-hour, wilderness first aid course may be required for professional guides). Other occupational-level first aid courses may require even more time. As a minimum, one or more people in a party should have a current emergency first aid certificate, with wilderness first aid preferred.

Map, compass and GPS navigation courses.

Survival course, basic, with a one-overnight field component.

Survival course, intermediate to advanced, with at least a two-overnight field component.

Survival course, winter, with a field snow-shelter component.

COMMUNITY RESOURCES

Clubs: hiking, climbing, skiing, canoeing and kayaking, natural history, general outdoors, snowmobiling and many more. Ways of accessing such resources include regional or municipal government offices; local newspaper community announcements of upcoming events; seasonal local recreation publications; and word of mouth – just ask around. Some clubs may be members of provincial or national federations, which can open doors for you when travelling. And of course, an online search for a community of interest will find almost everything, as most serious outdoor clubs now have websites.

Continuing education courses offered by school districts, community colleges and universities, as well as privately offered courses.

Volunteer search and rescue groups and other volunteer opportunities in the community.

NOTES

1   Fred Van der Post grew up in the Jura region of wartime France, where he learned early about the elements of survival. He came to Canada in 1961, and after a brief sojourn back in France, he returned to Canada and has worked in the bush ever since as a forester, often alone, with countless adventures under his belt. For nearly 20 years I worked in the same office building as Fred, and whenever I passed him as he was heading out to the bush he always had something positive to say about the day no matter what it was like, an important hallmark of a survivor. Between 1971 and 1982 Fred undertook three major solo snowshoeing treks across north central and northern British Columbia. The first was work-related, and following this experience he undertook two longer trips for his own personal experience and satis-faction. Following one of these, he received a personal letter from Prime Minister Pierre Trudeau, which closed with: "Connaissant un peu ce sport, j'imagine facilement combien cette randonnée vous a demandé de courage, vous donnant cependant un plaisir et une satisfaction que bien peu de gens peuvent soupçonner. Tous mes bons voeux vous accompagnent." ("Knowing a little about this sport, I can easily imagine how much courage this jour-ney demanded of you, yet giving you pleasure and satisfaction that few can imagine. All my best wishes are with you.")

2   Mike Nash, *The Mountain Knows No Expert: George Evanoff, Outdoorsman and Contemporary Hero* (Toronto: Dundurn Press, 2009).

3   Gordon Hamilton, "Death rate drops as BC loggers embrace safe practices on the job," *Vancouver Sun*, Apr. 25, 2011, D3.

4   Laura E. Middleton et al., "Activity Energy Expenditure and Incident Cognitive Impairment in Older Adults," *Archives of Internal Medicine* 171, no. 14 (July 25, 2011): 1251–1257.

5   Thomas Homer-Dixon, *The Ingenuity Gap* (New York: Knopf, 2000).

6   David Deutsch, *The Beginning of Infinity: Explanations that Transform The World* (New York: Viking, 2011).

7   Jeff Kerley, "Safe and Dry: Winter Cruising on the BC Coast," *BC Forest Professional* (Jan/Feb 2011): 14–15.

8   Toru Ishikawa et al., "Wayfinding with a GPS-based mobile navigation system: A comparison with maps and direct experience," *Journal of Environmental Psychology* 28, no. 1 (March 2008): 74–82.

9   Thea Pretorius et al., "Thermal effects of whole head submersion in cold wa-ter on non-shivering humans," *Journal of Applied Physiology* 101, no. 2 (August 2006): 669–675.

10   Canadian Red Cross, "Drownings and other water-related injuries in Canada: 10 Years of Research. Module 2" (April 2006).

11   See, for example, Wayne Giles and Barbara Robertson, eds., *Canoeing and Kayaking BC's Central Interior: A Guidebook* (Prince George: Northwest Brigade Paddling Club, 2002).

12   *Exploring Prince George: A Guide to North Central BC Outdoors* (Calgary: Rocky Mountain Books, 2004, re-printed 2007), 252–261.

13   Stephen Herrero et al., "Fatal at-tacks by American black bear on people 1900–2009," *Journal of Wildlife Management* 75, no. 3 (April 2011): 596–603.

14   Mike Nash, *Exploring Prince George: A Guide to North Central BC Outdoors*: 240

15   "The Fang Cave Rescue." Regional and Provincial Cave Rescue Coordinators'

Reports, *BC Caver* 23, no. 3 (Fall 2009): 18–25.

16 Geoff Powter, "Death on the Wapta," *explore magazine* (June 2007): 59.

17 Jack Boudreau, *Crazy Man's Creek* (Prince George, BC: Caitlin Press, 1998), 31.

18 See Mike Nash, *The Mountain Knows No Expert.*

19 See, for example, Murray Toft, "Willi Pfisterer: Deconstructing avalanche decision-making," *Alpine Club of Canada Gazette* 21, no. 3 (Fall 2006): 16–17.

20 Cited in Appendix C under "Transport Canada bulletins."

21 Gibson, Hugh F., Commissioner. "Report of Board of Inquiry into Accident at Toronto International Airport, Malton, Ontario, to Air Canada DC8 CF-TIW Aircraft on July 5, 1970" (Ottawa: Information Canada, 1971).

INDEX

ABOUT THE AUTHOR

Mike Nash has more than 40 years of experience in the Canadian outdoors, much of it in north central British Columbia. For five years after moving to BC in 1978 he was a volunteer member of the Prince George Search & Rescue group. In ensuing years, he led trips for Prince George outdoor clubs and has written about and taught outdoor safety, survival and leadership in the Prince George community. He held three industrial first aid

JUDY LETT

tickets during a five-year period in the 1980s; led a site evacuation team for ten years for a forest industry employer in the 1990s; and held a wilderness first aid certificate in the early 2000s.

For over 25 years, Mike has served on many public advisory groups related to the outdoors, including forestry, wildlife and backcountry recreation. He wrote a community newspaper column on the outdoors from 1995 to 2005, and his first full-length book, *Exploring Prince George: A Guide to North Central BC Outdoors*, was published in 2004 and reprinted in 2007. After a friend of his died in a grizzly bear encounter in 1998, Mike spent several years working on a biography, *The Mountain Knows No Expert: George Evanoff, Outdoorsman and Contemporary Hero*, published in 2009. After giving a series of safety workshops for students and staff at the University of Northern BC in the early 2000s, and later addressing a forest service safety day seminar in 2005, Mike organized the highlights of the extensive outdoor safety material he had gathered over several decades into a publication that might help others be safer in the outdoors. This book is the result.